Coming of Age
in U.S. High Schools

Economic, Kinship, Religious, and Political Crosscurrents

Sociocultural, Political, and Historical Studies in Education
Joel Spring, Editor

Coming of Age in U.S. High Schools

Economic, Kinship, Religious, and Political Crosscurrents

Annette B. Hemmings
University of Cincinnati

LAWRENCE ERLBAUM ASSOCIATES, PUBLISHERS

2004   Mahwah, New Jersey   London

Lawrence Erlbaum Associates, Inc., Publishers
10 Industrial Avenue
Mahwah, New Jersey 07430

Cover design by Kathryn Houghtaling Lacey

Library of Congress Cataloging-in-Publication Data

Hemmings, Annette B.
Coming of age in U.S. high schools : economic, kinship, religious, and political crosscurrents / Annette B. Hemmings.
p. cm.
Includes bibliographical references and index.
ISBN 0-8058-4666-2 (cloth : alk. paper)
ISBN 0-8058-4667-0 (pbk. : alk. paper)
High school seniors—United States—Social conditions—Case studies. 2. High schools—United States—Sociological aspects—Case studies. #. Educational anthropology—United States—Case studies. I. Title.

LC205.H46 2004
373.18'0973—dc22   2003049328

Books published by Lawrence Erlbaum Associates are printed on acid-free paper, and their bindings are chosen for strength and durability.

Printed in the United States of America
10 9 8 7 6 5 4 3 2 1

To my first teacher, fellow traveler,
dear friend, and mother,
Gloria Alban Biederwolf

Contents

Preface

There has been a succession of reports and research on U.S. public high schools that are largely concerned with issues and problems related to academic achievement. In my own prior research, I was especially interested in how high-achieving Black students formed academic identities and were poised to "do" or "not do" the academic work assigned to them (Hemmings, 1996, 1998). But whenever I entered the field, I was struck by the observation that high schools and the teenagers who attended them were involved in much more extensive cultural work. Academic achievement was important, but it was not necessarily a primary concern of adolescent students who were struggling hard to come of age in high schools that have been historically established to ease their passages to adulthood in the broadest, most comprehensive cultural sense.

I also noticed how adolescent passages were complicated by the fact that there is not and never will be a common, shared American culture. Culture in the United States is a dynamic seascape with a myriad of crosscurrents comprised of conflicting discourses and practices that can cause terrible confusion for, or open up creative possibilities to, teenagers. These crosscurrents converge in high schools, where students' cultural navigations may be fairly smooth or extremely treacherous. Such observations were not lost on anthropologists during the first half of the 20th century, but they have been overlooked in recent decades, especially among school ethnographers who are rendering culture into bounded systems or binary oppositions in studies that focus rather narrowly on differentiated patterns of academic achievement.

At the outset of the 21st century, it struck me as critically important to refocus high school research in ways that capture the actual nature and complexities of adolescent coming-of-age processes. Research of this kind is crucial for educational researchers, graduate students, policymakers, teacher candidates, and in-service practitioners, who seem more perplexed then ever about how to address the perennial educational question of what high schools in the United States ought to be doing to enrich individual human potential and allow young people, regardless of their backgrounds, to achieve a good life. This question imbues the larger purpose of the ethnographic research presented in this book. The more specific aim of the study was to describe and analyze how 10 graduating seniors, their friends, and many of their classmates came of age in three urban and suburban U.S. public high schools. The seniors who volunteered to serve as research participants included Black inner-city teenagers, White working-class youths, affluent middle-class suburbanites, a Mexican American girl, an Asian American boy, Christians, Jews, Muslims, mothers, mothers-to-be, gays, and lesbians. They attended Jefferson High, a racially desegregated school; Ridgewood High, a predominantly White, middle-class school; and Central City High, a school in an impoverished Black urban neighborhood.

Coming of age is conceived as a two-pronged process of identity formation and community integration. Identity formation is psychocultural work where adolescents attempt to form and situate a multifaceted enduring or "true" self. Community integration involves the particular strategic adaptations adolescents make as they navigate conflicting discourses and practices in multilayered cultural crosscurrents flowing through economic, kinship, religious, and political domains of American life. Among these currents are dominant culture, liminal trends, popular culture, undertows, ethnic tributaries, local family worlds, and youth cultures and sub-cultures.

This framework reacknowledges anthropological precedents while recognizing more contemporary (post)anthropological trends. It also forefronts the voices and observed experiences of the graduating seniors who participated in the research. I found that the stories these students told about how they formed a true self and pursued a good life in the particular contexts of their high schools provided extremely insightful, sometimes disturbing commentaries on the American cultural seascape. Although, all of them managed to reach the shores of adulthood, many of their passages through the crosscurrents flowing through their schools were marked by tragic setbacks, heroic comebacks, and triumphant endings.

Chapter 1 sets the stage for the study. It includes an overview of anthropological precedents and (post)anthropological perspectives on adolescent coming-of-age processes. This section is followed by a more detailed discussion of the study's conceptual framework. The chapter also includes sections on fieldwork methodology, reflexivity, and literary tropes.

General impressions of school life are presented in chapter 2 as contextual surfaces for more in-depth explorations of how graduating seniors came of age in the three high schools. The 10 seniors who served as key participants are introduced as they guided me through corridors and classrooms.

The next four chapters delve into how seniors viewed and navigated crosscurrents as they came of age in economic, kinship, religious, and political community domains. Each of these chapters includes a description of the facets of the enduring self that constituted the core of seniors' identity work. They are otherwise organized into analytical descriptions of crosscurrents in the four community domains and how teachers and school staff facilitated, and students experienced, coming of age within the contexts of their schools.

Cultural crosscurrents are summarized in chapter 7 as part of a general overview of how coming of age unfolded in the high schools, as well as how each school sought particular answers to the perennial educational question. The last section provides a reflexive look back at how graduating seniors accomplished what in the final analysis was truly remarkable identity and integration work in U.S. public high schools.

ACKNOWLEDGMENTS

I acknowledge with deep appreciation the help and support of high school contacts, reviewers, mentors, and family members. I thank Lynn Kitchen, Nikela Owens, and Lea Brinker for helping me to gain entree into, and recruiting such wonderful student participants within, the three high school sites. Your genuine concern for students and their welfare was truly inspiring and an impetus for the study.

I am grateful for the incisive feedback that Reba Page and Pamela Bettis provided on the early drafts of the book manuscript. Having such intelligent, busy scholars devote that kind of time and effort to my work is more than I could ever expect, much less reciprocate. I also appreciate the assistance I received from Naomi Silverman, her assistant, Erica Kica, and other members of the editorial staff at Lawrence Erlbaum Associates. Your masterful diplomacy in the negotiation of substantive revisions was grand. Patricia Ferenbach deserves the highest praise for the fabulous copy-editing, and Debbie Ruel, LEA Production Editor, for typesetting and final production of the book. And I thank Dawn Bellinger, who as my graduate student assistant handled my correspondence, proofread and critiqued manuscripts, and made sure that I was up to speed on the latest trends in the literature.

I also would like to acknowledge the guidance of my graduate school mentors especially Mary Metz, my major advisor, and George and Louise Spindler. Mary taught me about the value and methods of "doing" qualitative research in secondary schools. I would not be the scholar that I am without her wise counsel and supreme example. The Spindlers as visiting professors at the University of Wisconsin–Madison, introduced a handful of us to the fascinating world of educational anthropology. Much of my own thinking about how identity and integration work unfolds in schools was, and continues to be, inspired by their pioneering ethnographic research.

I want to thank my husband, Bill Hemmings, for his patient support, excellent copyediting, and honest opinions about the ideas presented in this book. And, thanks, Ma, for your abiding presence as I was coming of age through the obstacle courses of my own academic (and adolescent) passages. It is to you that I dedicate this book in loving appreciation of all that you are and have done for me.

—*Annette B. Hemmings*

1

New Age for Coming of Age

There are longstanding cultural assumptions in the United States that adolescent coming of age is fraught with difficulties and that public high schools often do not go far enough to ensure smooth passages to adulthood. It was Margaret Mead (1928) who popularized the belief that American teenagers go through an especially turbulent period of "storm and stress" made worse by a culture "woven of so many diverse strands [and] numerous contradictions [that young people confront] a confusing world of dazzling choices" (p. 204). She was quite pointed in her criticism of high schools for failing to transmit cultural certainties to young people who are uncertain about how to adjust to adult life.

The assumptions remained, prompting another anthropologist, Robert Redfield, many years later, to pose the question "What should education in the United States do in order to enrich the human potential of every single individual and to allow each person to achieve the good life?" (1963, p. 71). The query challenged educational anthropologists to explore the cultural development of children and youths more thoroughly and to think about how schools might do a better job of facilitating cultural processes that nurture individual potentials and create genuine opportunities for young people to live good, meaningful lives.

Now, at the beginning of a new millennium, adolescent passages to adulthood are just as perplexing and, some are convinced, much more troubling. There is growing concern that public high schools, especially those in impoverished urban areas, are less than effective in their original mission to provide some kind of a common cultural grounding for young people with widely diverse backgrounds. The question Redfield asked has

1

become much harder to answer in what appears to be an even more confusing world of dazzling choices.

But that does not mean that such questions should not be revisited or that more contemporary answers should not be sought. Public high schools have been and will continue to be primary staging areas for adolescent coming of age. Teachers, administrators, policymakers, and educational researchers need to wrestle with the question if they are truly committed to preparing teenagers for adulthood. Before the question can be addressed, however, there needs to be more comprehensive knowledge about how coming-of-age processes actually unfold in high school settings. Such knowledge needs to extend well beyond student achievement in standard academic subjects and include rich ethnographic descriptions and analyses of whether or how adolescents are forming identities and integrating themselves into economic, kinship, religious, and political community domains. And it needs to acknowledge the complexly fluid nature of American culture.

The research presented in this book provides a broad yet highly particularistic descriptive foundation on which this cultural knowledge base may be built. It includes extensive ethnographic case studies of how diverse adolescents came of age in three U.S. public high schools. Coming of age is conceptualized as a two-pronged process of identity formation and community integration with attention to anthropological precedents and emergent post-anthropological thinking. Identity formation is construed as a process of working through and situating a multifaceted enduring self that reflects adolescents' most deep-felt psychocultural commitments. Community integration involves the particular strategic adaptations adolescents make as they navigate conflicting discourses in multilayered cultural crosscurrents flowing through community domains of American life.

These processes are described as they unfolded in research sites selected as representative of public high schools in urban and suburban America. Although the schools shared similar educational missions, they varied enormously as contexts for adolescent coming of age. Jefferson High,[1] the first site, was a racially desegregated urban school serving middle- and working-class youths. Most of the Black students were bussed to the school in compliance with a court-mandated desegregation plan. Ridgewood High was located in a predominantly White, upper-middle-class suburb, whereas the last site, Central City High, enrolled mostly Black students living in poverty in the most economically depressed neighborhoods in the district.

Graduating seniors were invited to serve as key research participants because they were at a juncture in their lives where they could look backward at their passages through adolescence, look closely at their current circumstances, and look ahead toward their future as adults. They also had profoundly different backgrounds as boys and girls; Whites and youths of color; low-, working-, and middle-class teenagers; European Americans, African Americans, Mexican Americans, Asian Americans; and sexually straight and homosexual. Adam Willis was a White working-class boy at Jefferson High. His classmates were David North, a middle-class Black honors student, and Lona Young, an underachieving working-class Black girl. Lona was a central figure in a large, unusually mixed peer group that included gay, lesbian, and bisexual students, single mothers, and a disabled boy with a traumatic brain injury.

The seniors who participated at Ridgewood High were Cassandra Sommers, Christina Sanchez, Peter Hsieh, and Stuart Lyon. Cassandra was a Black single mother. Christina, a Mexican American, and Peter a Taiwanese-American, were second-generation immigrants. Among Christina's friends were other immigrants, including her best friend, from Japan, a Russian girl, and a Muslim from Pakistan. Stuart was a White Jewish boy from an affluent family.

Monica Reese was among the Black seniors who participated in the research at Central City High. She was an ambitious high achiever who lived with her single mother in a low-rent housing project. Michael Meyer, the senior class valedictorian, was a working-class boy who was among the small minority of White students who went to the school. Nay Wilson was a low-income Black girl who resided in the same apartment complex as Monica.

These 10 students, their friends, and other peers had qualitatively different adolescent experiences as they came of age. I found that in their identity and integration work they were absorbers of traditions, barometers of contemporary trends, and harbingers of change. Despite painful setbacks and daunting obstacles, most managed to make passages through the torrential crosscurrents of U.S. culture and did so with great hope for ages to come.

(POST)ANTHROPOLOGY

Coming of age in the United States has evolved and so, too, have the ways in which cultural processes have been conceived by anthropologists. Van Gennep (1960) was the originator of the classic notions that coming of age is a linear, three-phase series of developmental transitions or rites of adolescent passage. Teenagers during the first phase undergo rites of separation where they experience symbolic breaches with their families and communities. Breaches are followed by a turbulent phase of margin or liminality marked by mounting crises between youths and adults. Eventually adolescents reenter the community fold as culturally integrated adults through rites of reaggregation.

The second liminal phase was regarded by Turner (1969) as being of most crucial importance. Adolescents going through this phase are "betwixt and between the positions assigned and arrayed by law, custom, convention, and ceremonial" (p. 95) and are at heightened risk of being a loss or danger to their communities. They are much more attuned to, and critical of, cultural systems than are adults who have long accommodated to them. Turner (1977, 1982) in his later works went a step further with the thesis that societies as a whole pass through liminal periods often instigated by young people attempting to liberate themselves from oppressive cultural values and norms. As people break out of the normative structures of prevailing social statuses (what Turner termed *antistructure*), they sow the seeds of social and cultural change.

Public high schools in the United States are established to monitor or at least curb the excesses of adolescent passages. They are supposed to transmit common cultural knowledge and accommodate the cultural changes that come about as people with new knowledge come into contact (Singleton, 1974). Much of the common culture constituting the curriculum is a reaffirmation of Anglo-American, Western-European, middle-class traditions. Teachers convey this curriculum in incremental stages as they guide and judge individual students' progress from one level of instruction to the next. Their efforts are almost always augmented by extracurricular activities, ceremonial rituals, and other symbolic rites that ultimately culminate in students' "graduation" to adulthood.

Such conceptions of rites of passage and the roles schools were expected to play in facilitating them were shaken in the 1980s by a "crisis in representation" that called into question classic anthropological frameworks and methods of ethnographic research (Marcus & Fischer, 1986). The crisis eroded norms of objectivity, notions of social life structured by fixed rituals and customs, and the authority of the ethnographer to represent and interpret the lived experience of "other" people (Denzin & Lincoln, 2000; Lincoln & Denzin, 2000). Anthropologists no longer could assume the stance of detached observer and value-neutral researcher. They now had to acknowledge their subjective biases and privileged positions as individuals who construct social rather than definitive texts.

The crisis is being spurred on by post-modern/structural movements in the social sciences. Instead of conveying certainty, clarity, and wholeness, these new intellectual "posts" are fostering a sense of ambiguity, relativity, fragmentation, particularity, and discontinuity. The movements for many scholars are ruptures with the past. But for others they remain in broad continuity with intellectual traditions. They represent a logical succession in thought rather than the latest thought in succession through time (Crotty, 1998, p. 185).

The (post) anthropology that I am using to frame the research in this book acknowledges past precedents while pushing the bounds of how identity and integration work is conceived in coming-of-age processes. It places the examination of cultural discourses at the forefront of inquiry because of how they shape adolescents' social, cultural, and psychological realities. Much contemporary research analyzes discourses as language systems imbued with disciplinary practices and discursive modes of surveillance that inscribe what it means to be normal or abnormal.[2] In my analysis, I focus on the substance of the commonsense beliefs, values, norms, and other meanings comprising discourses, as well as attendant cultural practices. I examine the meaning systems of discourses as multilayered and affecting identity and integration work through the discursive pressures they exert. Such examinations were crucial for framing the more particular ways in which the teenagers in this research unleashed their individual potentials and pursued versions of the good life in community domains.

FRAMEWORK FOR STUDY

The more particular analytical framework I constructed for this study renders U.S. culture into a seascape with multilayered cultural meaning systems or *crosscurrents*. Crosscurrents are construed as discursive streams brimming with commonsense discourses and ordinary disciplinary and other practices. To represent U.S. culture this way is to recognize the fluid, intermingled, often conflicting nature of meanings, how meaning systems envelop people and carry them off in disparate directions, and the fact that individuals must respond and adapt to meanings as they work to define their identities and integrate themselves into the community.

Coming of age is furthered refined in my metaphoric view as identity formation and community integration accomplished through symbolic navigational work. Youths, in their identity work, struggle to produce and situate identities revolving around a multifaceted, psychocultural self. As they work to integrate their selves into the community, they navigate the discourses and practices comprising crosscurrents flowing through economic, kinship, religious, and political domains of American life. They swim with the currents or against them and do so through a multitude of adaptations constructed in light of their historical social locations, individual subjectivities, and the nature and intensity of contextualized pressures. Identity and integration work are interrelated yet distinctive enough to treat them as two prongs of a complicated process.

Identity Formation

Anthropologists traditionally have studied the process of identity formation as enculturation accomplished through cultural transmission with attention to understandings of what it means to become a person in
particular cultural contexts (Hoffman, 1998). Some consider psychological factors along with cultural ones in their conceptual approaches
(Shweder, 1991; Spindler & Spindler, 1978, 1989, 1993). Most recognize identity formation as potential cause for conflict especially in culturally pluralistic societies like the United States where there is no shared
culture to bind individual selves into a communal whole.[3]

Conventional anthropological studies of identity, especially those conducted in educational settings, have become more problematic in the
wake of the representational crisis. Hoffman (1998) made an attempt to
salvage explorations of identity by encouraging anthropologists to make a
crucial distinction between the innermost self and external cultural pressures. She cited Jen (1997), who was concerned that scholarship focusing
on "defining 'truth' from the outside" often neglects influences on the inner self that may, in fact, "define 'truth' from the inside" (p. 19). The
Spindlers (1992, 1993) have long recognized the distinction and provided useful analytical tools for understanding the self as enduring, situated, and endangered. The *enduring self* is comprised of individuals'
innermost psychocultural commitments. It is a person's most deeply ingrained psychological orientation and culturally patterned ways of "relat-
ing to others; to the material, natural, and spiritual worlds; and to time
and space, including notions of agency, mind, person, being and spirit"
(Hoffman, 1998, p. 326). The enduring self is not fixed but continues to
develop as individuals and their circumstances change. It is not a unified
whole but a multifaceted entity. Despite its evolving complexity, the enduring self gives people a sense of continuity with the past while simultaneously providing them with an inner compass of meanings for
negotiating the present and charting the future.

The *situated self* is the outward expression of a person's understanding
of what activities are linked to what goals and how one must behave in order to reach desired ends. It is instrumental in that it involves practical,
outward demonstrations of cultural competence in particular contexts.
The expressions of the situated self shift from situation to situation as individuals adapt to different rules, norms, values, and other cultural pressures. Expressions boldly displayed in one context may be carefully
suppressed in another.

Attempts to situate the self may go smoothly or lead to intense internal
or social conflict. If the enduring self is violated too often by the cultural
demands of a situation, it may become an *endangered self.* These are real

risks for individuals in contexts with cultural pressures that "are antagonistic to the premises and behavioral patterns of their own cultures" or
that threaten their psychological orientations (Spindler & Spindler,
1993, p. 37).

The Spindlers' notions of the enduring, situated, and endangered self
acknowledge both the inner and outer truths of identity work. They are
somewhat but not entirely compatible with post-modern/structural conceptions that generally reject the humanistic idea of an essential self. Fragmentation, contradiction, and discontinuity rather than continuity are
the focus in these conceptions as individuals are constituted through and
by particular discourses (Davies, 2000). The agency or choices individuals make about who they are may be based on rational analysis, but desires
deeply embedded in various discourses may subvert rationality. Identity
work so conceived is:

> an individual's or a group of individuals' interpretation and reconstruction
> of her/his/their personal history and particular social location, as mediated
> through the cultural and discursive context to which she/he/they has/have
> access. (Raissiguier, 1994, p. 26)

When mediations go well, individuals experience a sense of self that en-
genders positive personal growth. When identity work goes badly, people
end up with a fragmented, unstable, or endangered self with extremely
painful psychological and social consequences.

There is no doubt that identity work is paramount in the lives of adolescent students. Youths have a "passion for identities" that are:

> made around nation, community, ethnicity, race, religion, gender, sexual-
> ity, and age; identities premised on popular culture and its shifting sets of
> representational practices; identities attached to fashion and new imag-
> ined lifestyles, to leisure and work, and to the mundane and the exotic;
> identities made in relation to place and displacement, to community and
> to a sense of dispersal, to "roots" as well as "routes." (Yon, 2000, p. 1)

Such work certainly was important to the graduating seniors in this research. I found that they had some sense of an enduring self and that most
of them had experienced fragmentation or painful conflict as they situated their selves in various discourses. They exercised agency as they came
to terms with their own desires while adapting to the desires of parents,
schools, society, and other discursive forces.

I also found that seniors in their school-based identity work went well
beyond the formation of an academic self. Many educational anthropologists who studied adolescents in high schools have noted the profound impact that identity has on academic achievement patterns especially

identity work around the central social categories of ethnicity, race, social class and gender. Although this body of research has provided invaluable insight into the relationship between identity and academic performance, it does not reveal how students view and express themselves as workers, family members, religious believers, or political citizens. Also, by emphasizing social categories in identity work, many researchers lose sight of how adolescents actually work on or out their identities. Identity formation is undertaken by most teenagers as work around the economic, familial/sexual, religious, and political facets of their selves, with ethnicity, race, class, gender, and sexual orientation operating as critical influences. Personal desires are central because it is in their patterns that possibilities for life lie (Davies, 2000). These facets of the self and the desires they contain were integral to what the seniors in this study regarded as the most salient, significant features of who they were and hoped to become. They also were integral to processes of community integration.

Community Integration

Parents in the United States generally hope that their adolescent offspring will find good jobs in the economy and become contributing members of families held together by strong, intergenerational bonds. Many also hope their children, as adults, will adhere to a religious faith and participate in American democracy as law-abiding citizens who get involved in local, state, and national politics. But such ideal expectations for integration into community domains are not easily realized in a society where teenagers encounter conflicting cultural crosscurrents streaming out of the wellsprings of the dominant culture, liminal trends, vulgar popular culture, seamy undertows, ethnic tributaries, local family worlds, and youth cultures and peer subcultures. Crosscurrents are depicted in Fig. 1.1 as concentric layers flowing through community domains, with dotted lines indicating the openness of boundaries where discourses flow back and forth.

The outermost layer represents the *dominant culture* grounded in middle-class Anglo- and Western-European values and lifestyles. This cultural stream is characterized by a tempered individualism where freedom of choice is widely touted but heavily circumscribed by disciplining economic norms, conventional nuclear family values and arrangements, mainline Judeo-Christian religious theologies, and nationalized political ideologies. The dominant culture is widely regarded as the most "mainstream," that is, as the most accepted common way of life for Americans, regardless of their backgrounds.

Dominant currents are destabilized by *liminal trends* that shift societal views on what is or is not accepted as part of the larger common culture. Liminal trends generated by rapid developments in electronic technol-

Ethnographic Data important to show patterns

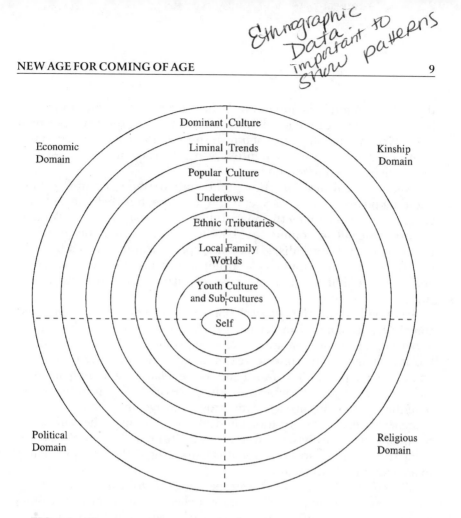

FIG. 1.1.   Crosscurrents in community domains.

ogy, a burgeoning service sector, and global exchanges of information have led to monumental changes in the economic domain. Young people in the liminal economy are "floating in a nebulous atmosphere" as they look over postindustrial employment opportunities and wonder whether or how to take advantage of them (Bettis, 1996, p. 115). Liminal trends also are altering the kinship domain, where the traditional nuclear family is becoming a personal choice rather than a cultural given as divorce, single-parenting, homosexual domestic partnerships, and other alternative living arrangements gain more acceptance. Conventions that once governed sexuality and sexual activity, child-bearing and child-rearing, and the roles of men and women are now openly challenged in ways unknown or unheard of in the past. Momentous changes also are occurring within the domains of religion and politics. The authority that mainline churches once held over their congregations has lost its grip as more individuals insist on constructing their own personal belief systems and pursuing their own spiritual journeys. United States politics has been transformed into a system focused more on special interests than the common interest.

Dominant cultural traditions and liminal trends occupy a commanding position in the U.S. cultural seascape, but their currents are constantly crossed up by the powerful forces of *popular culture.* Popular culture is the vulgar, commodified, industry-driven common culture of everyday life (Dimitriadis, 2001). It is spread through media by fashion, film, television, music, and other industries. And it is packaged and sold to a public eager to wear, watch, listen to, and otherwise consume its products.

Seething beneath the layers of dominant currents are *undertows* that constitute the cultural underside of what a community values most. When the values of economic success and competition are elevated, so, too, is the temptation to pursue wealth through illicit means. An emphasis on personal happiness in familial and sexual relations is accompanied by an easing of constraints on sexual indulgences and other pleasurable yet potentially risky intimacies. Undertows emerge in political spheres, churches, and other institutions and meander through the darkest recesses of U.S. social divisions, where they incite prejudice and ignite intergroup tension. They are everywhere as tantalizing as they are threatening to a community's sensibilities.

Also crisscrossing the U.S. seascape are *ethnic tributaries* sustained by groups determined to preserve their most cherished traditions. Tributaries often revolve around a religious faith, but they also reinforce intergenerational patterns of family, economic, and political security. They flow apart from or alongside other cultural currents and are distinguished by varying degrees of autonomy. The most autonomous ethnic tributaries are those sustained by groups whose members band together in small, closed communities. Other groups, including many immigrants, practice native traditions at homes or other community centers while making accommodations to dominant cultural expectations at school or work. Some are reviving lost traditions or generating new ones. What they all have in common is a strong communal desire to hold onto or bring back time-honored versions of the good life constructed within their own ethnic enclaves.

Larger cultural currents filter into more particularistic *local family worlds.* Local worlds are cultural systems containing knowledge, skills, values, beliefs, norms, and emotional responses that are peculiar to members of particular families (Phelan, Davidson, & Yu, 1993, 1998). Shweder (1991) used the phrase "intentional worlds" when he referred to these

[handwritten annotation: Anthropology - how the culture unfolds w/ in the schools - Allows researchers to show whats going on in education rather than statistics]

systems because they contain highly specific cultural prescriptions intended to inform family members' thoughts and behaviors. Adolescents in their families encounter detailed prescriptions for how they are to perform domestic roles and responsibilities, relate to relatives and nonrelatives, act in gender-appropriate ways, dress, talk, work, worship, and play. They are "intentional persons" who actively absorb, mediate, invent, contest, and otherwise negotiate prescriptions. As intentional persons, they make choices about whether or how they are going to respond to pressures to conform to what can be characterized as highly localized discourses and practices.

Youth cultures and subcultures are currents produced by teenagers themselves and are the most direct expressions of the attitudes youths have toward cultural currents. Youth culture denotes the general, distinctive, often antisocial patterns of adolescent behavior (Parsons, 1964). These patterns may signal alienation or social rebellion or reflect teenagers' desire to fit in by looking attractive, being popular, and having fun. Although youth cultures often appear to reject adult sensibilities, they actually derive much of their content and many of their practices from dominant meanings, media-generated popular culture, and other adult productions. They are forms of "symbolic creativity" where adolescents inject commonsense cultural material into uncommon yet widely shared expressions (Willis, 1990).

Youth subcultures are differentiated variations of youth culture produced by teenagers within the borders of their peer cliques. Subcultures are products of more refined processes of bricolage where particular groups of teenagers reorder existing meanings in a fashion that reflects their own personal predilections, cultural backgrounds, and social locations (Brake, 1980, 1985; Epstein, 1998; Levi-Strauss, 1966; Weinstein, 1991). Bricolage separates adolescents from the worlds of their families, schools, and other contexts while simultaneously maintaining symbolic connections with them. It occurs within private spaces away from the direct surveillance of adults. Subcultures are produced projecting a group image through styles of dress, hairdos, and adornments; a demeanor made up of facial expressions, gaits, and postures; and an argot or special language code for communication (Brake, 1985). They reflect the distinctiveness of the youths who manufacture them, often in an attempt to set themselves off from groups to which they are historically or personally opposed.[4]

At the center of the concentric seascape is the individual self, working hard to construct and project a viable identity while seeking integration into the community. For adolescents, much of this work takes place in high schools, where crosscurrents inevitably converge.

FIELDWORK

Site Selection

I chose Jefferson High, Ridgewood High, and Central City High as research sites because they followed similar approaches to education but were notably different with regard to their student populations. All three of the schools offered standard academic fare as well as programs in nonacademic areas related to my research interests. They also had common class schedules, instructional materials, graduation requirements, and other organizational features.

I chose the sites partly on the basis of statistical data on student population demographics summarized in Table 1.1. Whereas population demographics indicate general characteristics of communities, achievement patterns show the relationship between communities and schools. They indicate students' understanding of the place of formal education in their lives and also provide a sense of the resources that parents can bring to the task of assisting their children with their education (Metz, 1990). A good way to gauge achievement patterns is by examining dropout and graduation rates (Table 1.2).

TABLE 1.1
Demographic Composition of Student Population*

	Jefferson High	Ridgewood High	Central City High
White European American	44.35	88.9	18.20
African American	54.37	4.5	81.23
Asian/Asian American	0.52	5.1	0.10
Hispanic/Hispanic American	0.12	1.10	0.00
American Indian	0.00	0.00	0.10
Multiracial	0.64	0.4	0.37
Low-income**	49.36	2.83	63.60

* Percentages during period of data collection.
** Percentages of students enrolled in free and reduced federal lunch programs.

TABLE 1.2
Annual Dropout and Graduation Rates*

	Jefferson High	Ridgewood High	Central City High
Dropout rate	17.8	1.1	30.5
Graduation rate**	78.8	97.8	59.3

 * Percentages during period of data collection.
** Seniors in October who graduated by August.

Another way to gauge achievement patterns is to examine scores on standardized tests. Students, in order to graduate, had to pass a ninth-grade academic proficiency exam developed and administered by the state. There also was a twelfth-grade exam taken by seniors, but the state did not require passing scores for graduation. Students who failed all or parts of the ninth-grade exam could retake it until they passed. Ninety-five percent of seniors at Jefferson High eventually passed. But a sampling of their scores on the twelfth-grade exam indicates that many of them were not meeting the standards established for that grade level. Less than 45% passed the mathematics and science sections and 25% failed the reading test. Results were quite different at Ridgewood High, where students were ranked number one in the county in the number of freshman who passed the ninth-grade exam and where 90% of seniors passed every section of the twelfth-grade exam. The lowest scores were recorded at Central City High, where 15% of students had not passed the ninth-grade exam by the end of their senior year and less than 14% passed all required sections on the twelfth-grade exam.

Once the school sites were identified, I made arrangements to meet with principals to discuss the project. I received formal permission from them and the school districts to do the research. I also had my proposal for the study approved by the university's Institutional Review Board (IRB), which requires written informed consent from students and their parents. With approvals in hand, I was ready to recruit student participants and begin data collection.

Data Collection

I conducted my fieldwork at Jefferson High from late December, 1995 to early March, 1996; at Ridgewood High in the fall of 1996; and at Central City High in the spring of 1997. I spent at least 2 months at each site in order to get a good sense of the cultural "shifts and changes [and] contradictions and tensions" in corridors and classrooms (Yon, 2000, p. 23). Another advantage of the extended periods of fieldwork was that it enabled me to build rapport with students, especially the seniors who volunteered to serve as key research participants.

I recruited the 10 key participants (Table 1.3) with the help of teachers, principals, or other staff. We looked for graduating seniors who represented a cross section of the student population in terms of racial, ethnic, and gender demographics and academic achievement.

I went to school with each of the seniors for at least 2 weeks (3 days per week) in order to observe them and document their schools' everyday cultural patterns. I accompanied them to class, traveled with them through corridors, ate lunch with them, and hung out with them and their friends before and after school. I wrote copious field notes on what I saw and heard at the end of every observation day.

TABLE 1.3
Graduating Senior Participants

Pseudonym	School	Demographics	Achievement
Adam Willis	Jefferson High	White male Working class	Average achiever
David North	Jefferson High	Black male Middle class	High achiever
Lona Young	Jefferson High	Black female Working class	Low achiever
Cassandra Sommers	Ridgewood High	Black female Working class	Average achiever
Christina Sanchez	Ridgewood High	Mexican American female Middle class	Low achiever
Peter Hsieh	Ridgewood High	Taiwanese American male Middle class	High achiever
Stuart Lyon	Ridgewood High	White male Middle class	Average achiever
Monica Reese	Central City High	Black female Low income	Average achiever
Michael Meyer	Central City High	White male Working class	High achiever
Nay Wilson	Central City High	Black female Low income	Low achiever

As I accompanied seniors, I asked them to talk about themselves, their pasts, present circumstances, and future plans in order to collect data on their identity work. I adopted this autobiographical method to capture what Munoz (1995) refers to as "stories of identity where we tell ourselves and others who we are, where we came from, and where we are going" (p. 46). I also asked them, their friends, and other seniors to explain and interpret what I was observing. Much of the data on students' impressions of corridor life and what and how teachers taught in classrooms was gathered this way.

I conducted one-on-one, semistructured, tape-recorded interviews with all of the key participants in order to capture their thoughts on cultural crosscurrents. I used the same interview guide (see Appendix) with open-ended questions grouped under economic, kinship, religious, and political domains. As is customary in ethnographic interviewing, I asked probing questions during the course of the interviews in order to clarify or enrich responses about the dominant, liminal, and other layers of U.S. culture. Each interview lasted for about 2 hours and was conducted after school or during periods of free time during the school day.

I also arranged four focus-group interviews with key participants' friends and some of their classmates. At Jefferson High, I interviewed members of Lona's clique and also conducted an interview with Adam and his friends. I tried to set up focus-group interviews with seniors' friends in other schools but was unable to work out the logistics of getting everybody together. I did, however, manage to set up sessions with other seniors who were not adequately represented by key informants. I interviewed seven White students at Ridgewood High who belonged to a Christian club and eight Black and White seniors at Central City High who were much more disillusioned with their school and life chances than were key informants.

I also spoke informally with administrators, teachers, security guards, and other school staff. I engaged in conversations with them about student characteristics and the major issues young people faced as they enter adulthood. These conversations usually took place during idle times in hallways or before classes began. School staff had a wide range of opinions about students in their particular schools and about youths in general.

By the time my fieldwork was completed in May, 1997, I had completed more than 2 months of field observations in each school, tape recorded the voices of over 30 seniors, and documented the thoughts of dozens of other students and staff. Because my data collection procedures were consistent across research sites, I was able to triangulate data to discern commonalities and disparities in how diverse seniors came of age in different schools.

Reflexivity and Literary Tropes

The crisis of representation is changing the positionings of social scientists in their research. Researchers are now having to represent themselves through reflexivity or ways of demonstrating to readers their historical and geographical situatedness, the personal investments they have in the research, how the research has affected them, and the "literary tropes" they have chosen to lend rhetorical force to the research report (Gergen & Gergen, 2000, p. 1027).

My particular interest in, and approach to, how adolescents come of age in public high schools stems from my own story of identity. I am a White woman who was born in the late 1950s into a Roman Catholic family. As a child growing up in a city near Detroit during the culturally turbulent years of the 1960s, I saw firsthand how liminal tensions could lead to race riots, war, and other divisive acts of violence, as well as to socially constructive changes through peaceful civil rights movements and other collaborative endeavors. My family moved to Wisconsin, where I went to college, left the Catholic church, became quite liberal in my ideological leanings, and eventually became certified to teach secondary social studies.

As an idealistic teacher in her mid-20s, I was hired to instruct American Indians in an Upward Bound Program. The Ojibwa, Menominee, and Winnebago students in my classes opened my eyes to the devastation that White conquest had wreaked on their cultures, identities, and prospects as Indian people. I took what I learned from them to graduate school, where I sought to explore how and why cultural differences and social factors had such negative effects on the educational experiences of historically marginalized high school students and their teachers.

For my dissertation, I decided to conduct ethnographic case studies of high-achieving Black students in urban high school contexts (Hemmings, 1996). Like American Indian students, I found that inner-city Black achievers were struggling hard to make it despite overwhelming odds against them. I also discovered that there were students from other walks of life who were surmounting social and cultural obstacles. Now, as a professor in an urban university working with school teachers, administrators, and other adults deeply committed to the education of young people, I have even stronger incentives to be with, and listen to, young people as they navigate cultural crosscurrents in their journeys through the public school system.

With the interests of youths in mind, I adopted a literary trope that foregrounds the emic experiences of research participants. My written texts include numerous verbatim excerpts from transcribed interviews and field notes that convey graduating seniors' perspectives and their actions as individuals, as members of groups representing different racial, ethnic, class, gender, and sexual locations, and as an adolescent collective. These data are enhanced by written commentaries and material drawn from an extensive body of literature. I also adopted a straightforward, accessible style of prose and refrained from constructing a thick overlay of abstract interpretation that might distort seniors' own ways of making sense out of their experiences. The seniors who participated in this research were quite conscious—indeed, acutely aware—of the content and consequences of the cultural pressures swirling around them. They were often more incisive in their critiques than many adult researchers. And much more insightful.

2

Surface Depths

American depictions of high schools are replete with images of home-coming dances, pep rallies, athletic games won and lost, and students draped in medieval caps and gowns at graduation ceremonies. Classrooms are recalled as places where teachers deliver their subject matter in dull or inspiring ways and students amuse themselves with playful antics as they learn more serious lessons. Underlying the imagery is what Metz (1990) refers to as a "basic common script for 'The American High School'" (p. 77). Students, according to the script, are offered similar classes where they are taught standard curriculum, differentiated according to their abilities and interests. Their roles and those of teachers are similarly defined, as are the outlines of classroom plots.

Common images of the American high school extend into corridor spaces, where students spend about an hour a day in hallways, lunch-rooms, and bathrooms. Teachers, security guards, and other school staff are supposed to supervise these spaces, but they tend not to intervene unless events get noticeably out of hand. Left alone in relative freedom, students form tight-knit cliques, intimate dyads, and divisive rivalries, and they play out their relations in undirected scenes where actors take most of their cues from one another.

Taken together, these images and conventions make school actors feel like participants in a "Real School ... rich with symbols of participation in a cultured society" (Metz, 1990, p. 83). And yet, teachers take great liber-ties with the common educational script as they deal with building ar-rangements, resources, and other tangible material factors, as well as the more intangible demands that society and local communities place on schools (Hemmings & Metz, 1990; McNeil, 1983, 1986; Page, 1991). Their classroom performances are affected by—indeed, ultimately dependent on—the characteristics of students (Metz, 1993). Students are major players not only in the staging of classroom plays but also in the production of corridor scenes.

The dramas of school life were so profoundly different among the research sites that they are surveyed in this chapter as contextual surfaces for later, more in-depth explorations of coming-of-age processes. Surface descriptions are based primarily on graduating seniors' general impressions of their schools. They also are informed by conversations with school staff and, of course, my own observations of what actually occurred in classrooms and corridors.

JEFFERSON HIGH

I began my fieldwork at Jefferson High on a bitterly cold, winter day in December, 1995. As I drove down the long, winding road to the school, I passed rows of small houses and apartment buildings that were owned or rented mostly by White working- and middle-class families. Most of the teenagers living in the area, as had been the case with their parents and grandparents, went to Jefferson High. When I entered the parking lot, I saw several yellow buses filled with Black students who also attended the school.

The exterior of Jefferson High's main building was regal, with tall, majestic windows framed by a neoclassical facade of pillars and a red-tiled roof lined with pointed spires. Another, less ornate building had been added to the school in the 1970s to house vocational/technical education programs. Although the addition was not as architecturally grand as the original structure, it did not detract from the school's impressive outward appearance.

As I entered the school, I was immediately struck by how dismal the interior was in contrast to the building's exterior. Corridors were dimly lit, cement-gray passageways with gothic-like arched ceilings. There was a tunnel connecting the main classroom building to a lunchroom where hundreds of students gathered in overcrowded shifts during the noon hour. Other passageways led to classrooms cluttered with piles of discarded books and broken supplies. Desks were ancient, with wooden tops covered with graffiti, profanity, gang signs, and hearts with lovers' initials carved in the middle. Chairs wobbled. Clocks did not work. Windows were clouded with grime. Student bathrooms were in disrepair, with stalls that had missing doors or out-of-order toilets. Among the bright spots in the building were a state-of-the-art computer room and well-equipped labs for technical education. They were educational sanctuaries in a school that otherwise was crumbling with neglect.

Students and teachers blamed the dilapidated interior state of Jefferson High on budget cuts resulting from voters' refusal to approve increases in tax levies. Not only had funds been cut for building maintenance, but several teachers were laid off, programs were eliminated or scaled down and there were never enough textbooks. Conditions were less than ideal as students traversed corridors on their way to and from classrooms.

JHS Corridors

Adam Willis was the first senior to show me around Jefferson High. He was a thin White boy with close-cropped light brown hair, a moustache, and half-shaved stubble on his chin. He was an average achiever who hung out with White students enrolled in Advanced Placement (AP) and other college-prep classes. He had a girlfriend, Mary Carter, who was an AP student and the news editor of the school newspaper. Mary's best friend, Katie, was the newspaper's editor-in-chief. Other members of the clique included Katie's boyfriend and a few other White girls.

On the day that I met him, Adam was wearing a sweatshirt with a picture of "Dopey," a cartoon character, printed on the front. He explained that he often wore cartoon shirts to let everyone know how much of a "joke" the school was. Adam then proceeded to guide me through corridors where hordes of teenagers leaned against lockers, strolled or scurried to various destinations, shoved or hit one another, or held each other in passionate embraces. We passed security guards at various sentry points. Their activities and those of students were carried out in a deafening din of loud talking, laughter, and shouting and shrouded in air filled with the aroma of marijuana, cigarette smoke, and occasional whiffs of perfume.

Adam, as we walked along, gave me his impressions of corridor life in a soft-spoken, pointedly serious tone of voice. He warned me to "be real careful around here" and then described student relations as being marred by hostilities:

> Kids don't get along here. Some of them hate each other. There's order here but no discipline. You can see the hallways are crowded and that all kinds of bad stuff is happening. Kids fight, they steal, they get high. I'm not afraid but I know how dangerous things can get. It's a tough school, like what I mean is that this is a tough place to go to school. You have to be a tough person to survive.

He conveyed more detailed impressions of students as we continued our journey. I saw clean-cut boys who wore pressed khaki pants and polo shirts and girls wearing nice slacks, modest blouses, or pull-over sweaters. Adam told me they were "preppies" who were "middle-class types like the kids I hang around with." We went past "jocks" involved in high-profile, extracurricular sports. Many of them wore school letter jackets, expensive athletic shoes, sports jerseys, and other emblems of their status as athletes. Preppies and jocks were "into school," according to Adam. This was not the case with White, working-class youths who formed their own cliques with names like "skinheads," "head bangers," or "grunge." Skinheads were boys who shaved their heads, tattooed swastikas on their arms, and otherwise emulated extremist White neo-Nazi hate groups. Head bangers mimicked rogue motorcycle gangs with their shiny black leather jackets draped in chains. Grunge looked like prison inmates with their over-sized jeans that sagged and drooped low in the behind. Teenagers in all of these groups pierced small gold rings through their ears, noses, lips, eyebrows, and, I was told, genitals. We passed Black students congregated in groups with their own distinctive styles. Many of them wore sports-team or name-brand overcoats throughout the day. Others preferred designer clothes that carried Tommy Hilfiger, Nautica, Versace, and other expensive manufacturing labels. There also were real and pseudo street gangs. One was an all-White gang known as Gangsters with Drama or "GWD." Another was a racially mixed gang called "PHP" or Prentice Heights Posse. Each displayed special colors, insignia, and other signs of their affiliations. There also was an artistic group of kids who looked and acted like 1960s hippies. Known as the JHUBWT (Jefferson High Underwater Basket Weaving Team), they wore tie-dyed shirts and bell-bottomed jeans and smoked marijuana. Most other students were categorized by Adam as "normal" kids who wore regular blue jeans, moderately priced athletic shoes, t-shirts, sweatshirts, and other neutral apparel.

The impression that Adam conveyed was that students in his school had taken on distinct, somewhat antagonistic roles on the corridor stage. They literally wore their differences on their sleeves and did not, at least from his standpoint, show much respect for people who were not like themselves.

The corridor scene was interpreted in an entirely different way by David North. David was a Black high achiever who had a preppie, almost scholarly look about him. He wore wire-rimmed glasses, cut his hair short, and came to school wearing nice pullover sweaters and pressed slacks. He also sported a small diamond earring in his left ear in order to "to ice any impression that I'm a total geek."

David's best friend and constant companion was Cory Duncan. Cory, like David, was an honors student who took mostly advanced classes. In corridors they would walk side by side, talking and laughing about things they had done or seen. They especially liked to compare notes on pretty girls which, David explained, was an interest stimulated by an "overdose of the male hormone." Along the way, they would exchange cheerful greetings and conversation with other students. They enjoyed a popularity that ultimately got David elected as the senior class president.

David acknowledged social divisions, especially racial divides in student relations. But the separation was not due to racism, according to him, but because "that's who our friends are." David, for his part, went out of his way to get along with everyone. "I used to be bad and fight and all that," he said. "But now I'm a new man and don't have any good reason to get into it with anyone unless they get into it with me."

Lona Young had yet another take on the corridor scene at Jefferson High. She was a tall, overweight, 19-year-old African American who wore flannel shirts, blue jeans, and well-worn athletic shoes. Although her outward appearance was nondescript like "normal" students, she did not locate herself within well-established social boundaries of cliques split along racial gender, achievement, and other lines. She was a unusual person who exuded what one of her friends described as a "magnetism" that attracted "very, very strange people" to her.

Lona's magnetism eventually drew an unusually diverse group of teenagers together into a peer clique that won the vote as the "weirdest" for the yearbook. Among the members of the clique were lesbian and gay students. Ashley, Lona's best friend, was a White lesbian who had a partner named Beth. Paul was a gay youth who, according to Lona, was one of the "sweetest" kids in the school. The clique also included DeeDee, a White girl with a baby daughter, and Carole, an African American who was pregnant with her first child. Dee Dee had a White boyfriend named Stevie (not the father of her daughter), who was a high achiever that Lona described as a "computer geek too geeky even for geeks." Randy was a disabled White boy with a traumatic brain injury incurred in a bus accident. He talked incessantly about what Lona termed "crazy things." Ricky was a White boy who dyed his hair purple. Naomi, a White girl, came to school dressed like a U.S. Marine with camouflage pants and t-shirts with the *Semper Fi* logo on the front. Jennifer, another White girl, was regarded as the most normal person in the group. Not wanting to be different, she insisted that she was just as abnormal as everyone else. There were other members who I did not get to know. But the more time I spent with Lona and her friends, the more I realized that almost all of them were troubled or had been in trouble throughout much of their adolescence.

When I asked Lona and her friends to talk about their general impressions of students at Jefferson High, most of them painted a rather bleak picture. Jennifer said students were "obnoxious, loud, pushy, slow, and unlikely to graduate," a remark that made everyone laugh. Everyone, that is, except Ashley, who said that Jefferson High was the "shit school" where kids who "don't give a shit" go. No one, she continued, really cares about students at her school:

> Nobody cares about kids here so kids don't give a damn. Kids stand in your way and if you try and say something or push them out of the way, there's always a bad attitude thrown up in the air. They don't care about you or school or anything but themselves because nobody cares about them. The security guards don't care because they're just standing around getting their paychecks. Some teachers care, but a lot of them are so afraid of kids that they just stand back and let students take over.

Paul had more positive things to say about the situation. The school had been a good place for him because of all of the nice people he had gotten to know. "I've met a lot of nice people here. My friends are real nice. They look after me which is saying a lot. School is going too fast and I'm going to miss it because of all of the people I met."

Lona had the final say with one of her many insightful views on students. "Every person in the school is different," she said, "and everyone is changing all the time. Every kid is good, bad, crazy, unique, whatever. One thing about this school is that it made me more open-minded about people. You can't throw them all together and say they're the same when they're not. They don't even stay the same, you know, like sometimes they're well adjusted and other days they go all to hell. That's how it is."

And that's how it was in the corridors of Jefferson High.

JHS Classrooms

Jefferson High, like other comprehensive public high schools in the district, offered an array of academic and vocational programs. Students were assigned to various academic tracks in special education, remedial, and regular-level programming and Advanced Placement. They could enroll in technical or school-to-work programs housed in the building that had been built as an addition to the school. According to the student handbook, the school's overall curricular philosophy was to provide students:

> with a wide variety of educational and extracurricular opportunities to prepare them for a lifetime of academic and social learning. The school's intent is to foster responsible citizenship in a democratic society and to reinforce traditional values of honesty, tolerance and dignity of work in the community, home and family.

The philosophy encapsulated the dominant ideal of public expectations for schooling. But the instructional patterns that emerged in classrooms were less than ideal as teachers wrestled with the reality of students who challenged their approaches to the basic common script.

One of the teachers I observed taught the English class in which most of the seniors in my study were enrolled. Day after day, for nearly 2 months, I watched as the teacher tried to convey standard curriculum. While half the class went along with her directions, the other half would continually crack jokes, talk or fool around with their friends, complain loudly about assigned tasks, or spend entire class periods in somnolent repose. The teacher would maneuver around the room firing off questions, calling on individuals to read passages or do writing assignments, and demanding that students "be quiet," "pay attention," or "get to work." She would shake students who had their heads down on their desks and send the most disruptive ones down to the office. Despite her stubborn resolve to move every single member of the class through the curriculum, there were students who simply refused to budge. Among them was a Black boy who arrived every day yet literally slept through class. The teacher would wake him up and threaten to fail him up if he did not pay attention. The boy would raise his head, stare blurry-eyed into space, and fall back to sleep the moment she left.

A few teachers tried to relate to students by appealing to what they considered to be adolescent interests. Adam's Advanced Placement psychology teacher would lecture about "theories of love," sex, and other somewhat off-color topics. Although some students found his approach amusing, others, like Adam and his friends, thought it was disgusting. Amused or not, everyone agreed that the class was a waste of time.

Then there were teachers who simply gave up. They would use up class time talking about nonacademic topics. Or they would hand out seat work, retreat to their desks, and let students do whatever they wanted so long as nothing and no one got hurt. They, in effect, abdicated their instructional responsibilities. Fortunately, these teachers were a minority in a school where most faculty members did what they could to ready students for adulthood despite the on-going dilemmas students created for them. The challenges they faced were very different from those at Ridgewood High, where students were growing up in what seemed to be an altogether different world.

RIDGEWOOD HIGH

Ridgewood High was located outside of the city limits in a predominantly White, upper middle-class suburb. To get there, I drove along a tree-lined boulevard with grassy medians accented with flowers planted by local volunteers. The boulevard went through a quaint downtown area with up-scale restaurants and specialty shops and meandered past parks, a town hall, a new fire station, and a public swimming pool. I turned onto the road that led to the school and drove by large, expensive homes with landscaped yards. United States census data in 1990 listed the median household income in this section of the suburb as $46,339 and the median housing unit value as $101,900. By 1996, the year that I conducted my fieldwork, a booming economy had boosted these figures to all-time highs, spawning housing developments with homes retailing at a quarter of a million dollars or more. Signs of affluence were everywhere in the places where people lived, purchased goods, worshipped, and entertained themselves. They were very evident in local public schools, like Ridgewood High, where children were sent to be educated.

The school was built in the 1970s on the side of a forested hill. The two-story, brick building was originally designed with an open classroom layout that was partitioned over time. I entered the school through a door next to a parking lot filled with cars, many of them owned by students. The door opened onto a spacious second-floor foyer with rows of lockers painted in bright school colors. The foyer and hallways were covered with brand-new, rust-colored carpet. As I walked to the administrative offices, I passed dozens of students standing or sitting on the floor. Some were gathered in the middle of the building where there was a large opening surrounded by a chest-high wall where people could lean over and look down into the cafeteria and library on the first floor. I noticed that there were no security guards. Instead, the hallways were monitored by teachers who stood idly by until the bell rang signaling the beginning of classes.

I passed by classrooms grouped together into departmental suites demarcated in colorful letters on the walls as mathematics, science, language arts, and other academic subjects. Most classrooms had small, two-person tables and chairs that faced the front of the room where the teacher's desk was positioned. All of them were well equipped with state-of-the-art computers, audiovisual equipment, books, and other supplies. There were no signs anywhere of vandalism or graffiti or garbage or grime or discarded or outdated curricular materials or broken objects and windows. Rooms were clean, modernized, and aesthetically appealing, with large rectangular windows exposing picturesque views of the woods surrounding the school.

I arrived at the office where I was scheduled to meet the assistant principal, Dr. Grayson, and the seniors who volunteered to be in the study. Dr. Grayson was a petite White woman with a soft, reserved manner. She greeted me with a warm, welcoming smile and introduced me to Stuart Lyon, Cassandra Sommers, Christina Sanchez, and Peter Hsieh. I explained my study to the students and asked if they still wanted to participate. I handed out parental consent forms after they all assented with an enthusiastic "yes." We then decided that Stuart would be the first to lead me through corridors and classrooms at Ridgewood High.

RHS Corridors

Stuart was a six-foot-tall White Jewish American. He had short auburn hair, penetrating hazel eyes, a trimmed goatee, and two earrings in his left earlobe. Most of the time he came to school wearing t-shirts, athletic shoes, and khaki slacks or jeans. He looked and acted like a "preppie," who, in contrast to Jefferson High, were what the majority of students identified as the most dominant peer grouping. Preppies were students being groomed for college and ultimately for high-status, middle-class positions. Like many other preppies, Stuart was from an affluent family. He clearly enjoyed his place in a group that literally dominated the student social scene.

Stuart loved being the center of attention. He especially liked the attention of girls, with whom he was thoroughly preoccupied. "I date a lot of girls," he said, "because I haven't found what I want yet. I like sweet girls. I like strong girls who can rein me in. I'm food to girls because I take them to nice places. They eat me up."

But not every girl ate him up. He had been dating a girl named Carrie who suddenly began to avoid him. The first day we were together, Stuart went on a single-minded mission through corridors to find Carrie or at least find out why she was avoiding him. He took me to places where she usually waited for him. She wasn't there. He asked her friends what was wrong. They didn't know. He finally concluded she was angry because he hadn't been "playing the phone game." Stuart explained how the rule of the game was to call a girl every night and "bullshit" her. When I asked why he was so determined to find Carrie, he said it was not because he wanted to go steady but, rather, to be the one who breaks off the relationship. "I can't tolerate the thought of a woman leaving me before I'm completely through with her."

Stuart was candid about his desire to "control relationships with women" (his exact words) and, for that matter, with people in general. His friends also came off as controlling preppie White boys. When I met them at lunch, I asked them to give me their impressions of themselves and other students at Ridgewood High. One of them said, "Kids here are totally stuck up. Kids are stuck up like they are into themselves. Sometimes you think you have a friend and then they turn on you. Suddenly you're no use to them so they abandon you."

Another boy said everyone tries to have a "distinguishing mark." He pointed to a boy wearing a football jersey. "That guy is the quarterback of the football team." Then he moved his finger around the cafeteria pointing at other students. "That guy is a genius, that girl is a cheerleader. That one is a musician." He then turned to me and explained how vitally important it was to have a distinguishing mark. "If you don't have it, you're a complete nobody. Everybody has to feel important like they are somebody who's known for something. It's starts at home and goes on from there."

As I trailed Stuart through the hallways, I spoke with other students with similar impressions. I chatted with a group of girls, one of whom saw the situation this way: "Kids are stuck up and snobby because they are rich and they're competitive about GPAs and things. They are told from day one by their parents that they are special and you better be smart and go to college or you're worthless." Everyone was under pressure to be self-promoting, socially successful, academically competitive, and, above all else, in control.

Peter Hsieh certainly felt the pressure. He was an Asian American about 5'9" tall with a solid, athletic build. His slicked his short black hair down with gel and had several gold rings pierced through his ears. He wore preppie garb such as khaki slacks, blue jeans, and sweatshirts with university logos on the front. A straight-A student, Peter's ambition was to enroll in a university ROTC program and become an Army officer.

Peter, like Stuart, talked about "playing the field" with girls and his ability to control people with his eyes. "There's a sucker born every second," he told me. "Just look at their eyes and that's how you find out what you can get out of them." But although he came off as a controlling preppie, Peter actually existed on the outskirts of the preppie social scene. His marginal status was more than apparent as he raced through corridors trying hard to interact with others along the way. I watched as he ran up to students and greeted them with a friendly "How's it going?" or attempted to start a conversation. Most of the time, his advances were rebuffed with frigid stares or out-and-out rejections. It did not take long for me to figure out that Peter was a social outcast searching desperately for social acceptance. He had no close friends even though he was a member of the track team, the cofounder of a student organization called the Asian U.S. Ambassadors, and in the Army reserves. Something about him caused other preppies to keep him at bay.

Like many outsiders who want to be insiders, Peter was a keen observer, especially of the teenagers with whom he longed to belong. He described Ridgewood High students as "superficial" in that they were "nice in public but suspect when people aren't looking." Students had a public image of well-behaved teenagers who did well in school, got along, followed rules, and contributed in meaningful ways to their communities. This image was reinforced by a number of facts. Students' standardized test scores were among the highest in the metropolitan area. Fights in school were infrequent and disputes, when they did occur, were usually resolved through some kind of staff intervention or by students themselves. Kids from different racial and ethnic backgrounds coexisted peacefully. They cooperated in classes, played sports together, and often accompanied each other to dances, parties, and other social events. Thefts, assaults, and other types of criminal activity were rare. Peter could not recall any arrests or incidences where police had been called out to the school. The only time he ever saw police at Ridgewood High was when they came to talk about D.A.R.E., a drug intervention program, or to direct traffic.

But students behind the scenes and out of public sight could be ruthless in their competitiveness. Kids jockeyed for positions in a social hierarchy where jocks and "white caps" (Peter's term for preppies) were at the top and "druggies, dirties, and White trash" were at the bottom. Black kids segregated themselves in the midst of the competition. There was a section in the far corner of the cafeteria that was packed at lunch with Black boys and girls from all grade levels. Much of the rest of the cafeteria was occupied by White students, who separated themselves into smaller, more exclusive cliques. Gender relations were marred by incidences of harassment and unwanted predation. "Guys," Peter said, "got this thing about hassling girls. Some girls get picked on more than others, but the hassling is pretty constant. It happens at colleges and everywhere else, so who cares. Like a guy will tell a girl, 'Hey, I saw what you were doing at that party.' Or 'You look like you want to have sex with me.' Lots of sexual stuff. Mostly sexual stuff but other stuff, too."

Students also indulged in illegal drugs. As a recovering drug addict, Peter was quite familiar with the drug scene. Most kids were casual users. Some, like him, became hooked. He explained how easy it was for rich kids to get money to buy drugs. "They get it from their parents or part-time jobs. They don't have to resort to stealing or violent crime like low-income kids in the inner city." Most drugs and alcohol were acquired and consumed at unsupervised parties or private gatherings. "In some ways," Peter said, "We're no different than the street gangs you see on TV except we can afford it and they can't."

Cassandra Sommers had much more positive things to say about her school. She was an African American who loved Ridgewood High precisely because she could be a preppie. On the day we met, she had on a nice black-and-white sweater, designer jeans, and a brand new pair of shoes. Her hair was tied back into a neat bun and she had a pair of glasses that she wore during class. Not only did Cassandra dress like a preppie, but she also acted her part on the preppie stage as an upwardly mobile Black woman with a real opportunity to secure a decent, middle-class life for herself and her son.

Cassandra was glad to be a student at Ridgewood High for other reasons that came to light as I accompanied her through the hallways. Several

Black students, Asian Americans, White boys and girls came up to her as we walked along. Cassandra always took the time to talk and listen to them. She was a popular girl who very much enjoyed what she described as a "relaxed" social atmosphere. "I would say it's real relaxed here. Our administration doesn't have to worry about kids bringing guns to school, fights happening everyday, and stuff like that because basically we get along. Basically we're all preppies."

Christina Sanchez, unlike Cassandra, purposefully distanced herself from the preppie scene. A petite Mexican American girl with long silky black hair and big brown eyes, Christina was a dissenter who, along with other girls in her clique, purposely positioned herself on the margins. Corinna, her best friend, was Japanese American. The two were inseparable, often walking arm-in-arm through the hallways. Her other friends included a Pakistani Muslim girl, a Russian immigrant, and a girl from India. Christina said the girls had become close friends because they came from families that were different from those of preppies. "Our families are really, really strict about things. Like we're not allowed to go on dates and church is the center of our lives. Preppie kids can go to parties and have cars and things. If I go to a party, I have to crawl out the window so my parents don't know. That's true for all of my friends."

Christina's clique had strong ethnic affiliations and family loyalties. But they also identified with fringe groups. Many of these groups adopted styles meant to upset middle-class sensibilities. They sported odd haircuts such as Mohawks or long pony tails sprouting from the tops of their heads with shaved scalps along the bottom. One group dressed entirely in black. Another group of girls went "totally gothic" with black lipstick and white facial makeup. Christina and her friends were attracted to artists on the fringe. They signed up for art courses where they painted pictures, carved sculptures, molded clay, and created their own self-portraits. Christina created a 1960s pop-art image of herself by wearing tie-dyed t-shirts and bell-bottomed jeans that she covered with holes and patches. Her friends were not so boldly attired, mostly because their families forbade such apparel for women.

Christina also claimed to have ties with the underworld subcultures of druggies. Although she did not actually use drugs, Christina liked druggies' antipreppie stance. "Preppies," she said,

> are the biggest hypocrites 'cause they look down on people then turn right around and copy them. They think they are so superior but are so hypocritical. Take druggies for example. Druggies smoke pot and stuff and know how to do it. They know when to do it so that no one is bothered or finds out. Preppies are into the drug trend but don't know what they're doing. They get into trouble and before you know it their parents send them to

rehab centers. Their parents come to school and want administrators to get rid of druggies. It's like they blame druggies for getting their kids into drugs when it's not true. It's preppies who copy druggies. Druggies don't copy preppies or even want to be around preppies.

Christina carried her antipreppie stance one step further. She was an underachiever who flunked math three times and barely passed her other classes. But somewhere along the line she seemed to have internalized preppie aspirations. "I want to go to college even though I don't do my homework very well. I get scared when I think about going off to college and being on my own, but then I sort of like the idea, you know, the idea of having a college degree and being on my own."

Other seemingly contradictory subjectivities began to emerge as I got to know Christina. She was trying to deal with a number of pressures including one that weighed very heavily on her and her classmates. This pressure, which permeated classroom instruction, was the expectation that students, regardless of their aspirations, were destined to go to college.

RHS Classrooms

Most Ridgewood High seniors signed up for classes in U.S. government, world literature, British literature, physics, chemistry, precalculus, and/or Algebra II. Some took electives in art, creative cooking, military history, or marketing. but the main thrust in their class schedules was to put the finishing touches on their preparation for college. Few teachers, or students for that matter, saw it otherwise. Ridgewood High was a school where over 80% of graduating seniors went on to 4-year colleges and universities. Going to college was more than an expectation. For most students, it was a given.

I observed teachers as they dedicated themselves to the transmission of college-prep curriculum. Some were methodical in their approaches, like Peter's precalculus teacher who plodded step-by-step through problem after problem pausing only to answer questions. Others were much more entertaining, like Mr. Samuels, a chemistry teacher, who was quite theatrical in his scientific demonstrations. This teacher came to class on Halloween dressed like Count Dracula and proceeded to conduct a series of what he called "spooky experiments." Students were spellbound as he told ghost stories while mixing chemicals to create witches' cauldron flames and change clear liquids into colors like "animals who in their search for light in the darkness burned themselves on the sun and stars."

Students liked their teachers and felt they were good if not exceptional. Yet they sat through many of their classes in an agitated state of restlessness that rippled across the otherwise smooth gloss of instruction. Students would talk quietly, giggle occasionally, pass around notes, or read magazines and newspapers. But despite what often looked like blatant inattention, students were quite tuned in to what their teachers were doing. When teachers called on them to repeat something or answer a question, most were able to provide the correct response. Almost all of them turned in homework assignments and studied for tests. They did what they were expected to do, I was told again and again, because they were extremely grade conscious. Although they may not have been personally interested in school work, they were very interested in earning high GPAs so they could go to college.

Academic classes at Ridgewood High were augmented by weekly counseling programs. Administrators believed there was such a high number of students with nonacademic problems that they decided to provide counseling that could be incorporated into class schedules. Cassandra was heavily involved in these programs as both a recipient and deliverer of services. She got involved in peer mediation as a sophomore and eventually became a mediator herself. She credited the program with helping her become a better student and "a somebody":

> Through peer mediation I learned how to work on my problems better. Basically what I learned is that I am somebody. That they care about me here and don't just want to suspend me. They want everybody to be somebody.

The language of being somebody (or having a distinguishing mark) was clear in Cassandra's interpretation of the overall purpose of peer mediation. "The whole idea," she said, "is to be proud of who you are, not let anyone push you around, and be a leader not a follower."

Cassandra also was a member of the "grieving group," which she joined after the death of her father. Peter belonged to the "mixed relationship group" set up for students having problems with relationships. Peter said the group was for "dysfunctional people" and that he had been a member for over a year and a half. There were other groups for recovering alcoholics and drug addicts, pregnant teens, and kids suffering from depression. Whether or not these programs fostered higher self-esteem or better relationships or solved other personal problems, they certainly complemented an instructional trajectory geared toward moving students into the most privileged centers of middle-class society. They helped adolescents to stay the course no matter what obstructions they hit along the way.

CENTRAL CITY HIGH

To get to Central City High, I drove along a heavily congested interstate highway past manufacturing plants, warehouses, office buildings, and dozens of other commercial enterprises. I headed downtown where sky-scrapers towered over newly constructed athletic stadiums, restaurants, and condos. The visual scenery out of my window was that of vibrant urban renewal spurred on by a booming economy. But it evaporated the moment I got off the exit ramp and entered the street that led to the school. I suddenly found myself in a world of grinding poverty in the midst of great prosperity.

One side of the street was lined with low-rent housing projects comprised of four-story brick apartment buildings with names like The Courtyards, Red Bush, and Riverside. They were enclosed within steel chain-link fences that were littered along the bottom with empty liquor bottles, beer cans, cigarette butts, disposable diapers, and other trash. Most of the families who resided in the projects were African American. Some were White Urban Appalachian. On the other side of the street were small businesses, a store-front Jehovah's Witness church, a Catholic elementary school, an adult vocational center, and a police station. Central City High stood on the corner across from the police station. Together, these places formed the nucleus of a community of neighborhoods known as the Upper Banks.

In 1996, 25% of the city's population lived below the poverty line. There were 1088 cases of murder, rape, and other violent felonies and over 6520 reports of property crimes. Much of the poverty and crime were concentrated in the Upper Banks, where unemployment rates were among the highest in the city and where neighborhoods ranked at the top in all categories of crime and crime service calls. The area was especially besieged with criminal activity perpetrated by young people between the ages of 14 and 25. Many of these youths were or had been students at Central City High.

As I approached the school, I was struck by how much it resembled a prison complex. The parking lot and playing fields in the back were surrounded by a chain-link fence with barbed wire strung along the top. The plain, red-brick school building had five sets of doors that were locked except for those in the front facing the street. Security guards were posted at the front doors, screening everyone who went in and out. Windows were covered with bars and student bathrooms had stalls without latches and often without toilet paper.

The prison-like layout reinforced Central City High's public reputation as a dangerous school overrun with Black hoodlums. The principal, Mr. Cole, was an African American administrator who did whatever he could to offset the school's bad image. He kept up good appearances by making sure that hallways were kept meticulously clean and decorated with colorful artwork, pep rally posters, and enlarged framed photographs of students and teachers at school events. Classrooms were painted pastel yellow, light green, and other cheerful hues. Although some rooms were cluttered with books and supplies, most were kept neat and in fairly good repair. Gang signs and graffiti would occasionally appear on walls but were quickly erased by a diligent maintenance crew. It was Mr. Cole's determined hope that such fastidious attention to the school's interior would help to allay the widespread belief that Central City High was a real prison full of young offenders.

Students were well aware of their school's bad reputation. Monica Reese, one of the three graduating seniors who participated in the study, agreed there were lots of "thugs" in her school, but she also insisted that there were a lot of good students, too. "All of these kids," she said, "make this school what it is."

> Because if you have a school full of thugs which probably has happened in Central's history, you know, people who don't care about school or don't care about themselves, then you get all of the stereotypes that we have. But we have students who come through that do care about school, do care about self-respect. They get the bad end 'cause everybody has it in their head that this is a bad school. It's unfair to them that people think that way but, you know, it's up to us to change how they think.

Although Monica felt students were being unfairly stereotyped as bad kids, she also acknowledged that many of her classmates made certain adaptations in order to survive in the Upper Banks. Nowhere was this more visible than in the corridors.

CCH Corridors

Graduating seniors constituted a small proportion of students at Central City High. Only 95 students out of over 500 who entered as freshman made it to the twelfth grade. Out of that number, only 67 had the credit hours and passing state-exam scores necessary for graduation. Almost 80% of the original class of 1997 had moved away, transferred, been expelled from, or dropped out of school. The rest were survivors.

Among the survivors was Michael Meyer, who was the first senior scheduled to show me around. Michael arrived late to school the day we were supposed to begin. I tracked him down with the help of Amber Solomon,[5] an African American advisor for the CASE school-to-work program, who worked in the school. As we headed to Michael's first-period class, I noticed several students milling around the hallways. Amber said kids were constantly in corridors and that security guards did little or nothing about it. "We have a situation here," she explained, "where people know each other well, almost too well." Student and staff relations were characterized by an intimate familiarity that, in Amber's opinion, greatly undermined professional conduct:

> I'm appalled at how unprofessional the staff is. Teachers have their hearts in the right place but they try to be cool with kids so their classes are comfortable. They lower their standards to the point where classes are a joke. Security guards get too friendly with kids. Some of the girls flirt with them and I see guards going right along with it. I've counted seven guys walking around who aren't students. They come off the streets and sell drugs or whatever. Guards let them in and don't check them like they are supposed to.

Lax adult control over students was evident in corridors where students constantly wandered around talking casually with peers or guards, eating snack foods, or doing other things. As we passed by students, I heard many of them speaking local hip-hop street lingo heavily laced with obscenities. Most of them were dressed in the latest, hippest fashions. The idea, according to Amber, was to "be cool." Images of coolness varied among students, but there were distinctive types such as boys known as *playas* who emulated the mack-daddy personas of street hustlers and *fly girls* who were playas' female counterparts. There were other students who were not as flashy as playas and fly girls, but they nevertheless paid careful attention to their outward images. The last thing they wanted was to be regarded as a preppie or "punk" who looked foolish, weak, or, even worse, like someone who was acting White.[6]

Despite their intimate familiarity and conformity to images of coolness, students developed intense rivalries. Amber said fistfights and verbal arguments were common as students settled disputes or sought respect. In the midst of their rivalries, kids banded together into tight-knit cliques and gangs. The kids who resided in the apartment projects formed cliques known as the Courtyarders, Red B's, Riversiders, or other derivatives of building names. A few belonged to well-organized street gangs like Vice Lords or to more loosely organized quasi gangs. Most of the rest stuck together in pairs or unnamed groups through good times and bad. Making the best of good times was what mattered most as students interacted during the school day.

Amber and I finally found Michael halfway through his first-hour AP English class. He was the lone White student in this and most of his other classes. He also was the senior class valedictorian with a 4.0 GPA. I wondered how it was possible for him to be an academically achieving White boy among street-wise Black youths. Michael let me know right away that he did this by associating with a certain set of students. There were, he explained, two sets at his school. The set he belonged to was comprised of good students who had been together since junior high. The other set included kids who were "too big" for school. "Kids in the other set are the ones who drop out, fool around a lot. They get too big for school, you know, they think they know all there is to know and leave. You see them driving fancy cars and wearing expensive clothes and then two years later they are on the street corners begging for money. I don't have a whole lot to do with them."

His set separated themselves from other kids by signing up for AP, AA, and other advanced classes. But cordoning himself off in upper-track classes was not enough for Michael. He also had to deal with his Whiteness in corridors, which he did by projecting in-vogue images of coolness. He came to school wearing baggy designer jeans and the exact same brand of athletic shoes worn by Black boys. He darkened and slicked back his light-brown hair with gel and wore gold necklaces, a gold ring with his initials spelled out in fake diamonds, and a brand new gold class ring.

He looked very cool. He also was astute enough to know that in his school, truly cool White kids hang out with Black kids. "Some White kids come here who haven't been around Blacks. They keep to themselves 'cause they're scared or don't know what to do. Black kids see that and think the kid is prejudiced or a wimp and before you know it, they start to hassle him. So what you got to do if you're White is get to know Blacks, don't be scared and don't be stand-offish."

Hanging out with Blacks meant acting Black, which Michael did with extraordinary deftness. He spoke to me in Standard English, but in the company of Black peers he would switch over to hip-hop speech codes. He blended in so well that his words and actions were virtually indistinguishable from those of his Black peers.

Nay Wilson also knew how to maneuver around streets and corridors, having resided in the apartment projects since birth. She dressed like a fly girl in short skirts and tight-fitting shirts and wore several gold chains and rings with fake diamonds. She had a gold front tooth and a tattoo of her name above her left breast. Although she looked like a fly girl, Nay, as she talked about herself, tried to create the impression that she was one of the good students even though her grades were low. Her stated goal was to finish high school, go to the nearby vocational school, and become a nurse.

Although Nay was quite forthcoming about her personal goals, she initially talked in vague terms about her classmates and school. The ice broke when she took me to an administrative office where she often went during her free periods. She let the office secretaries check me out before she clued me in.

The secretaries were united in their impressions of students. One of them told me, while the others nodded in agreement, that "Kids here aren't angels but they aren't all that bad either."

The more you get to know them, the more you have to love them. It's easy for someone on the outside to assume what's going on in here is bad. But they don't know what's really happening. If they came in here like you and get to know kids, they would have to love them because of what they're go-ing through. What I'm saying is that if people knew what these kids were going through, they would love 'em.

The secretaries stressed the importance of caring about kids in a man-ner that I did not hear at the other high schools. Their speech was imbued with an ethic of care as they told me how they dealt with kids who con-fronted incredible hardships. As one of the secretaries put it, "Someone has to stick up for these kids. We care about kids in this school 'cause no one else does. It's like a battle. We stick up for them while it seems every-one else in the country wants to throw them in jail. It's no wonder they get into so much trouble."

Nay listened for a while before stating her own opinion. "Kids," she said, "also have to care. There are too many kids who don't care about themselves or what they're doing. There's girls having babies who don't care about having any money. A lot of kids don't care about school and it's not because their mamas aren't home. As for myself, I'm going to do it right. I'm comin' to school and will not have a baby until I can afford it."

Monica Reese certainly cared about school. A good student with a 3.6 GPA, she had already been accepted to a college. She had a part-time job in a marketing firm where she worked on computers. And she had accom-plished all of this despite the fact that she had been raised by a "poor momma" in the apartment projects. "You're probably thinking I'm one of the lucky ones," she quipped. "But I'm telling you that I worked for what I got and no one can take that away."

Monica was blunt in her opinion about my research on teenagers. "It's teenagers this and teenagers that," she said. "Everything you hear is about teenagers and all their problems but you seldom hear about what is going on with little kids. I'm telling you the problems start when kids are small. I feel it's all over for them when they become teenagers. They get hardened. They've already messed up bad or are making it somehow. We need to start worrying about the ninth graders on down and make sure it's okay for them because it's too late for teenagers. Way too late."

She felt there were a number of students at Central City High already "hardened" and on their own because parents couldn't take care of them:

Parents are on welfare, can't get jobs, or don't know what the hell to do to make money so they leave it up to kids to take care of themselves. It's got-ten to where a lot of teenagers are taking care of their parents. I know this guy who was real smart in school until he dropped out to sell drugs. He pays his momma's rent, buys stuff for his kids, and doesn't see any other way to make it big. His momma says "You just keep doing what you're doing," so he's like the man of the house and he's only eighteen.

Students, as far as Monica was concerned, did what they had to do to handle the situations in which they found themselves. She certainly did what she felt she had to do to survive in the streets and get through school. Like Nay, she came to school dressed like a fly girl in skin-tight dresses with skirt lengths that rose half-way up her thigh. She adorned herself with gold jewelry and had tattoos on her breast. But unlike Nay, Monica was much more successful as a classroom achiever. She adapted well to the ways in which teachers adapted to students.

CCH Classrooms

Central City High instituted a team-teaching approach to instruction. Teachers who taught mathematics, English, and other subjects were grouped together into teams and assigned the same group of students for the duration of their years in school. The philosophy of the approach was to facilitate effective professional collaboration among faculty while fostering a sense of community for students. Team members ideally collaborated in ways that promoted academic achievement. But they faced such obstacles in their work with students that even the best-laid plans and most determined joint efforts often yielded limited results.

The teachers who worked with the senior class were known as the Blue Ribbon team. Members included three White women who taught English, mathematics, and history and a White man who taught science. There were other teachers in other subject areas who were not core members but often attended daily team meetings. I went to some of these meetings and listened as teachers discussed ways to deal with students who cut classes, were chronically tardy, or hadn't been in school for days. They talked about parents who were upset because their son or daughter was not going to graduate, a boy who had just been arrested, a girl who had been sexually molested, and about other kids in crises.

I also observed team members in their classes. They wanted to follow educational scripts but were continually stymied by highly social teenagers. Students would talk, yell, laugh loudly, sleep, pass notes, swear, eat, hug, hit, and play around despite their teachers' efforts to rein them in. This also happened in Advanced Placement classes where Monica said kids had been together so long and knew each other so well that they "just can't shut up. "

Most members of the Blue Ribbon team tried to take control of the situation by striking some kind of balance between the ethic of care and strict discipline. One of them told me how teachers had to be caring or students would stop coming to school. "Kids come because they want to and not because they feel they have to. Parents won't make them come to school so if they show up it's because they choose to be here. We teachers have to be pleasant and caring to convince kids that school is a wonderful place to hang out during the day. If it's not wonderful, they won't come. Period."

She also said that a caring approach was absolutely necessary because kids were not getting the care they needed at home. The teacher sounded like the secretaries when she said, "If we don't care, then God knows what would happen to these kids. They probably would end up in jail or something."

Teachers also talked about the necessity of being disciplinarians in full command of instructional activities. One of them discussed the importance of discipline and how it was something that students both needed and craved. "These kids, these young people understand the importance of discipline but they don't always get it at home or anywhere else. They don't have adults in their lives setting up boundaries or laying down the law. They want that. They crave it. Even though they fight it, they know deep down inside that discipline is important."

Providing care and enforcing discipline turned out to be much easier said than done. Michael, Nay, and Monica were all enrolled in the same AP English class so I saw quite a bit of Ms. Hathaway, the teacher. Day after day, Ms. Hathaway would greet students entering her class with a warm, welcoming smile and kind words. She would show care by asking students how things were going for them or if they had any problems she could help them with. A few students responded to her expressions of care. Most walked right past her into the classroom, where they sat down and began talking with their friends. Once the class officially began, Ms. Hathaway would change gears and try to implement more take-command, disciplinary practices. But her attempts at taking control were inevitably challenged by students who had their own agendas.

Whereas Ms. Hathaway agonized over her disciplinary tactics, most other teachers settled into a routine where they maintained a semblance of care and discipline by being pleasant to students and assigning easy desk work. Teachers would pass out worksheets or tell students to write out answers to textbook questions. They would then sit down at their desks, wander quietly around the room, or otherwise fade into the background. Students would talk as they did their work, glancing up and down at their papers as they chatted back and forth with each other. It was not at all uncommon for them to copy someone else's paper, often in full sight of the teacher. I observed only one student who always did assigned work quietly and on his own. That student was Michael, the senior class valedictorian, who was the lone solitary exception in an intensely social crowd.

3

Economic Domain: Il/licit Pursuit of Mobility

There is perhaps nothing high schools in the United States promise more than a chance for young people from all walks of life to pursue upward mobility. Formal education has long been touted as a ticket out of poverty, as a conduit for passing along affluence from one generation to the next, and as an otherwise reliable means for achieving success within the highly competitive, capitalistic American economy. The graduating seniors in my study all agreed that adults without at least a high school education are at a great disadvantage if they hope to amass wealth, find meaningful, personally gratifying work, and live a good, lucrative life. But whether or how they pursued mobility within their particular high schools depended on how they were geared in their identity work toward economic opportunities as well as how they were positioning or being positioned for integration into the job market. Through it all, they were very much caught up in the il/licit discourses of money and occupational gratification flowing through crosscurrents in the American economic domain.

DISCOURSES OF MONEY AND OCCUPATIONAL GRATIFICATION

Sociologists since the middle of the 19th century have emphasized social class as the single most powerful factor explaining and predicting people's position within capitalistic economies. But whereas social class is a focal point in sociology, it is not emphasized among ordinary Americans. As Ortner (1991) noted in her reading of America, people in the United States generally do not flaunt inherited ranks or present themselves in class terms. What they do instead is express a discourse of money, the main tenet of which is that money really is power. People who have money have the power to buy goods, services, status, freedom, happiness, and more power. With the expansion of the global economy and the explosion of consumerism, there is even more reason to believe that money will, in fact, purchase a better life.

Accompanying the discourse of money is the discourse of occupational gratification. Americans in the past may have looked upon work as a duty or necessity to be performed regardless of whether or not it was self-fulfilling. But such stoicism has receded as more people, especially young people, are encouraged to find jobs that are fun and interesting, prestigious and important, that put them in charge or allow them to do other things they want to do. To be trapped in an occupation that is not personally gratifying has become many Americans' idea of oppression.

The discourses of money and occupational gratification, like others discussed throughout this book, are ensconced in a more fundamental notion of individualism. Individualism, as Bellah, Madsen, Sullivan, Swidler, and Tipton (1985) explained, is a "habit of the heart" comprised of common understanding so basic to the American identity that it cuts across cultural traditions:

> Whatever the differences among traditions and the consequences of differences in their understandings of individualism, there are certain things they all share, things that are basic to American identity. We [Americans] believe in the dignity, indeed the sacredness, of the individual. Anything that would violate our right to think for ourselves, judge for ourselves, make our own decisions, live our lives as we see fit, is not only morally wrong, it is sacrilegious. (p. 142)

It is in tension with the equally cherished American value of the common good. But as a defining discursive orientation, individualism shores up discourses in the economic domain by exalting the ideal that every person, regardless of his or her background, may choose to pursue whatever economic goals he or she desires. Everyone agrees that such pursuits begin with the economic self.

THE ECONOMIC SELF

Children in the United States are frequently asked the question, "What do you want to be when you grow up?" Most know full well that the questioner is not interested in what they will become in some existential sense. They understand that the question they are really being asked is, "What are your economic ambitions?" Children learn fairly early in life that they are expected to form an identity with an economic core self that can prosper in a highly competitive, capitalistic system. The economic self, simply defined, is comprised of the subjective, psychocultural commitments that position, direct, and discipline people in their economic pursuits. In the United States, it is constructed and expressed in terms of personal aspirations aimed at economic success (making money) and as orientations toward work.

Pressures to construct a viable economic self mount during adolescence. Some teenagers' aspirations become so well defined that they know exactly what careers they want and how they will go about pursuing them. Many are ambivalent, diffuse, or uncertain about their goals. Others are decidedly entrepreneurial in their orientations. A few teenagers may experience a calling or divinely inspired mission to perform work where they are subsumed into a community where activities have meaning and value in and of themselves. Or they may be opportunistically poised to take advantage of whatever good prospects happen to come along.

How adolescents go about constructing an economic self is guided by their innate dispositions, personal life histories, and real or perceived work opportunities. It is affected by their race, ethnicity, class, gender, sexual orientation, and other social locations. And it is influenced by conventional workplace roles deemed normal for them and by movements that upset the status quo. Economic self formation is thus shaped by a range of pressures that can reinforce, constrain, or crush economic desires.

But when I asked graduating seniors what they wanted to be when they grew up, most of them spoke as if such pressures did not matter at all. They sounded like young, upwardly mobile adults who were fairly certain about the directions they planned to take and their good prospects for the future. A number of them aspired to follow new career paths being ushered in by advances in computer technologies. David North, a Black student at Jefferson High, wanted to become a computer engineer specializing in "hardware and software-specific operating systems." Monica Reese was a Black girl at Central City High, who despite the fact that she was living in poverty, saw no reason why she could not become a computer programmer. "Nothing can stop me except myself." Her White, working-class classmate, Michael Meyer, had plans to become a mechanical engineer with "excessive computer skills." Cassandra Sommers, a working-class Black student at predominantly White, middle-class Ridgewood High, said she "loved computer marketing" and believed she would have no trouble being a marketer because businesses would always need them. "As long as people have businesses, they're going to need marketing and retail to be there. We're going to have to sell products to keep people going. So I think there will always be marketing jobs, especially for people like me who aren't afraid of computers." Adam Willis, a White, working-class boy at Jefferson High, decided to enter the horticulture field and become a landscaper. He, too, felt it was important to know something about computers. "Computers are what it's all about in today's times," he said. "If you don't know how to use computers, you don't know how to do anything."

Not everyone jumped on the computer band wagon. Lona Young, a Black girl at Jefferson High, regarded herself as a natural-born counselor and thought she would like a career where she could help people with "big problems." Nay Wilson, a low-income Black student at Central City High, wanted to be a nurse. Christina Sanchez, a Mexican-American girl at Ridgewood High, thought she might enter a helping profession and be a professional artist. "I guess I could do both, you know, help people and be an artist."

Peter Hsieh, a Taiwanese-American at Ridgewood High, had ambitions of becoming an infantryman in the U.S. Army. His goal was to achieve the rank of colonel in command of "planning stages of war." Stuart Lyon, an upper-middle-class White boy, wanted to become an environmental litigator, which meant going to college, law school, and "probably some kind of grad school." Other seniors were much less sure about their economic aspirations. But certain or not, there was common agreement that it was ultimately up to them to form their own economic self and to integrate that self into the economic domain. As a Black boy at Central City High put it:

> To make it in this country, well, it's all in your own mind, the individual mind. You choose what you're going to do. You think about the pressures on you. You take it all up here [in your head] and think about how you're going to do this or that. You make your own decisions, then you use your will to get it done. It's your will that gets it done because in this country you're on your own.

But making it on one's own turned out to be much easier said than done, as was made evident during more in-depth explorations of how graduating seniors navigated economic crosscurrents within their schools.

DOMINANT CURRENCIES

Hard Work Through Least Resistance

High schools in the United States are expected to endorse dominant economic discourses as they prepare youths for various economic opportunities. They are to pave the way for money-making, personally gratifying pursuits through the transmission of knowledge, skills, and other cultural currencies deemed necessary for success in college or the workplace. High schools also promote the belief that success ultimately depends on adherence to the American work ethic.

The American work ethic is all pervasive. It encourages people to eschew lifelong financial dependence on relatives, the government, or other sources of income by committing themselves to the disciplinary practices of hard work. These practices are marked by competent performance; compliance with workplace rules, standards, and procedures; deference to, or exercise of, legitimate authority; and punctuality, efficiency, and productive time on task. Those who abide by the ethic and its practices understand that their economic goals may take a long time to accomplish. They come to accept the fact that gradual accumulation of money and delayed occupational gratification are probable, if not likely, consequences of an orientation that ultimately holds individuals responsible for their own economic gains and losses.

The work ethic is so familiar, so hegemonic, so deeply ingrained in the American psyche, that every high school senior in my study recited it as an integral part of their own orientations. All of them discussed the ethic in terms of the individual economic power they believed it would eventually give them. David was emphatic that anyone, including Black men like him, could achieve personal prosperity if they worked hard enough. "I think anyone in this country is in a good position to make it as long as they work hard. Like, you can be from the lowest of the low and really bad off and still work hard and get lots and lots of stuff."

Nay, who grew up in poverty, constantly referred to the ethic. She talked repeatedly about her determination to go to work "even if it means standing on my feet for eight hours 'cause I don't see no other way to stop being so poor." Stuart, who came from an affluent White family, had every intention of putting forth "maximum effort" in his quest for success. "My parents can pay for my college education or maybe I got a rich uncle who gives me a business loan. But if I don't cut it in college or make the business successful, then it's my fault. I'm the bottom line."

Although seniors described themselves as adherents of the work ethic, many of them did not adopt the ethic's strict disciplinary practices, especially the ones typically associated with schools. As students, they were expected to go along with what could be a very ungratifying schoolwork regime with few choices in job assignments and limited material rewards. They were required to sign up for classes in English, social studies, the sciences, mathematics, and other subjects regardless of their personal interests. They were to follow teachers' dictates as they learned curricular material and subjected their work to assessment procedures intended to evaluate and rank their levels of mastery. The schoolwork regimes students encountered were not solely about the transmission and learning assessments of cultural currencies. They also were about control. Teachers, when they assigned work tasks, did so with classroom management in mind. They would direct students to fill out worksheets, listen quietly to lectures, and participate in other instructional routines not so much because they facilitated optimal learning but, rather, because they effectively controlled student behavior (McNeil, 1983, 1986). Although teachers adjusted instructional scripts in response to various factors, most of the regimes established in classrooms were well within recognized parameters for defining and regulating the daily production and management of student work.

Graduating seniors accepted and even defended the schoolwork regime. But they also experienced it as tedious, overly difficult, too time consuming, or unfair. Although most of them viewed regimes as important for their futures, they also felt there were times when regimes impeded their progress. They were simultaneously supportive of, and repulsed by, the work practices that were supposed to ensure their integration into the economy and other American community domains.

Abundant literature exists on how high school students purposefully reject schoolwork as acts of resistance against an educational system that does not appear to serve their economic or other interests.[7] Students, especially working- and lower-class White youths and youths of color, have resisted schooling in a manner that has caused them to fail, fall behind, or drop out. But this was not the tack taken by the graduating seniors in my study. They had come a long way through school and were not about to give up their chances to graduate. What many of them did instead was follow paths of least resistance where they limited their actual adherence to the work ethic in their adaptations to the schoolwork regime. They became "minimalists," described by Peter Hsieh in an interview as kids who do just enough work to make it through their particular schools.

> **Peter:** People think that I'm a guy who spends 12 hours a day on homework but that's crap. I'm a minimalist. I do only minimal homework to get good grades.
>
> **AH:** Are other kids "minimalists?"
>
> **Peter:** Oh, yeah. Yeah. Most kids are. Like in this school [Ridgewood High] everyone expects us to go to college. They want us to bust our butts, but most of us just kind of coast, you know, take it easy even when the going gets rough.

Minimalists follow paths of least resistance by investing minimal amounts of time and effort into assigned work or by minimizing assigned workloads through tactical ploys intended to loosen or usurp teachers' controls. Although least resistance was apparent at all three research sites, there were distinctive variations in patterns that reflected the kinds of pressures that were placed on students to go along with dominant discourses.

Compliance with dominant discourses was intense at Ridgewood High, where "preppies" were under enormous parental pressure to earn high grade-point averages and meet other criteria for admission to college. As youths being groomed to keep their middle-class status, they were primed to accept the authority of teachers to control the nature and pace of schoolwork.[8] In spite of such pressures, they nevertheless attempted to assume some control over teachers' control by placing limits on the work they actually did. I observed several classes where students insisted that teachers spell out precisely how many math problems they had to solve; how many pages, paragraphs, and sentences they had to write; how many correct answers they needed to get an A; and other exact minimal expectations. If expectations were too stringent or time consuming, students would dicker with teachers or find other ways to make assigned tasks less demanding. Occasionally, they would resort to cheating, as was the case with Stuart who, in one of his classes, would copy the work of a girl sitting next to him. "She likes me," he said with a smirk. "Who am I not to take advantage of that?"

Patterns at the other schools were driven more by students' desire to finish high school than by pressures to get into college. Lona and most of her friends at Jefferson High had gotten off to a bad start as freshmen and continued to experience academic problems well into their senior year. Lona talked about how she had gone to a Catholic elementary school, where she earned good grades and was a "holy child." Then in the seventh grade she entered a public middle school where she "went to hell." Lona failed eighth grade and was on the verge of flunking out of high school in tenth grade when she suddenly "saw the light" and decided it was in her best interest to graduate. But doing schoolwork, even minimal amounts of it, was difficult. She blamed herself for many of the problems she had with the completion of assignments. But she and her friends also blamed their difficulties on teachers who, they said, "don't give a damn" and on curriculum that was "out of touch with reality." By far the biggest issue for them were classroom assignments that one of them described as turning "unsuspecting kids into mindless nerds." They simply did not like or see much reason in doing the particular work tasks they were asked to do. So as was the case with many of their classmates, they ended up following paths of least resistance that caused teachers to drastically lower their standards and otherwise compromise their control over the content and pace of instruction.[9]

Jefferson High students loosened teachers' grip on the schoolwork regime by talking, laughing, or fooling around with their friends as they hassled or complained to teachers about assignments. Most adopted more passive tactics such as putting their heads down on desks, staring out the window, doodling, or writing notes to their friends. Teachers did what they could to regain control and put students to work. I watched an English teacher as she pranced around the classroom trying to motivate her classes by lifting students heads off their desks or threatening to sanction those who refused to do their assignments. Others attempted to make schoolwork more palatable, like an art teacher who asked students to write a "movie review" of a colorful slide show she presented on African-American painters or a psychology teacher who would ask student to write essays about the slightly off-color lectures he delivered on sex and theories of love. Although Jefferson High teachers utilized a range of instructional techniques, most ended up making significant concessions to students. They watered down the curriculum, made it much simpler to achieve passing grades, and, of particular interest to students, meted out quick-and-easy schoolwork. Members of Lona's clique took full advantage of the minimization of teachers' controls as they inched closer and closer to high school graduation.

The schoolwork regime was at its minimalist best (or worst) at Central City High, where teachers made huge concessions or surrendered altogether to students who spent entire class periods cavorting with their friends. It was not at all unusual for seniors to be given work that took only a few minutes to complete in class and to leave class without any homework. "We have it pretty easy sometimes, like sometimes," Monica said. "But we're doin' the work, I mean, some of it, maybe not all of it, but some of it."

There were, of course, seniors who worked very hard. They were extremely conscientious although they were inclined to hide the fact. Despite Peter's claim that he was a "minimalist," his outstanding academic achievements suggested otherwise. But he was careful not to reveal how much time and effort he actually devoted to schoolwork in accordance with another, antiwork ethic. This ethic makes it socially inappropriate for anyone who is a hard worker to show off, or show up, those who are not. Students who openly flaunt maximum effort in their schoolwork run the risk of being ostracized as social misfits, labeled a "nerd" or other derogatory names, or subjected to abuse. Being pegged as someone who publicly "sucks up" to teachers was, according to Michael, the "kiss of death" at his school and, for that matter, in other schools. If a student does decide to work hard, he or she better hide it, deny it, or in the case of Michael, weave it into everyday routines as if it were as natural as eating, sleeping, or engaging in casual conversations (as Michael occasionally did) with acquaintances.

The extent to which students put the American work ethic into practice was affected by pressures from parents and peers as well as by the schoolwork regimes established by teachers. But it also was influenced by how they were being positioned, or hoped to position themselves, within dominant divisions of labor.

DOMINANT DIVISIONS OF LABOR

Upward mobility in the U.S. economy is often conceived of as a ladder with stratified divisions of labor. High school seniors certainly recognized the existence of labor divisions. But rather than discuss these divisions in hierarchical, class-based terms, they spoke of them as a patchwork of occupational traditions. Their perspectives were much more in line with social anthropologist Cohen (1974), who theorized that capitalistic economies in pluralistic countries like the United States are divided into bounded niches inhabited by different groups. Groups monopolize or vie for economic positions within these niches through elaborate social networks and cultural systems that offer certain advantages to their members. Members not only tend to share similar social class locations, but they also are joined together by cultural understandings providing assurances that they and their descendants will succeed within their own or other groups' economic niches.[10]

Cohen focused particular attention on how ethnic groups secure economic positions through social ties and the transmission of traditional cultural prescriptions. Numerous ethnic groups in the United States have sustained intergenerational strongholds in various occupational niches by carving out cultural tributaries that enabled them to secure and sustain their particular livelihoods. Amish farmers for centuries have maintained an economically viable way of life through a stable, agrarian-based cultural system. Other ethnic groups have incorporated newfound economic skills into age-old traditions. There is a Mohawk Indian tribe in New York that became well known for its expertise in the construction of skyscrapers after members incorporated modern ironwork skills into the fabric of their tribal culture. Whereas economic strongholds have worked to the benefit of some groups, they have contributed to the perpetuation of stereotypes that may or may not provide advantages to other groups.

Peter Hsieh, as a Taiwanese-American, was well aware of how people of Asian descent are often stereotyped as "model minorities" who excel in science, engineering, and other careers requiring advanced mathematical and technical skills. When I asked if Taiwanese culture had anything to do with this stereotype, Peter said, "Culture has everything to do with it. My family's culture is basically Chinese and Chinese people are taught to work real hard, especially in school. You're supposed to work hard and not complain. If you fail you bring shame onto yourself and your family, which is very bad. So, yeah, the stereotypes are there as long as the culture is there."

Although other seniors noted the impact of ethnic traditions, most were inclined to regard race and gender as much more powerful determinants of how groups in the United States are positioned within the patchwork of dominant economic niches. This was especially true among Black seniors, who saw Black people as having been historically relegated to low-wage, subordinate jobs that offer little in the way of individual advancement. Their talk about these positionings rubbed up against some of the other stances they took within dominant currents. Recall David North's emphatic insistence that individuals, regardless of their backgrounds, could fulfill their chosen economic goals through hard work. Yet he was just as adamant that race has been and continues to be the most significant factor affecting who has access to the most lucrative and prestigious occupations. Upper- echelon jobs, he said, "are owned by Whites. The reality is that big companies and corporations are mostly White owned, White operated, a White board of directors, like White-operated businesses. As long as Black people are minorities, we have to put up with that. It's not fair but it's reality. Sometimes I get angry, but anger for me is like a motivation to do my best even though everywhere I look I see White people."

Monica Reese also recognized how White people monopolized the best jobs. But she offset this view with the belief that it was possible for Black women like her to achieve upward mobility in the business world by accommodating to (White) corporate culture. Monica saw "proper style" as key to her success. "I know that if I'm going to succeed I have to have proper style. I have to talk proper [standard American] English and wear business suits. I have to act like I'm educated so that people think I know what I'm doing. Some people would say I'm acting White but to me it's just acting properly, you know, like a professional lady with style."

Both Monica and David regarded White-dominated occupations as offering the most in the way of monetary gains and gratification. But whereas Monica felt confident that accommodation to dominant White corporate culture would lead her to the centers of economic power, David was convinced that Black people would continue to find themselves in "po Black folk jobs."

> **David:** We were janitors, garbage collectors, cleaning ladies, and stuff like that. Things have gotten better for Black people, but there's still this lingering thing that all Black people are good for is po Black folk jobs.
>
> **AH:** What are "po Black folk jobs?"

David: You know, I know you know. It's waiting on people, White people.

Gender also was identified as a significant factor in sustaining dominant divisions of labor. Seniors recognized the highly gendered, unequal nature of workplace relations. All of them agreed that men were much more likely than women to hold positions of authority. Michael Meyer explained how most bosses are men who prefer "other guys around than put a lot of responsibility on a woman." Monica observed how the women where she worked rarely assumed leadership roles even if they were more qualified or did more work than men:

> I know this woman at the place where I work who has a masters [degree]. She's the only person with a masters. The boss is this man who puts a lot of work in her bin. It piles up in her bin and she does it and he's not doing anything except taking credit for it. She makes jokes about it but it makes me mad because she's the one who's got more education and gets things done, but she's not the boss and probably never will be.

Monica's analysis of workplace discourses of male authority reveals how abnormal it was for the women in her office to give orders, make important decisions, or receive credit for a job well done. This impression was augmented in other seniors' observations by a "culture of femininity" that encourages women to accept subordinate positions where they are treated as "sex objects, on the one hand, and as [workplace] wives and mothers, on the other" (Valli, 1983, p. 214). These positions include jobs as retail clerks, restaurant waitresses, receptionists, and others involving face-to-face customer services. Women, as many of the girls observed, are convinced that physical attractiveness and other indications of femininity are necessary to get and keep such jobs. One of Lona's friends, who was employed in a fast-food restaurant, complained bitterly about how the best work hours went to the sexiest girls. "There was this other girl who was maybe a year older than me. She's real skinny and tall. She was prettier and a lot sexier than I am. The manager chose her to work more hours than me because she looks better. There was no other reason that I could see."

Other jobs for women include child day care, cleaning services, nursing, pre- and elementary school teaching, counseling services, and other virtual extensions of their domestic roles as caregivers. Most of the women Lona knew had jobs where they took care "of people's dirt, brats, and diseases." Although she regarded many of these jobs as "crappy," she envisioned herself in a caregiving occupation where she could exercise her "God-given gift" for helping people. "A lot of kids I don't even know would come up to me with big problems. One thing I could do was talk to them, and I realized I had this God-given gift. I got this insight thing that everyone wants." She thus positioned herself in an occupational niche deemed appropriate for women even as she complained about how women get stuck in crappy jobs where they have to take care of other people's problems.

As women find themselves relegated to jobs deemed acceptable for them, men compete for jobs they believe are rightfully theirs. Not every man has a job that puts him in a position of authority. Nor are men necessarily in a position to pursue high-status careers. Many men, especially those from working-class backgrounds, are much more oriented toward manual labor that pays decent, livable wages and provides other kinds of benefits. Nay Wilson talked about how most of these jobs are considered by men to be theirs and theirs alone. "I know some construction is only for men and men, drive trucks and load things and build roads and all that. I know some women do those things, but not too many 'cause it's too hard for them and men don't want them around anyway."

Men until the late 1980s were able to find good, blue-collar jobs in manufacturing plants, semiskilled trades, and other industries. The most sought after jobs often went to White men who were major beneficiaries of employment in the industrial labor market (Fine & Weis, 1998). Men of color were more typically hired to do the dirtiest or most dangerous jobs, but many of them also managed to earn a decent income. Masculinist attitudes arose within these occupational niches as male workers asserted their manhood through machismo displays of physical prowess, crude manners, and sexist put-downs of women. They let it be known that a "real man" was someone who worked with his hands, the sweat of his brow, and to the limits of his strength. He was the undisputed head of his household and could hold his own in any dispute with another man. These attitudes were handed down from father to son, as was well documented in Willis's (1977) classic study of working-class boys in an English comprehensive high school. The lads, as the boys called themselves, strongly identified with their manual-laborer fathers. Manual labor for them was the ultimate expression of masculinity, whereas mental labor was ridiculed as feminine or for "ear'ole" classmates who let teachers pour worthless knowledge into their empty heads. The lads were content with where they stood economically in the 1970s and might very well have continued to do so if good, blue-collar jobs were still around today.

Working-class boys, ethnic minorities, Black people, women, and other groups were all viewed by seniors as being positioned in dominant divisions of labor in culturally stereotypic or monopolistic ways. High schools have reinforced these divisions in their long-standing practice of sorting adolescents into differentiated occupational tracks. Students designated as college-bound and destined for middle-class careers are placed in advanced academic courses. Others are channeled into vocational education programs where they are prepared for working-class jobs. In either case, young people are directed toward occupational niches deemed most appropriate, if not desirable, for them.

OCCUPATIONAL TRACKING

Most American high schools have some kind of process where students are placed in differentiated academic and vocational tracks that, among other goals, are geared toward various occupations. Academic tracks are usually divided into three or more levels. Upper tracks include Advanced Placement (AP) classes, honors sections, or other advanced academic courses for high-ability, college-bound students. Middle or regular tracks are for students with average ability who may or may not go to college. Remedial, basic, and special education classes constitute the lowest tracks and are for students who have learning problems or disabilities.

High schools also offer vocational education programs that prepare students for entry into the workforce. Whereas academic tracks generally do not correspond in a direct way to particular occupations, classes in vocational education are usually tied to specific types of trades and jobs.

Tracking has been roundly criticized over the years as perpetuating socioeconomic inequalities through the reproduction of dominant divisions of labor. Abundant evidence has been gathered on the notable discrepancies between which groups of students get assigned to different tracks and the types of instruction that are offered (Gamoran, 1987, 1992; Gamoran & Berends,1987; Lucas,1999; Oakes, 1985). Studies indicate that students in upper-track classes are disproportionately White and middle-class. The education they receive is likely to emphasize critical thinking, complex problem solving, and other higher order academic knowledge and skills. A significant percentage of those placed in the lowest tracks are low-income, working-class, and/or students of color. These students are taught through methods that emphasize rote learning and tight behavioral controls. Their experiences have been compared to factory production lines where the work is repetitive, tedious, and intellectually deadening (Bowles & Gintis, 1976). But as Page (1991) observed, what happens in different tracks within a particular school are variations of common curricular and instructional themes. Much can be inferred about the educational experiences of students in a school by examining upper tracks as representative of overarching pedagogical patterns.

Upper Tracks

Upper-track classes in high schools are usually regarded as courses of study for college-bound students who demonstrate high levels of cognitive ability and motivation to master advanced academic curriculum. Students are presumably exposed to the most rigorous forms of instruction, yet the upper-track classes I observed revealed striking variation in pedagogical patterns between schools that had significant educational consequences, including those related to economic endeavors.

Advanced Placement and other upper-track classes at Ridgewood High were quite rigorous despite students' attempts to minimize the demands teachers placed on them. They also were taught with middle-class professions in mind. Peter's AP chemistry class was set up by the teacher to resemble a real chemistry lab. Students used authentic scientific equipment to carry out experiments where they were required to calculate and record results through complicated mathematical procedures. The teacher told me that 30% of students in his chemistry classes received the highest marks of 5s and 4s on the AP chemistry exam. Most of the rest got 3s. This pattern of instruction was evident in other upper-track classes where teachers and students followed similar scripts for advanced academic study.

Instruction in upper-track classes at Jefferson High could be just as challenging. David signed up for several AP classes, including advanced calculus. The calculus class was taught by a veteran teacher who marched students through a curriculum that was just as demanding as any I had observed at Ridgewood High or any other school. The teacher managed to quell the most disruptive behavior, but, like many of his colleagues, was unable to put every student to work. I noticed that two of the boys, one White and one Black, constantly had their heads down on their desks. Several other students sat in passive silence. They did not take notes or otherwise appear to be paying attention. The teacher told me after class that AP calculus had been combined with a regular math section because of budget cuts. "You can tell," he said, "who the lower kids are. They don't do the work."

At Central City High, the teachers who taught upper-track classes had students who relished their designation as good students but were extremely minimalist in their work. Ms. Hathaway was an AP English teacher who tried hard to instruct students who were more interested in socializing with their friends than in mastering the curriculum necessary to earn high marks on the AP exam. Several times I heard her tell students they were going to fail the exam if they didn't settle down and learn the material. Most ended up not taking the exam at all. Those who did received few points or no points at all. The pattern was much the same in other upper-track classes. In an advanced AP European history class, I listened to the teacher present a fascinating lecture on the Russian revolution. She spun a gripping tale of how Tsar Nicholas sought the counsel of the evil monk Rasputin and the mystery of his murder by the Bolsheviks.

While I sat transfixed, most of her students were noticeably bored. At one point, the teacher walked over to a student who was sound asleep. She put her hand on the student's head and asked, "Are you alive?"

Nay, Michael, Monica, and about 15 other students signed up for every upper-track class offered at Central City High. Monica said the group had been together since middle school when they were identified as academically gifted. They kept enrolling in advanced classes in part because they wanted to steer clear of students who "do not care about school." Michael alluded to this situation in his description of the two sets of students in his school. "The set I'm in, we've, we've been together for years. We take the same [advanced] classes and pretty much stay away from the other set."

Upper-track classes were safe social havens for Michael and other seniors and also very much reinforced their own economic self-images as upwardly mobile. Teachers recognized the reasons behind their positions, but they were deeply concerned about the lack of effort students put forth in their studies. Ms. Hathaway talked about how AP kids were "madly in love with the idea of being the best and the brightest" but refused to act the part. She would actually tell them in class that they were not behaving like "real" college-bound students. I heard another teacher tell students how woefully ill-prepared they were for college. "The hard classes in this school," she told them, "are remedial classes in the suburbs. It's you guys who are making them that way."

Students agreed that they were not studying as hard as middle-class kids in middle-class schools. If they were concerned about whether they would be able to compete in college and professional occupations, they did not talk about it, at least not to me. They had, after all, made it through high school and there was no reason for them to believe they would not continue to make it after graduation. "I know," Nay said, "that it gets harder after high school, especially this high school, but I don't see nothin' stoppin' me, ain't nothin' stoppin' me now."

Students in vocational tracks were caught up in completely different discursive veins. They were much less content and even angry about how they were being prepared for, or stopped within, occupations that offered them few monetary rewards and limited opportunities for personally gratifying work.

Vocational Tracks

Whereas upper-track classes are theoretically geared for academically advanced students destined for higher education, vocational education programs are intended to ready non-college-bound students for direct entry into the workforce. Vocational education has been offered as an alternative to college preparatory tracks since the 1930s. When voc ed programs

first appeared, they were explicitly geared toward sorting students into occupations on the basis of their gender, race, and other social locations.
Girls had the option to enroll in textile, culinary, and clerical programs or,
as was often the case for young Black women, in courses that trained them
for paid domestic service. Boys took shop classes and could sign up for
more advanced training in carpentry, auto mechanics, or other trades. Although gender- and race-specific vocational programming is less common
today, high schools continue to offer vocational tracks that feed into
working-class occupational niches.

Such was the situation at Central City High where the school district,
in collaboration with local corporations, introduced a school-to-work program. The program, entitled Career and Academic Success Education
(CASE), was set up to facilitate the transition of the school's mostly
low-income Black student population into local jobs. The model and
much of the funding for CASE were provided by the Carl D. Perkins Vocational and Applied Technology Education Act of 1990 and by the
School-to-Work Opportunities Act of 1994. This federal legislation has
turned traditional vocational education into school-to-work initiatives
based on a model of "incremental economic development" (Fitzgerald,
1997; Smith & Rojewski, 1993). The transition from school to work is
conceived not as a single event in the lives of American youths but, rather,
as a series of milestones that typically begins with part-time jobs and pro-
gresses to full-time employment. Teenagers, in other words, are integrated
into the workforce in direct, incremental stages.

With the backing of the school district and corporate interests, the
CASE program became an integral part of most students' educational experiences at Central City High. The majority of students enrolled in the
four-year CASE curricular sequence where, in addition to standard academic subjects, they received career counseling, exposure to career opportunities through job shadowing, and paid job internships. During the
internship phase, students were usually placed in unskilled, minimum-wage jobs in health care facilities, fast-food restaurants, the telephone company, nursing homes, and other local businesses. One girl I met
was placed in a motel where, she said in a sarcastic voice, "I got intensive
training in how to clean rooms."

Every CASE student in his or her junior year was assigned an advisor.
The main responsibility of CASE advisors was to help students with their
internships. But other responsibilities accrued as the needs of students
mounted. Amber was an advisor who did everything from driving students to internship work sites, settling disputes between kids and their
bosses, teachers, or parents, testifying at juvenile court, taking girls to hospitals to give birth, and handling "every other unimaginable problem."
She and her colleagues went even further in their advocacy. Collectively,

they were young college-educated men and women who felt that the CASE program did not go far enough to empower poor, Black students. They felt, as one of them stated in a group interview, that the program should "empower kids to be life forces and future leaders instead of slave labor." They voiced strong objections to the program's limited model of incremental economic development that placed kids in minimum-wage jobs, then left them there. They hoped to take students to the upper tiers of the economy by promoting an ideology of empowerment through higher education. An African-American woman with a degree in social work talked about how CASE advisors were in a unique role as adults who could empower Black youths:

> I like to think a part of this process is to empower these kids. That's an everyday thing with us. We have to do that because sometimes we are the only person, the only adult who is neutral enough to say, "Man, we want to empower this person." We don't owe allegiance to anybody except to these kids.

Another CASE advisor explained how empowerment meant allowing kids to negotiate their present realities while repositioning themselves for a "better tomorrow":

> We empower kids by allowing them to retain their own survival skills they need to live in this community. We can't just de-quip survival skills because that's reality down here in the streets. So we allow that but then get them to see how the rules of the streets aren't going to win them the game in the long run. We get them to see through society's game and how to play the game. We don't just tell them stuff, like we actually get college applications and show them how to fill them out. So our approach is to allow them to survive for today but show them how to play the game for a better tomorrow.

Students, for their part, were skeptical about the CASE program's emphasis on incremental integration as well as CASE advisors' visions of empowerment through higher education. When I asked a group of seniors if CASE was beneficial, a boy said that although the program was billed as providing an "escalator edge," it actually put kids in the "basement." "Whereas other kids have to walk up the ladder, they make us think we're going up an escalator. But, man, all I can see is them puttin' us down there in the basement." He quit the program after being sent to a hospital where he was assigned to maintenance services. "We might be kids," he said, "but we ain't blind. I could see that I was a long, long ways from being a doctor."

Other students were more appreciative of CASE although, like the boy, they suspected that the program was really positioning them in jobs with few avenues for advancement. A Black girl was delighted with her placement as an office clerk in a telephone company. But she was not at all convinced that she would eventually move up the ranks within the company. "Black people don't move up like other folks. A lot of kids including me aren't sure if this program is gonna get us anywhere or is just a way to get us into those jobs that no one wants." She clearly echoed what David North said about "po Black folk jobs." As a poor Black girl, she felt like she was being funneled into dead-end jobs.

Students also had reservations about going to college. College, from their vantage point, was too expensive, took too many years to get through, and had no real guarantees that it would pay off. "It takes a helluva long time get through college," a boy observed. "Like it takes 4 or 5 years to get the first part done and then sometimes another 4 years to be a lawyer or doctor or whatever and, man, you're like paying for it the whole way." Michael was someone who had every intention of going to college. But he, too, was aware of the potential costs and risks involved. He could understand why kids in his school considered college as well as the CASE program as less than optimal routes to economic success. "I can see where kids are coming from. Like what's in it for them? College is expensive and it's more school and there's no guarantee it will amount to anything. They get jobs with CASE but they don't pay much and what they do pretty much sucks. Kids are like, 'Man, which way should I go 'cause neither way is great?' I can understand that."

Whereas the CASE program was an integral part of schooling for many students at Central City High, vocational programming at Jefferson High was an entirely separate track, housed in a separate building. Students throughout the city could apply to Careers for Tomorrow (CFT), which was Jefferson High's version of a school-to-work program. Careers for Tomorrow offered courses and placements in aircraft technology, automotive technology, building trades, culinary arts, and graphic arts. Or, if students so desired, they could sign up for classes in "intercity bus driving."

None of the seniors who participated in my study were enrolled in CFT. But they did occasionally visit a job placement office located in the building that housed the program. One afternoon, I accompanied David and his best friend, Cory, to the office. We went there because Cory wanted to find an after-school job. The woman who ran the office told him about a dishwashing position and another opening requiring fluent knowledge of Spanish. Neither job appealed to Cory, who walked away muttering about "lousy choices" and "stupid jobs where you can't even speak English." David told me later that Careers for Tomorrow and the placement office were supposed to be for kids who "detested school and wanted to go out and work." But what they really did was put kids in low-paying jobs with high turnover rates. "It's like the employers have figured out that they can come to our high school and get a constant supply of workers for their crappy jobs." David was especially incensed about the fact that most of the students enrolled in Careers for Tomorrow were Black. "See," he said, "that's how they get us into those po Black folk jobs. Now if they could only figure out how to keep us there."

The overwhelming educational thrust at Ridgewood High was preparation for college and professional careers. This was true even for students who were not enrolled in upper-track classes. What little the school did offer in the way of vocational programming was condensed into a handful of electives in Industrial Technology and Home Economics. There were a total of eight industrial technology courses in drafting, architectural drawing, power mechanics, engineering design, and woodworking. The home economics department offered classes in "Fashion Expression and Design," "Contemporary Clothing Construction," and "Advanced Fashion Design." Students saw these classes as supplementing academic curriculum rather than as an alternative to them. Vocational electives were quite peripheral to the educational experiences of the school's clientele.

Ridgewood High did have a Career Center. Every school day, the Center would post listings for part-time jobs, mostly in fast-food restaurants, mall retail stores, child care, and yard work. Cassandra got a job at a McDonalds fast-food restaurant with the help of the Center. We had lunch where she worked and I listened as she spoke in glowing terms about how wonderful the McDonalds' company was and how much she was benefitting from her job. Cassandra felt that working at McDonalds was a good first step in a series of steps that would eventually lead her to economic success. "Like, I don't plan to stay at McDonalds all of my life but it's a beginning, like a good beginning. It's a good company and I could probably be a manager, but I'm going to do other things, but this is a good beginning anyway."

It was not at all unusual for other students at Ridgewood High to seek and accept minimum-wage jobs as "good beginnings." Unlike their poor and working-class counterparts in other schools, they did not suspect that they were being shunted into the least profitable, most ungratifying lines of work. They believed they had a genuine chance to advance well beyond part-time jobs into college and on to more prestigious, full-time careers. As current or aspiring members of the middle class, the discourses of incremental economic development and empowerment through higher education flowed together into an ideally straightaway path to success. What made the difference in the perspectives of many Ridgewood High students was the availability of financial support, sponsorship through social networks, insider cultural currencies, and other resources that make moving into or staying within middle-class niches much, much easier to accomplish. Dominant discourses worked well for them and for others who have benefitted the most from dominant divisions of labor. But these benefits have become less assured in an economy that is changing and changing fast.

LIMINAL PROSPECTS

The foundations of the dominant economic order are being rocked by torrents of liminal streams that are opening up new prospects for some while undermining the occupational advantages of others. A rapid succession of technological inventions beginning with the telegraph and onward to the telephone, radio, television, mainframe computer, photocopier, personal computer, video cassette player, fax machine, camcorder, compact disk player, cellular phone, video teleconferencing, and other devices has propelled the U.S. economy into an electronic state of flux. These devices have ignited an explosion of consumerism as goods and services of all kinds are made more readily and globally available. And they are radically altering the workplace.

Fast-food restaurants, shopping malls, walk-in clinics, quick-stop convenience stores, drive-up banks, and thousands of other consumer businesses have cropped up and multiplied across the country. Jobs in industries requiring skilled and semiskilled manual labor are drying up as positions requiring interpersonal and computer skills are flooding in. The new working classes are employees who have the people skills and technical know-how necessary to provide merchandise and services to people in ever-expanding marketplaces.

Professional sports, movies, musical performances, amusement parks, and other entertainments have burgeoned along with other consumer demands for pleasure in leisure. Americans, during their free time, want to enjoy themselves, and entrepreneurs have responded by erecting a massive entertainment industry. Popular entertainers such as high-profile athletes, top-10 bands, and headlined movie stars are becoming multimillionaires while countless other people are finding employment in subsidiary jobs (e.g., concession stands, ticket sales, security, and so forth) that pay considerably less.

The net result of these changes is that the material conditions of the industrial age of production that so intrigued Marxists are giving way to a postindustrial era of communications and consumerism that is revolutionizing the workplace. Youths no longer expect to get many of the jobs held by their parents. Nor do they expect working conditions to be the same. They are looking ahead at liminal prospects for money and occupational gratification in an economy that is literally "betwixt and between the old and new economic and social order" (Bettis, 1996, p. 106). Although these prospects are cause for excitement, they also are catalysts for conflict as young people struggle to retain past advantages while taking advantage of emergent opportunities. Perhaps the most powerful force unleashing liminal prospects is the tremendous influx of electronic technologies. Technologies have ushered in a screen age of innovations that is captivating young people as they contemplate the direction of their own future economic pursuits.

Technological Screen Age

Electronic technologies have had a profound impact on the economic orientations of young people. Teenagers are reorienting themselves as "screenagers" in an expanding technological world projected and marketed to them on computers, televisions, movies, videos, and other illuminated screens (Douglas, 1996). They are anticipating jobs where much, if not all, of their work will take place in front of computers. Such anticipation was more than evident in seniors' responses to my question about what they thought the best jobs would be in the future. Every single one of them talked about occupations involving computers.

> **David:** The next 10 years will be definitely in computer technology-related industries especially since America is moving toward a technological society. That maybe doesn't make sense because we have vast lands and the economy should be agriculture based but technology is where the bucks are. That's where we're moving toward.

> **Adam:** Most everything will be technology jobs, you know, that deal with computers.

> **Michael:** I think mainly a lot of jobs are going to revolve around computers. It is going to be more or less if you don't get adept at computers, you're gonna be left out.

> **Lona:** It's gonna be a lot of computer jobs 'cause there's so much stuff on computers now. You go to a record store and order something by computer without anybody else's help, you know, touch screen stuff, so I think it's gonna have a lot to do with computers.

> **Christina:** Mostly computers and technology and stuff like that which I'm not really interested in anyway. I mean everybody's looking for the new things like computers. Like everything is high tech now.

> **Cassandra:** I think the good jobs will be dealing with computers. Basically, you see, they are trying to run the world by computer.

Even though there was agreement that knowledge about computers and other electronic devices was critical for integration into the emergent economy, there was considerable variation in the extent to which seniors were exposed to such knowledge in their high schools. Students at Ridgewood High were literally surrounded by computers in classrooms, the library, and offices. They were given classroom assignments requiring word processing, spreadsheets, graphics, or the production of other computer-generated products. A few teachers experimented with online Internet instruction, whereas others assigned creative projects where students used camcorders to make videos or compact disk burners to produce CDs. Like it or not, students were being thrust headlong into the powerful currents of technological discourses that promised even greater economic advances. Although students liked what these devices could do, some of them sensed a dark, potentially destructive side to them. Cassandra believed that electronic technologies were the "mark of the beast" heralding the end of the world:

> Computers are the mark of the beast. I can't believe any other way 'cause that's ... how I was taught in the book of Revelations. I think they are going to run everything until God comes and wipes everything out. 'Cause they are corrupt and bad. I don't see any change. I see on TV that somebody's dead, somebody's getting killed, somebody's getting robbed, somebody's getting raped. I see the same thing on video games, movies, you name it. That's all the sign of the mark of the beast.

Peter was concerned about the dehumanizing effects of technologies:

> I think in the 21st century and onwards, it will be too technological. People will begin to lose their humanity if they haven't already. They won't know what it's like to be a person anymore because there won't be much face-to-face contact. They won't know what it's like to be an individual because they're all going to be turned into numbers and digitized profiles. This is going to go on until some kind of religious fervor gets into people and they start wrecking their machines.

And, like Cassandra, he had an apocalyptic vision of computers falling into the hands of evil people out to destroy the world:

> With the fall of the Soviet Union and other empires, there are going to be lots of unchecked dictators popping up all over the world. They are not

likely to use computers correctly or to help people. They'll use them to invade countries and destroy everything in sight. You never know there might be hackers who figure out how to get into government computers and press the button that blows everything up. I don't know, but anything could happen.

Students at Jefferson High were much more concerned about their lack of exposure to computers. The school did have a state-of-the-art computer room, but most students never ventured into it. Adam assumed that he would spend time on the computers when he signed up for a class called Computer Awareness. The class was described in the school's handbook as an introduction to "computer technology and the use of computers, ... commercial programs and their applications as well as simple programming." But rather than convene the class in the computer room, students were assigned to a large classroom filled with antiquated typewriters. Day after day, week after week, Adam and his classmates were given "keyboarding" assignments where they typed sentences and paragraphs printed on handouts. I heard the teacher tell students not to worry about spelling and punctuation because the main purpose of the assignments was to give them "a feel" for what a computer was like. Adam never did get a chance to use a real computer. "I know I have to have some computer training," he said with irritation in his voice. "But I guess they don't think I need it."

David's experience was entirely different. He was part of a "select group of hardcore geeks" who spent a great deal of time in the computer room. *Geek* was students' term for kids who were utterly absorbed by computers. Hardcore geeks like David not only became adept at software applications and Internet usage, but also mastered the intricacies of computer hardware and programming. They were deeply immersed in, and the staunchest defenders of, postindustrial technological trends. David and about 20 other hardcore geeks signed up for a cluster of advanced computer classes taught in the computer room. The room, which was located in a secluded corner off the main hallway, became their own exclusive enclave where they were inducted into the "select" technological classes.

Students at Central City High used computers sporadically if at all. There was a room on the third floor with several outdated, mostly Apple computers. Computer courses were offered but none of the seniors took them nor knew anyone who had. Few teachers incorporated computers into their instruction. When students did use computers, it was mostly to type papers or check out the Internet. The focal point of students' lives at Central City High otherwise was not computers. Students stood on the edges of a technological revolution that was rerouting the direction of economic progress.

Equalizing Equal Opportunity

Another liminal current is the equalization of equal opportunity. Equal opportunity in the United States is a much-heralded discourse premised on the principle that all citizens, regardless of their background, have the right and freedom to compete for whatever economic pursuits they desire. Equal opportunity means equal competition based on natural talent and hard work rather than on inherited ranks and social status. Those who demonstrate the ability and effort necessary to do a job well ought to get and keep the job.

Despite its widespread appeal, equal opportunity has long been more of a myth than a reality in a capitalistic economy characterized by divisions of labor bounded by ethnic, racial, gendered, and other sociocultural borders. Crossing the borders surrounding occupational niches solely on the basis of individual merit has not been easy in a country that for centuries has had few effective sanctions against workplace discrimination. But borders are beginning to open up or disappear altogether in a liminal economy where both the field and rules of competition have been altered.

Jobs in manufacturing and other sectors are being replaced by ones geared toward the production and marketing of information, communications, consumer goods, and services. These trends have changed the field of competition by opening up new opportunities for employment and closing off others. The rules of competition also have been changed by policies intended to curb overt and covert forms of discriminatory employment practices. Beginning with the authorization of Affirmative Action in the 1960s, a progression of executive orders, civil rights legislation, and court rulings have been issued to truly equalize equal opportunity. Employers have responded to these policies by adjusting their hiring practices to create a more numerically balanced workforce of people representing racial, ethnic, and gender diversity. These changes may have lifted some of the barriers that blocked or hindered the mobility of certain groups of people, but they have left other groups behind. Among the most hardest hit groups are working-class White boys.

Fine and Weis (1998) studied the lives of poor and working-class youths in the postindustrial age. They found that working-class White boys were becoming mired in a discourse of loss brought about by the decline in the "truly masculine jobs" that provided their male forebears with enough money and manly status to secure dominant positions in their homes and other social spheres (p. 39). Job losses among White men are being compounded by the policies aimed at the equalization of employment opportunities for people of color and women. This confluence of economic forces has caused working-class White boys to feel decentered, under siege, and no longer able to get jobs they believe are rightfully theirs.

Shifts in employment opportunities and policies are decentering White boys, but they are not necessarily changing the positions of boys of color. Fine and Weis (1998) found that African-American and Latino boys had great faith in the dominant belief that hard work yields economic rewards and that it is their fault if they don't succeed. But the boys also felt that their progress was hindered by discrimination, racism, and disinvestment in the places where they lived. Equalization policies did not go far enough to end inequality in the workplaces that were closest to them. Their economic outlook was that although hard work is necessary for advancement, obstacles still stood in their way.

These opposing points of view came through loud and clear during interviews I did with Adam and David. Adam, in his answers to my questions, talked about how much tougher it was for White men to get good jobs. He was totally against Affirmative Action and felt the policy was wrong because it gave Blacks and women an unfair edge. Proven ability, he insisted, should be the main qualification for hiring decisions.

AH: What, in your opinion, should be the main qualifications for getting a job?

Adam: Like jobs and stuff should be based on your skills, on your ability to do the work and not on race or color. It should be that. It shouldn't have anything to do with race or sex like it seems to be right now.

AH: So you're against Affirmative Action?

Adam: Yeah. Completely. Like my brother wants to be a cop. There's several problems running against him. He's not female. He's not a Black female. He's not a Black male. That's going to work against him. If he can do the job, he should be hired. Even if there is a Black guy that's going in for it but if he can't do the job he shouldn't be there.

AH: You're a White male. Do you feel that in some ways you're being discriminated against?

Adam: Yeah, oh yeah. Because some of the companies don't have enough Blacks and they got to have an equal balance. If there was less Blacks and a lot of Whites and they need to hire more Blacks, I probably wouldn't get the job.

AH: How do you feel about that?

Adam: I feel bad. I don't like it at all. It's not fair. It's not fair to me 'cause I got the ability to do it.

AH: You perceive discrimination?

Adam: Yeah. Definitely. It's wrong. It's definitely not fair.

David had a diametrically opposed perspective. He talked about how his family and other African Americans had made significant strides into middle-class occupations. But he felt that educated White men remained "number one" in a system that, despite Affirmative Action, continues to discriminate against Black men.

David: White males with an education are number one. They get the best jobs. Next are young White females and then young Black females. At the bottom of the ladder, you have Black men. It's not because of lack of numbers but because one in three of us are in jail. The problem is lack of education that's still left over from the days when they didn't give Black people good schools. Those days in a lot of schools are still here. Like the system is against Black men more than anybody.

AH: So what's going on? Why after 25 years of Affirmation Action are Black men still at the bottom?

David: Affirmative Action has helped the wrong folks. It helps Black females and White females because they are minorities and women. You had like the feminist movement in the early seventies. It helped them. The politicians in the early seventies maybe felt they could knock out two birds with one stone if they used Affirmative Action for young females in general and Black females. When you have a Black female it's like you hire two minorities. That leaves young Black men like me out in the cold.

AH: Do you think that's fair?

David: No, no. It's not fair, but life's not fair. It's not fair at all. Black men have to always constantly improve themselves. That's what they're told. No else has to improve but us. You never hear they have to improve schools or bring jobs to where Black men are. You never hear that.

Affirmative Action policies also were being applied in local public schools. The district had magnet schools offering popular programs in performing arts, Montessori, and other specialty areas. All of the schools had admission policies intended to create racially balanced student populations. Adam pointed to the policies as another example of discrimination against Whites because, in his estimation, "a lot of the Blacks who get in aren't qualified."

David, on the other hand, was a strong supporter of Affirmative Action in education. He did not think that it led to preferential treatment for Blacks:

> People think, they think that when Black kids get admitted to, say, Harvard they're there only because they're Black. No way. Harvard wouldn't admit someone who isn't smart. Fewer Blacks than Whites apply, like, there might be two thousand Whites and two hundred Blacks. So more Whites are getting turned down because there are more Whites in the first place. When they get done admitting students, lo and behold the majority of Harvard students end up being White.

Job shifts in the liminal economy and the equalization of equal opportunity have fueled contention between working-class White boys and Black youths who see their future prospects in the American economy as threatened or hardly changing at all. Whereas boys were being repositioned in or cut out of the economy, girls felt they were being pushed into it. Of all liminal trends, none is more momentous then the large-scale entry of women into the U.S. workforce.

Women's Work

There was a time when the dominant cultural ideal for married women with young children was for them to stay home and out of the workplace. Women were to depend on men for financial support and if they did go to work, it was to supplement the family income rather than to fulfill personal ambitions. Those looking for jobs encountered limited access to the high-income, high-status employment opportunities available to men. They often found themselves channeled into positions with comparatively low wages, little or no fringe benefits, and few avenues for promotion. These positions were regarded as "women's work" from which men gladly excused themselves.

Several forces have combined to change the employment situation for women. The Black civil rights movement in the 1960s inspired women to organize their own movement for equal rights, including the right to compete with men for good jobs. The movement, known as *women's liberation,* was one of the political forces behind the passage of federal legislation that enforced equal opportunity in employment for women and other historically marginalized groups. The government established the U.S. Equal Employment Opportunity Commission (EEOC), which has as its stated mission the promotion of equal opportunity through administrative and judicial enforcement of federal civil rights laws as well as through education and technical assistance. Among the statutes the commission enforces are those that prohibit employment discrimination on the basis of race, color, religion, sex, and national origin. It also prohibits the practice of paying women lower wages than men for similar work under similar conditions.

The women's movement did not stop there. It progressed under the leadership of feminists who set their sights well beyond the liberal cause of enforcing equal rights. Women are now encouraged to seek financial independence from men and empower themselves through self-gratifying careers. Ideally, they are to escape the oppressive patriarchy of domestic life by venturing forth into workplaces where they can acquire individual liberation, if not a bank account of their own.

Radically new cultural ideals are not the only forces propelling women into the workforce. Technological advances in home appliances have drastically reduced the number of hours women spend on housework. Women now have the time to take advantage of job opportunities in a liminal economy that is especially suited for them. Wilson (1996), in his comprehensive study of urban poverty, pointed out how most of the new jobs for workers with limited training and education are in retail and other customer/client services held disproportionately by women. There also are a number of jobs for educated women in health care, preschool and elementary education, welfare agencies, and other female-dominated social services. Other trends, such as the rise in divorce rates and single parenting, have caused both uneducated and educated women to look for jobs to support themselves.

These forces have led to a dramatic discursive shift in whether or how women ought to work. Affluent women, whose major economic contributions used to be as spending consumers, are now encouraged to enter careers just as lucrative and prestigious as those of affluent men. Poor and working-class women are getting the message that they can no longer depend on welfare programs or other long-term public assistance. They are under enormous pressure to find jobs that will make them more economically self-sufficient. These pressures are piled on top of dominant expectations that continue to position women as primarily responsible for taking care of children and domestic housework. Rather than feel excited about their burgeoning prospects for employment, most of the girls in my study resigned themselves to the likelihood they would be working both inside and outside of their homes. Their adaptations were more about accommodating to women's expanded roles in a changing economy than about directing or challenging them.

Girls at Ridgewood High were the most optimistic about jobs and careers as avenues for women to achieve the good life. Cassandra, as an upwardly mobile Black preppie, was quite enthusiastic about the economic progress of women. "Women," she said with confidence, "are definitely going to have more power."

AH: How will women have more power?

Cassandra: Power making more money and being equal. Guys are looking at us as equals, which means more power for us.

AH: Guys are giving women more power?

Cassandra: They might not see it that way but they are 'cause they are like seeing us as equals and don't mind if we make our own money.

Cassandra not only identified expanding money-making opportunities as a reason for why women will have more power, but she also noted men's changing attitudes toward women's equality. Such attitudes, in her opinion, were causing men to give up power, albeit unwittingly.

Boys at Ridgewood High did claim to accept women as equal contenders for employment opportunities. But they certainly were aware of the real or perceived erosion of men's economic power. After summarizing the "egalitarian model" in the United States, Peter joked about returning to the days when "male chauvinists" ruled. "The model is like women and men are equal in everything. I say let's bring back the male chauvinist kind of thing. Let's go back to the 50s and 60s when this country ran pretty good. Now things are going to hell because women are trying to be equal with men. I say men take over the world and put women back in their place!"

Other boys were less sarcastic but just as cognizant of the impact that women's economic empowerment has or might have for men. Some, like Stuart, had no problem with women moving into positions of power so long as the rules of entry are fair and, most importantly, did not shut him out of the competition. Stuart didn't care if women got good jobs so long as he got a good job. Some kind of economic power sharing was an acceptable ideal for him and, perhaps, for most other preppie boys at Ridgewood High.

Whereas Cassandra reveled in economic discourses that promised more wealth and power for working women, other girls at Ridgewood High were more concerned about finding ways to juggle the demands of paid employment with the responsibilities of family life. A girl in a group interview I conducted with White seniors said that although it was important for women to set their own career goals, they also needed to strike a balance with their families. "I think it's important that women strive for their goals; if that's what they want to do, then that's what they should do. But there's got to be some sort of mean in between where your family, where you can take on the responsibilities of your family." She and other White girls in the group believed they would be performing some kind of balancing act between work and family. All of them were from well-to-do families where their mothers could choose to remain at home, pursue full-time careers, or hold part-time jobs. They were thus primed to approach the balance as a decision among various options rather than as a perpetual dilemma with no clear resolutions.

The girls presented several scenarios for their own decisions, most of which were premised on the assumption that they would be married to affluent men. A couple of the girls said they wanted to work for awhile and then stay home to raise children. Another one had what she described as a "schedule for my life. I definitely want to educate myself as much as possible. I'd like to be an architect for a few years and then either work out of my house or do missionary work with my husband."

Yet another girl planned to go into politics unless it interfered with her family life, at which point she would go into the "business place." "For my career, I'd probably say politics, like run campaigns and stuff. But I also, family is very important so I'll get into politics up to the point where it's interfering with that. If it's dirty stuff and I don't want to do it, I'll just go into the business place and get away from it."

Boys in the group went along with the scenarios and their projected roles as backers or backups for their wives' choices. One of them said that his wife, "whoever she is, can do whatever she wants to make herself happy." He seemed confident that he would have the financial wherewithal to fund his wife's aspirations, whatever they happen to be.

The economic scene was much harsher for low-income and working-class girls at Jefferson High and Central City High. I interviewed girls in these schools who had watched their mothers as they shouldered the burden of job losses and displacement among men. Men in their scenarios were portrayed as worthless or abusive or as having lost their grips as principal breadwinners and undisputed heads of households. Women were forced to take center stage after coming to the realization that they simply could not rely on men to provide them with financial support. They became more independent, or as a White girl in Lona's group explained, less dependent on men:

> Woman around here, like, nowadays they have to make sure they can be stable and on their own and stuff. They just cannot depend on any guy. 'Cause I see like moms taking all this crap from men because they can't make it on their own. Sooner or later they learn to depend on themselves.

The girl's own mother had learned painful lessons about relying too much on men:

> My mom's been through a lot. She's been married three times. Her first two husbands were alcoholics and they left her high and dry. She had four kids and worked from seven in the morning until nine, ten just to support us. We lived in a house and we weren't on welfare or anything. She's telling

us don't hit on a guy because she doesn't want us to go through what she went through. She wants us to make sure we can support ourselves and, like, to hell with guys 'cause they can really screw you.

The mother passed these lessons down to her daughters along with other advice that can be characterized as working-class women's discourses of economic independence in the absence of men. Girls were taught that work, for them, was a practical necessity and not an optional choice. They also learned that men are not always good sources of income and may even be detrimental to their economic pursuits.

Nay, who lived in poverty, took the discourse a step farther. Women, in her opinion, should not ask for money from a man even if the man is the father of their children. Her reasoning was that if women got money from men, then men would end up getting much more money from women:

I'm just saying that girls, just because their baby's daddy has some money, doesn't mean they should ask him to bring it in all the time. It's not their money. It's the man's money. The woman's money is her money and she's got to keep it. What I'm saying is that the man might be thinkin' he can give her a little money and that she has to give him back a lot of money.

It was not, in other words, in women's best interest to participate in a system of monetary exchange with men who may not pay them back or will figure out other ways to exploit them. It was perfectly acceptable for women to pool or share their resources, especially within kinship networks formed for the mutual care of families. It was not a good idea to give money to unscrupulous men who might, after all, "spend it on another woman."

The most surprising revelation for me was girls' adamant opposition to publicly funded welfare programs. Much national attention was being focused on welfare reform during the period of my fieldwork. Although the girls had different opinions about how programs might be improved, all of them were opposed to long-term monetary benefits for able-bodied mothers who did not work. A White girl at Jefferson High had very strong objections to the existing welfare system because of what she had heard in school. "I mean they're just giving [welfare] to anybody. There's girls in this school that have kids and they're on welfare and all I hear is like, you know, the more kids you get, the more money you get. That's ridiculous. If they're able to have kids, they're able to work."

Nay, whose mother received food stamps and monthly AFDC checks, also felt that long-term welfare had to end. She knew several women on welfare who had never gotten used to going to work. "That," she said, "ain't right and they're going to find out pretty soon. Too many mamas on welfare ain't going to work. I know they don't want to go to work 'cause they ain't used to havin' a job standing on their feet eight hours a day. They ain't used to that. They used to sittin' down, watchin' TV. That money they get ain't that much so they got to stand on their feet. Way things are going, they won't have a choice but to stand on their feet."

Welfare and other forms of financial dependency were thus being eliminated by a surge of negative public opinion and other factors carrying women out into the workforce. Some of the senior girls in my study were enthusiastic about the rise in opportunity for women. Many of the other girls were being swept along by pressing, practical need. Then there were those who could not resist the glitter of the underground economy.

FAST MONEY, INSTANT GRATIFICATION

The Underground Economy

Seething below dominant and liminal economic currents are the seamy undertows of the American underground economy. Hustlers run businesses within this economy as manufacturers and dealers of drugs, sex, pornography, and other vices. Others work to acquire cash and goods through thievery, robbery, or other acts of criminal extortion. The underground economy is replete with high-risk ventures that can have dire consequences for both the perpetrators and their victims. Yet youths are drawn to it by the irresistible allure of fast money and instant gratification.

The underground economy seeped into my school research sites, where several students sought to enrich themselves through illicit practices of rapid acquisition. They acquired fast money and sought instant gratification through means deemed illegal or illegitimate in the dominant economic order. Most of these practices were deployed in hallways, bathrooms, lunchrooms, and other corridor spaces where there was little or no direct adult surveillance. Out of sight of adults, students learned and applied economic lessons that rejected dominant modes of economic mobility (Hemmings, 2000a). These lessons constituted a hidden corridor curriculum that taught youths how to become rich and powerful through quick, exciting, occasionally violent endeavors.

Seniors at Jefferson High were well versed in the lessons of the hidden corridor curriculum. One of Lona's friends summarized what she and her classmates could learn "free of charge. You can learn how to use a knife to hold people up. How to pick a lock. You can learn to sell drugs without getting caught. You can learn how to fraudulently reproduce documents, which I had that experience."

Adam learned some of these lessons the hard way. His locker had been broken into so many times that he no longer used it. "My girlfriend and I share a locker. The locker was broken into twice and our parents had to come in and change the locks. It got broken into again. I carry all of my stuff with me now. I don't even leave my dirty track clothes in the locker."

A security guard led me through the hallways and showed me places behind stairwells, in empty rooms, and other "hot spots" where illegal drugs were sold. She knew where drug dealers conducted their business, but usually did nothing to stop the transactions because they happened too fast for her or anyone else to do anything about it.

Discourses of fast money and instant gratification also snaked their way through the corridors of Central City High. Monica said her classmates were "money hungry" because money bought them "cute girls, cars, fancy clothes, and respect." Kids who were turned off by menial, low-paying jobs and the thought of going to school for extended periods of time were "more turned on by the glamour of fast money. Kids don't want to work at McDonalds or empty bed pans all their lives. They are thinkin' I can make two hundred dollars in 20 minutes selling drugs in the streets which is quicker than sittin' in school for 8 years. They know not even a high school education is enough to get a good job that pays better than that."

Monica said that the role models for many kids were flashy drug dealers, pimps, gang bangers, and other local hustlers. Hustlers appeared to be rich and in control of their lives as well as life on the streets. They flaunted their wealth by wearing expensive designer clothes, driving fancy cars, and covering themselves in gold. They exuded control by cultivating images of coolness that blended intimidating toughness with smooth savvy. Kids looked up to hustlers as individuals who had made it big without submission to anything or anyone, including the dominant economic powers that be.

I heard several stories about how hustlers robbed, conned, or bullied kids out of their cash and valued possessions. Some acts of extortion were so violent that they left permanent scars. A CASE advisor told me about a Black boy who had been robbed twice at knife point. An out-going student with aspirations of going to college, the boy became despondent after the second attack and was often absent from school. Not only did he lose his money, but he also paid a terrible psychological price from which he never fully recovered.

Incidences of violent attacks were rare at Ridgewood High. No one knew anyone who had been an instigator or target of extortion. But everybody knew somebody who used illegal drugs and engaged in underage drinking. "Getting high" was a form of instant gratification that stimulated the distribution of mind-altering substances to any Ridgewood student who wanted to buy them. The consumption of beer and other alcoholic beverages was standard practice at parties, dances, games, and other events. Drugs also were consumed, I was told, "as a matter of personal choice." Christina said organic drugs like marijuana were the usual drug of choice but manufactured drugs like acid (LSD) were growing in popularity. "Ecstasy" was just coming into vogue as a club drug with psychedelic pop. Unlike low-income students at other schools, affluent students at Ridgewood High were in a privileged position to acquire money through legal means. Yet they routinely violated laws that banned or placed strict regulations on the possession of drugs and alcohol. They used legally acquired funds to purchase illegal substances.

When I asked seniors why students used illicit practices to acquire cash and goods, some saw it as a rational response to severely limited job opportunities. Monica talked about how a lot of smart kids in her neighborhood entered the underground economy because they could see no other way to make money. She had a friend who had been a high achiever in school until he dropped out to become a full-time drug dealer. He figured out that selling drugs was the best way for him to provide for himself and his family. And so, for that matter, did his family. "I know this guy who was real smart in school but he dropped out to sell drugs. He pays his momma's rent, buys stuff for his kids, and doesn't see any other way to make it big, you know, get rich. His momma says, 'You just keep doing what you're doing,' so he's like the man of the house and he's only eighteen."

Poor people, in David's opinion, often resort to drug dealing and other illicit economic activities because they are trapped in an irrational cycle of mixed messages that tells them one thing, then forces them to do something else. The government tells them they are "stupid" if they don't go to work and then sets up programs to assist them and their children. Then the government turns right around and cuts programs and does other things to keep poor people out of work. Poor people end up thinking they have no choice but to find other ways to make money:

> It's like a trap for poor people, Blacks, you know, people who don't have much influence. Everyone makes you feel like you're stupid or it's going to hurt you if you don' get a job. But how can you get a job when you have to drop out of school 'cause you got a kid or aren't learning anything? So they set up programs like Headstart and Job Corps then they cut them back. It's like they're saying you have to go to work and we'll help you then they turn right around and do everything they can to keep you out of work. So kids feel like they have to sell drugs or something. Can you blame them?

Hustlers' Guise

As far as I could tell, the seniors in my study were not directly involved in the underground economy. But a few of them had gotten caught up in the hustler-glorifying currents of popular culture. Television, movies, and other media portray street hustlers, especially Black hustlers, as violent, predatory criminals ultimately destined for prison. In films such as *Boyz N the Hood, Menace II Society,* and *Clockers,* Black males and their female accomplices are framed as dangerous threats to society. "Within these films," Giroux (1998) wrote, "violence resonates with the popular perception that everyday black urban culture and the culture of criminality mutually define each other" (p. 31). To be Black is to be criminal.

A Black girl at Central City High lambasted popular cultural portrayals of Blacks and the corrosive impact that these images had on kids in her school. "I don't care what anybody says," she growled. "They stereotype Blacks real bad."

> These movies, they don't show the positive side to anything. It's like violence is glamourous and that's what's highly publicized on television. And then these kids I know they want to be like that. They want to be drug lords and gang bangers and all that. And then people who live out in the suburbs, who don't live close to downtown or close to the inner city, they see that stuff on TV, they don't even want to come down here. They teach their children not to, you know what I'm saying? Not to want to be around.

Despite the fact that popular cultural portrayals of Blacks and other youths reinforce destructive stereotypes, they were used by high school students as symbolic material for their youth cultural productions. At Central City High, boys known as "playas" adopted male hustlers' rhythmic gaits and their melodious, hip-hop street talk. They wore five-inch gold herringbone necklaces, gaudy gold rings, flashy gold watches, and capped their teeth in gold. "Fly girls" and "hoochies," playas' female counterparts, came to school looking like popular stereotypes of prostitutes with tight-fitting tops and hip-high shorts or miniskirts. They, too, draped themselves in gold.

White kids also were captivated by the images of wealth and power that could be acquired in the streets. There was a pseudogang of White boys at Jefferson High known as Gangsters with Drama or GWD. Members of GWD were described as "wannabes" who wanted to be like real gang bangers. Their gang colors were black and white—black for "bad" and white for "pure"—and they expressed their solidarity through hand gestures, group slang, and other signs. At Ridgewood High, "druggies" and "dirties" wore shirts with pictures of marijuana and other contraband and they pierced their ears, noses, lips, and other body parts with gold rings and studs.

Youth cultural expressions took different forms depending on the particular configurations of teenagers' subjective positionings and hopes and fears for mobility. For some middle-class students, like those at

Ridgewood High, youth cultural expressions were signs of resistance to intense parental pressures. They would challenge their parents' class values by adopting what they believed were the styles of lower-class youths. Jennifer, one of Lona's friends, could not figure out why suburban middle-class teenagers copied lower-class kids. "We used to strive to be more like them," she observed. "Now they're becoming more like us." But from the point of view of middle-class kids, imitating stereotypes of lower-class groups was a way for them to escape or seek relief from unrelenting pressures to remain at the top of the economic heap. Doing drugs served a similar purpose. "I think I did drugs," Peter said, "because I wasn't handling what my family, you know, what I supposed to be doing. It felt good to get away from it all."

Other Ridgewood students were from families who were upwardly mobile yet not as assimilated or welcomed into the centers of White middle-class society. Such was the case with Christina, the daughter of Mexican immigrants. Christina took issue with her White preppie classmates and their middle-class discourses that essentially looked down on or excluded people like her. She made a conscious effort to disassociate herself from preppies by cultivating the image of an off-beat 1960s artist and marginalized druggie. But she also imagined a future for herself as a professional artist. Her desire for achieving upward mobility without selling out completely to preppie values surfaced when we went to a slideshow presented by a recruiter for an art school in New York. Christina sat in awe as the presenter showed pictures of the school and the art work students had produced. "I'm not that good," she said after the show. "But it would be nice to be one of them, one of those artists who aren't like totally preppie."

Like Christina, most of the students who took on the guise of hustlers, gang bangers, and druggies did not go much beyond that. They looked but did not necessarily live the parts they played. But there were some who crossed the line between symbolic display and actual ploys for money and instant gratification. A few went a destructive step further in their productions of a youth culture of hostility (Hemmings, 2000a, 2002). Rather than direct their hostilities outward at the socioeconomic forces that were immobilizing them, they directed them inward at one another. They used dangerously hostile means to reach their desired ends by taking advantage of the most disadvantaged people in their neighborhoods. And they did so through knife-point robberies, brutal beatings, potentially murderous shootings, and other vicious acts of violence.

Monica had seen or heard about so much violence like this that she was numb to it. If she felt anything at all, it was excitement when it was happening. Like the excitement she felt when she heard gunshots while driving her car:

The other day I was driving by KFC and I could hear, I mean I know gun-shots. I was at the light and as soon as I turned the corner it's like a thou-sand people just running around the corner. So I got out of my car. I parked my car in the middle of the street and got out and ran. There was a boy standing on the street shooting I mean like it was nothing. A girl got shot. The guy was shooting at this one specific boy and he missed and hit the girl. You think he was going to hit him? I mean the guy he was aiming at was in the crowd with a thousand other people.

Monica knew the shooter and defended him. "Smokey, that's his name, is in a gang but he don't want to hurt nobody. If he does, you know, if he does hurt, shoot people it's because there's pressure on him, pressures on him 'cause he wouldn't hurt anyone on his own. He's not like that. Most people aren't like that."

As far as Monica was concerned, Smokey was a good person who was under a lot of pressure by fellow gang members to adapt in particularly de-structive ways to the harsh realities of life in a poor, isolated neighborhood where Black kids saw few job opportunities and much racial discrimina-tion and where they were bombarded by media images that essentially vil-ified them as public enemy number one. But for every young person like Smokey, overrun by the forces of undertows, there were many, many oth-ers who managed to navigate these and other currents in positively cre-ative and flexible ways.

4

Kinship Domain: Family (Dis)connections

Kinship studies flourished in anthropology until the 1980s, when they supposedly lost their popular appeal. To at least one notable scholar in the field, research on kinship, after decades of decline, is beginning to rise "phoenix-like ... from its ashes" as contemporary anthropologists rediscover its importance in explorations of cultural institutions (Schneider, 1995, p. 193). For others, this line of research has neither dwindled nor is experiencing a sudden resurgence in its former focuses of inquiry. Instead, it has been undergoing a steady transformation from investigations emphasizing genealogies, domestic group cycles, alliance, and descent theories to inquiries focusing on how people actually construct and utilize their kinship connections (Stone, 2001).[11] New directions, including those followed in this chapter, are being spearheaded by scholars who explore kinship in terms of sexuality, reproduction, and new forms of the family by "examining ideologies, using narratives, and placing the anthropologist among his or her subjects" (Lamphere, 2001, p. 42).

Although kinship studies have undergone significant transformations, high schools continue to be ignored as prime sites for fieldwork. This is curious given the fact that high schools have offered formal instruction on the family since the 1940s when "life adjustment education" was officially added to the curriculum (Kliebard, 1987). High schools also are where teenagers form intimate heterosexual and/or homosexual relationships; make love or abstain from sexual intercourse; use or don't use birth control; bear, give up, or abort children; become parents or forego parenting; and otherwise negotiate the discursive extremes and practices of kinship relations. I found that graduating seniors, in their negotiations, were coming of age in ways that connected them to, and disconnected them from, the many meanings of good family life.

FAMILY TRADITIONS

Seniors had notably disparate family backgrounds. Adam, David, Stuart, Christina, Peter, and Michael lived in what they described as stable, two-parent homes. Their mothers and fathers had weathered the ups and downs of family life through marriages that had lasted for years. Lona's parents had not fared so well. They were an unhappy pair who, according to Lona, "think communication is either fighting or not talking at all." Most of the rest of the seniors lived in homes headed by single mothers. Nay's parents were never married but maintained amicable relations. Cassandra's father passed away when she was 15, and Monica was estranged from a father she had never really known. Other seniors talked about having mothers who had a succession of husbands and/or boyfriends and fathers who were abusive, sporadically present, or altogether absent. A few had been abandoned by their parents. Some were parents themselves.

Despite the differences in their background, seniors' general outlook on what constitutes the ideal family was virtually the same. Almost all of them talked about the desirability of traditional family arrangements where men and women get married, have children, and live together as closely related kin. Christina, at Ridgewood High, felt "any other way would be odd."

> I would like to get married and have some children. I mean, that's what I'm used to. Any other way would be odd. I couldn't see myself being a single mother. I would like to have someone there. A man.

Adam, at Jefferson High, spoke about how students, over the course of his years in school, have come to the realization that the traditional "mother-and-father" family is the best way to go.

> Walking around school with other people for all these years, it seems like they're getting to know each other and getting to know where they know what they need to do. Like, they know that the family should probably be a mother and a father more than the divorce thing that's going on. So I think in a way it's, they're like trying to go back to a time when there were less divorces and more mother-and-father families. They're figuring out that's the best way to go.

David, from his perspective as a middle-class, Black student, presented an elaborate social/moral argument for why traditional family arrangements were ideal for minority and White families.

I don't really want to sound like some kind of racist but there's a difference between minority families and White families. It seems like White people are getting tired of getting divorced and they're moving towards staying together. On the other hand, minority families it seems like the father is never, ever present. That's like the root of most of their problems. Social problems. If everybody, the children, the products of this generation gets tired of that, if they don't want that for their kids, you might see a movement where they get married and stay together. But if they take the attitude of their parents, I can see where they don't have the advantage like in a family where a father is present, where it's a traditional type of family. I guess what I'm saying is that everybody's family should be more traditional because you have a stronger base. You have a stronger moral base.

Michael, a White boy, and Monica, a Black girl, at Central City High both agreed that mothers and fathers need to be around.

Michael: I think more families should stay together. Hopefully, I mean, that way maybe the kid will have a mother figure and a father figure around. They'll feel more confident instead of going home and wondering if they're going to see their dad again or their mom. I think it's relatively strange for a kid, in my opinion, to come home and have a mom who is like a dad figure. It's also kind of strange to come home to parents who have the same sex.

Monica: I think that two parents are what you need. My mom raised me. It was just me and her. But I think you really need a two-parent home. I mean if I had my choice, well, yeah, I'd have a father in the home because you need to see two different points of view. Like just with your mother you almost know what she's going to say. But you see your father and you never know because he comes home tired and he might say "no" or whatever.

These and other seniors were thus unequivocal in their affirmations of the dominant discourses that have structured American family traditions for centuries. Schneider (1968) presented what has become a classic cultural account of what these traditions entail. Basing his analysis on what he declared as "ethnographic facts," he explained the "order of law" and "natural order" of the family as if they really were facts. The most basic unit in the American kinship system is the nuclear family, where close unions of relatives are joined together by the laws of marriage and the biogenetic bonds of blood. Unions are forged by a legally married couple—a husband and a wife—whose relationship is symbolized by exclusive acts of heterosexual intercourse. The couple's sexual relations or "conjugal love" are legitimatized through universally accepted cultural standards.

> Of all of the forms of sexuality of which human beings are capable, only one is legitimate and proper according to the standards of American culture, and that is heterosexual relations, genital to genital, between man and wife. All other forms are improper and held to be morally wrong. (Schneider, 1968, p. 108)

The nuclear family also includes children. A married couple without children does not quite constitute a family as children are necessary to complete the family unit and for the continuation of intergenerational blood lines. Whereas spouses are related to each other by law, children (unless they are legally adopted) are related by blood to their parents, each other, and relatives on both sides of the family. A married couple may get divorced or otherwise end their relationship, but children are always related to them and other blood kin. Where marriage may be terminal, blood ties endure forever. Blood, in commonsense parlance, is thicker than water.

Everyday family relations are structured by behavioral codes of conduct that prescribe how homes are maintained, children are reared, and other household duties are performed. These codes are naturally divided into gendered roles and responsibilities. The natural endowment of women is to bear, nurse, and care for children. Men are more suited to protecting the home and providing the resources needed to support the family. Among other natural gender differences are the active, aggressive qualities of men and the more passive and accommodating characteristics of women. As Schneider explained:

> Men have greater physical strength and stamina than women. Men are said to have mechanical aptitudes that women lack. Women have nurturant qualities which men lack. Men tend toward an aggressive disposition said to be absent in women. (p. 41)

These differences in the qualities of maleness and femaleness put husbands into the natural position of head of household, whereas wives assume the more subordinate role of helpmate. These positionings and other traditions not only cohere around dominant notions of nuclear family arrangements, but also depend on individual members' sense of a familial/sexual self.

THE FAMILIAL/SEXUAL SELF

Schneider's (1968) account also included a discussion about the formation of a common family identity, especially among blood relatives:

People who are blood relatives share a common identity, they believe. This is expressed as "being of the same flesh and blood." It is a belief in common biological constitution, and aspects like temperament, build, physiognomy, and habits are noted as signs of this shared biological makeup, this special identity of relatives with each other. (p. 25)

The familial self is formed very early in the lives of children. Children, the moment they are born, are given names and surnames as signs of their inclusion into their parents' families. Surnames are especially potent indicators of membership in, and identification with, an extended family group. People frequently refer to themselves as being a "Smith" or "Jones" or belonging to some other named family lineage. Women, when they get married, traditionally assume the surnames of their husbands as they essentially exchange one named familial identification for another. For people who no longer identify with their families, dropping or changing their surnames is the most drastic way for them to sever ties.

The symbolic significance of family names was evident among seniors. Stuart was from a prominent family and loved it when people recognized his paternal surname, as an indication of his own good family connections. "I'll like go into a store and show them my credit card and the clerk is like 'Are you related to Dr. Lyon? Are you from that family?' That's pretty cool. It's cool to say 'Yeah, I am.'"

Such recognition clearly boosted what for Stuart was a rather strong sense of himself as a member of the Lyon family. Seniors at the other extreme were either inclined or forced to disconnect themselves from their families in name as well as through other means. Ashley, one of Lona's friends, when she came out as a lesbian, was abandoned by her mother and alienated from the rest of her family to the point where "I don't think they want to be seen on the streets with me. I supposed they'd like to disown me. I don't know. My dad kind of already did that. I don't even have his last name which is okay with me."

The disconnections Ashley described were partly a result of what she described as her true sexual self. The nature and origins of the sexual self have long been topics of dispute among American psychologists and anthropologists. Psychologists tend to trace sexuality and sexual preferences to genetic inheritance or external environmental influences. Anthropologists focus on how sexuality forms as individuals adapt to community values, norms, and practices. The most extreme versions of this view are promoted by those who believe that sexuality is completely a product of culture and therefore an "entirely arbitrary" form of human expression (Lipkin, 1995, p. 45). Then there are those who conceive the formation of the sexual self as identity work where cultural forces interact with innate biogenetic psychology. Hacking (1999) categorized such conceptualiza-

tions as "interactive kinds" where the manner in which people are culturally classified affects the way they experience psychological states:

> We are especially concerned with [cultural] classifications that, when
> known by people or by those around them, and put to work in institutions,
> change the ways in which individuals experience themselves... Such kinds
> (of people and their behavior) are interactive kinds. This ugly phrase has
> the merit of recalling actors, agency and action. The *inter* may suggest the
> way in which the classification and the individual classified may interact,
> the way in which the actors may become self-aware as being of a kind, if
> only because of being treated or institutionalized as of that kind, and so ex-
> periencing themselves in that way. (p. 104)

Individuals' expressions of their biogenetic sexual psychology are affected by how sexuality is culturally construed. Such expressions are discursively constructed renditions of sexual preferences and practices as
normal or abnormal, abject or acceptable, controllable or uncontrollable.
In dominant cultural currents, the "normal" sexual self is rendered in
terms of "straight" heterosexuality. Most of the graduating seniors, with
the exception of some of Lona's friends, were heterosexual. But how they
expressed their sexual selves—indeed, their combined familial/sexual
selves—was affected by a myriad of discursive forces including liminal
ones that are allowing people to venture out into once unimaginable directions in the (re)makings of their family lives.

FAMILY LIFE IN THE PUBLIC (RE)MAKING

In contemporary America, the cultural moorings that used to firmly an-
chor nuclear family traditions and the common familial/sexual self are
being dislodged by people no longer able or willing to go along with dominant currents. A liminal shift is occurring after a long, protracted history of public disapproval and laws that effectively suppressed,
stigmatized, or encouraged the outright condemnation of adultery, divorce, cohabitation of unmarried couples, children born out of wedlock,
homosexuality, and other deviations from nuclear family arrangements.
The tight constraints imposed by custom and legal pressures began to
loosen in the 1960s and 1970s when the civil rights movement was expanded to include the right of people to makes personal choices about
family-life styles. The movement opened the gates for more individual-
ized/istic discourses to flood into the public layers of the kinship domain. More and more people are now forming their own sense of a
familial/sexual self and (re)making the family to fit their own personal
proclivities and circumstances.

Far from being universally welcomed, the liminal shift has ignited ideologically charged disputes over what it means to live a good family life. Convinced there has been a dangerous erosion of traditional family values, conservative Americans have made the preservation of the nuclear family into a national political issue. They are waging media campaigns affirming the correctness of heterosexual marriage, the proper roles of fathers as providers and mothers as caregivers, and, in the most ultraconservative veins, the duty of wives to serve and obey their husbands. Feminists are countering with critiques of nuclear families as oppressive patriarchal strongholds where women are subjugated, silenced, or forced into submissive servitude. They focus on the unjust locus of power in marriages and other heterosexual couplings where men seek control over women in sexual relations as well as in the realm of domestic service. Activists among them are working to liberate and ultimately empower women by toppling male-dominated family structures or through the creation of women-centered family networks where men have little or no power over members' lives. Liberals fall somewhere in between with their ideologies of egalitarianism where spouses or sexual partners share domestic responsibilities as they pursue their own individual happiness. Power in their relations is to be evenly distributed as they bear and rear children, manage day-to-day household operations, and attend to their own careers. Gays, lesbians, bisexuals, and transsexuals have adopted the most radical stance. Historically stereotyped and mistreated as psychologically abnormal, sinners, or criminals, they are now counteracting heterosexist hegemony through tactics that celebrate homo-, trans-, and bisexual orientations and "queer" perspectives on intimate relations by troubling or unsettling the notion of stability in sexual identities.

Although most graduating seniors endorsed dominant family traditions and familial/sexual identifications in their talk on ideal family arrangements, they spread themselves across ideological positionings in our conversations about the future direction of the American family. In their thoughts about the future, they recognized what appeared to be an irreversible liminal shift in the public acceptance of once unacceptable family-life styles. Monica described how the public mentality had shifted dramatically from "marriage only" to "anything goes."

> About the only thing you could do in olden days was get married. Then people started getting out of thinking, of having the mentality where you have to be married to have sex, where you have to be a certain age to have children. Back in the old pioneer days, you could get married at thirteen and have a baby, then it got to where you were expected to be older, like in your twenties, but you still had to get married first. Now the thing is, like in the nineties, I believe in the eighties that's when girls started having babies in high school without being married. It wasn't long before fathers did not

participate in their children's lives. Some of them, can't speak for all of them, but a lot of fathers just flee the scene. Now it's like you can be a single mom and there isn't a stigma. You can be gay and, like, hire a woman to have kids for you. Man, it's like anything goes, whatever you want to do, just go ahead and do it.

Seniors stood firm or vacillated back and forth along the conservative-to-radical scale of public opinion. An admittedly conservative White boy at Ridgewood High believed changes were harming the family as it is only natural for men and women to get married and assume traditional gender-differentiated roles.

> When it comes to kids, I don't know, I suppose it's possible for men to stay home and take care of them. But I don't think it's the way we're created. Honestly. I'm not trying to be sexist, but we are like kind of like born natural leaders, like it's natural for us to feel responsible for protecting the woman and providing for the woman. I mean even a relationship in high school you feel that way. Women are like the caring ones, nurturing, the ones who like naturally take care of kids and the rest of the family.

David, in a much more liberal vein, felt that the best situation for husbands and wives would be one where both of them had gratifying careers and shared domestic responsibilities. "As much as possible," he told me, "it should be fifty-fifty so it's fair and they do other stuff they like."

Some of the girls were attracted to feminist positions in anticipation of expanded opportunities for them to elevate their status both in and out of the home. Monica said she would not be at all surprised if "more guys stay home while the woman goes out and work. I know a couple of families where the mother works and the father stays home. There could be more families like that. Probably will be because there are more working women. Work means money and more power and guys, you know, the husbands will be looking at us like equals or maybe superiors."

Other seniors were more radical in their outlook. For Lona and her friends, the ideal family had more to do with the quality of interpersonal relationships (loving, caring, sexually satisfying) than the biogenetic and legal nature of familial bonds. Paul was a young gay man who envisioned families in the future as units where people are conjoined primarily by how they feel about each other, rather than by blood. "To me, the ideal family are people who are related to you by how they feel about you. I don't see, I don't consider the word 'family' to be about blood. It should have nothing to do with blood. It's about love, all about love. I believe that we're all headed that way, the way of love." Love was thicker than blood in his imaginings, but that did not mean that nuclear family arrangements should be abandoned entirely. Paul saw no reason why traditional codes of conduct could not be incorporated into alternative family-life styles. "Gay men, lesbians, all of us should be able to get married and have kids. Gays can have surrogate mothers where, like, the gay couple would be the parents and the mother would also be present. I don't see why something like that couldn't be worked out."

Other members of Lona's clique totally rejected the traditions of the heterosexual nuclear family. They were or wanted to be lesbians with long-term companions, bisexuals with an assortment of male and female partners, single straights with multiple straight lovers, or loners existing, as one girl said, "all by myself in total, total freedom."

Then there were seniors like Cassandra, who shifted back and forth from one extreme to another. She spoke with the conviction of a staunchly conservative Christian about how families were being destroyed by "Godless" people who do not care about anything or anybody except themselves. Referring to the Bible, she condemned divorce as immoral, promiscuous sex as sinful, and homosexuality as especially nasty. "I think it's wrong. It's in the Bible. You ain't supposed to do it. You ain't supposed to do a lot of stuff in the Bible. I'm not going to quote that but I just don't think it's right. I think it's nasty, especially what homosexuals do." But although she thoroughly chastised people who deviated from nuclear family arrangements, she relished the growing public acceptance of out-of-wedlock births and single parenting. As an unmarried teenage mother, she was much relieved that women like her are no longer stigmatized for life. "Back in the old days if you were pregnant before you got married it was like 'oh, God, no, no, no!' If you didn't marry the father, you would be an outcast or everybody talked about you like you were a really wicked person. It was worse if you kept the baby and bad for the baby 'cause they'd come right up to him and call him a bastard. A lot of the time, they'd take the baby away even if the mother wanted to keep it. They'd take it away and put it up for adoption but they'd still be talkin' about her for the rest of her life. It's not like that anymore. People don't seem to care as long as you aren't on welfare or something. I'm glad about that."

So while Cassandra was vehement in her refusal to accept people who rattled the foundations of American family traditions, she was grateful for the destigmatization of her own once unacceptable family situation. Such was the contradictory yet potentially integrating mix of her and many other teenagers' stances on the public (re)makings of the American family.

LOCAL FAMILY WORLDVIEWS

Prescriptive Intent

While once unacceptable discourses on family life are being unleashed in the realm of public opinion, traditional family-life styles remain tightly fettered in private, local family worlds. Phelan, Davidson, and Yu (1993, 1998) used the term *world* to refer to the highly localized cultural systems produced within the boundaries of particular family units and other social groupings. These systems are intentional worlds because they contain cultural prescriptions intended to configure inhabitants' sense of self, place, and actions (Shweder, 1991). In the case of local family worlds (i.e., nuclear and extended families), prescriptions constitute an everyday scheme of things for family members to follow. Far from behaving in passive compliance to these schemes, family members are intentional persons who actively negotiate their worlds as they assert and situate their selves, define what they want their place to be or become, and determine how they will or will not act.

As I observed in a prior study, American teenagers grapple with local family prescriptions as they work to project or transform their identities (Hemmings, 1998). If teenagers experience family worlds as conducive to the realization of their self-images, they are likely to accommodate to the prescriptions intended for them. But if they perceive the expectations of parents or other relatives as oppressive or self-restricting, they will challenge prescriptions in a manner that often leads to intense cultural and psychological conflict.

In this study, I found teenagers, in addition to their identity work, were negotiating integrative family role positionings that were governed by prescriptive codes of conduct intended to control their actions and, just as importantly, their relations. I discovered that family (dis)connections were affected not only by the cultural scheme of things in intentional family worlds, but also by the individual intentions of teenagers drawn to other worlds of family-life possibilities.

"Good" Family Connections

Local world prescriptions in the broadest sense are intended to forge the kinds of "good" family connections that facilitate the day-to-day affairs of domestic life and ensure the reproduction and well-being of future generations. These prescriptions are directly shaped by the economic, cultural, and social circumstances of family groups. They are formed as families respond to conditions of wealth or poverty; the influences of ethnic and other cultural beliefs, values, and norms; and the nature of immediate interpersonal and larger social relations. There is no single local world scheme for ensuring good family connections. Rather, there are countless local family prescriptions resting on highly particularistic discourses and everyday disciplinary practices intended to define each member's familial/sexual self, role positionings, and actions. These prescriptions contain shared and/or contested messages about what family members ought to be and do, especially in relation to one another.

Adolescents, as intentional persons, engage in varying degrees of accommodation or resistance to local family prescriptions. Among the most accommodating adolescents in this study were Stuart Lyon, Nay Wilson, and Christina Sanchez. Although prescriptions for good family connections differed notably between their families, all three had strong familial identifications, were comfortable with prescribed codes, and bonded to parents and other relatives in long-lasting, mutually supportive relations.

Stuart clearly identified with his family, especially his father's side. His paternal grandfather was a renowned plastic surgeon who ran an extremely lucrative medical practice. Stuart's father and uncles had become quite successful in their own pursuits as professionals and business entrepreneurs. They and other Lyon relatives formed and sustained what Stuart described as "one big happy family. The Lyons are huge. Like it seems there are 300 of them, so many Lyons. Two families live here. One lives in Montreal. One lives in Boston. Another lives in Cleveland. We keep in touch. I'm close to them, like my cousins and I grew up seeing each other a lot. We have very snobby people in the family. We also have great people. But we like everyone, you know, each other."

Stuart was especially close to his grandfather who, he said, had taught him a great deal about success and happiness. "I'm very good with my grandparents. I respect them a lot. I respect my grandfather more than anyone in the world. So I go over there a lot and spend time with him. He tells me things like how to be successful. Like he stresses the importance of going to good colleges, working hard, but also of being happy."

Happiness was just as important as success. But success, especially monetary success, was clearly touted as necessary for happiness. Lyon family prescriptions not only stressed the importance of making a lot of money, but also of spending money on domestic services so that family members could do other, more enjoyable things. "My mom doesn't like to cook but she does like us to eat together on Sundays and Mondays. The rest of the time we eat out at restaurants. My dad's fun. He's funny, too. He likes to plan trips, go to games and stuff. He lets my mother do whatever she wants. He wants her to have fun, too." The essential prescriptive intent was to maintain good connections as one big happy family by accumulating enough wealth to release members from the drudgery and constraints of traditional familial roles and responsibilities. The goal was for every member to have fun in the collective yet highly individualistic pursuit of happiness.

The particular prescriptions for good family connections that governed everyday life in Nay's family were constructed in circumstances of extreme economic poverty and social isolation. Nay lived with her mother, other relatives, and hundreds of other low-income Black people in a sprawling, low-rent apartment complex. The complex included several barracks-like brick buildings surrounded by a tall wire fence that kept residents in as much as it kept other people out. Within the fence, women banded together in real and fictive kinship alliances as they worked to ensure their own survival as well as that of their children and other relatives.

The connections within these alliances were sustained by familial discourses of mutual aid observed among other low-income Black women (Hale-Benson, 1986; Hemmings, 1998; Stack, 1974; Ward, 1995). The mutual aid orientation not only is produced by Black women in response to the economic and social disenfranchisement of Black men, but also has deep roots in African traditions where female members of extended families are obliged to offer assistance, share resources, and provide other kinds of support wherever and whenever it is needed.

The main intent of the mutual aid orientation is the provision of care for children and other dependent family members. Of secondary importance is the individualistic pursuit of economic success and happiness. Nay wanted a career and to otherwise establish her independence, but she also valued her position as an integral member of the alliance formed by her mother and other female relatives. Within the alliance, Nay was obligated to participate in the daily activities of mutual assistance. Rather than resist these obligations, she willingly shouldered them, knowing they were intended for the collective good of the entire family.

Alliance members included Nay's mother, her sister who had four small children, female cousins who were single mothers, and close friends who, Nay said, "might as well be relatives." Nay said that the children were like her own babies. She spent a lot of time after school and on the weekends caring for them while their mothers went to work, shopped, and handled other affairs. The mothers, she said, would "dress the babies up and I like come and get 'em. I might take 'em to the mall or something but mostly I just take 'em home and look after them. I'm like their second mama and not just their aunt or cousin."

Although men were present, they were somewhat peripheral to the inner workings of the alliance. In Nay's imaginings, fathers should share equally in the financial support and care of children. "If it were up to me, both the daddy and the mama should work and bring in half the money. One should get a job in the morning and one should get a job at night. The daddy would help change the diapers. My attitude is that if I gotta change 'em, he gotta change 'em. If I got to stand the smell, he does to. We both gotta share." But the reality was that men either did not contribute in any on-going way to the family's upkeep or were purposefully kept at bay by women who did not trust them around the children. Although Nay's father had amicable relations with her mother, he offered little in the way of monetary support and he never changed diapers or performed other domestic chores. Like many other men in the neighborhood, he was essentially excluded as a full-fledged member of the alliance. Men often were cared for but kept on the margins as people who provided little or no aid, were inclined to drain rather than replenish scarce resources, and/or were threatening to women and their children. They were more of a burden than an asset in family networks that depended on cooperative assistance and personal sacrifice.

Good family connections in the families of Christina and other members of her friendship clique were forged within the tributaries of ethnic traditions. The clique included two second-generation immigrant girls from India and Pakistan. Another member of the group was Japanese. And, of course, there was Christina, who was the daughter of Mexican immigrants.

Although their cultural backgrounds were distinctive, all of the girls encountered restrictions on their relationships with men. None were allowed to date boys without the approval and supervision of parents. Premarital sex and out-of-wedlock pregnancies were strictly forbidden. Restrictions were even more stringent for the Pakistani Muslim girl, whose marriage was to be arranged by her parents. "Her parents will pick the boy for her," Christina explained. "But she does have the option to turn courtship and marriage offers down."

Whereas other American teenagers rejected such restrictions as oppressive, members of Christina's clique accepted them as beneficial for their families. "One thing is that we understand each other and how our families are. Like if one person can't go out, we understand. We aren't like, 'Well, why not? What's wrong with your parents?' We don't ask. We just know that the reason why things are the way they are is because it's for the family, you know, so we don't pick stupid boys, get pregnant, and like mess up the family. Other kids don't understand that. They don't get it. So we are minorities in this school and we stick together."

The girls not only understood how their relationships with men have consequences for their families as a whole, but also how the family itself is and ought to remain central in their lives. Maintaining a common familial identity and solidarity were all-important in Christina's home where "everyone is talking and doing things. My mother says that friends and boyfriends might leave, but family always stays. All of my brothers and sisters live at home. My oldest brother is 25. I think he should leave but he doesn't. My older sister left home for a couple of years but moved back in because she couldn't afford the rent. It's okay with my parents because they like having us all around."

Good family connections, in other words, rested on prescriptions intended to ensure that blood relatives remained close and close at hand and that spouses or other new nonblood members were deemed worthy enough to be absorbed into the family fold. That was "the thing" that set Christina, her friends, and their families apart.

In Defense of the "True" Self

Not every senior experienced good family connections. A few of them suffered through family-splintering disconnections that had terrible consequences for them. I heard stories about bitter divorces, the unsettling comings and goings of parents' boyfriends or girlfriends, and the travails of other adult relationships. But of particular interest to me were the disconnections instigated by seniors who openly challenged family prescriptions in order to realize their familial/sexual selves. Such realizations are possible but extremely difficult to accomplish. Teenagers who dare to defy intentional family worlds often end up becoming isolated within, or expelled from, those worlds (Shweder, 1991).

That is what happened to Lona and many of her friends (Hemmings, 2000b). Lona's clique was unusually mixed (or "mixed up," as Lona liked to say), especially with regard to members' sexual orientations. I conducted an interview with clique members during which I talked about a best-selling book about how teenagers develop a false self in order to get people to like them.[12] Ashley, Lona's best friend, spoke up and said, "I know exactly what that book is saying. A lot of kids do that, but we're not like that in this group. We're our true selves. We are who we are and don't care if other people don't like us."

When I asked what it meant to have a "true self," another girl, Jennifer, said, "It's the feeling of knowing who you are and what you want." Probing further, I asked the group to talk in more detail about their own true selves. Ashley suddenly sat upright and exclaimed, "Okay, I'm coming right out and telling you what it is for me and for a lot of us here in this room. It's got to do with sexuality and why a lot of people don't like us." She then came out with her lesbian sexual orientation, with Paul following suit with his own assertion of himself as a gay man. Both of them went on to describe how their mothers had evicted or abandoned them because they refused to conform to prescriptions intended to normalize their sexual identities.

Ashley spoke first. She told of how she was an only child raised by a single, working mother who never had a healthy relationship with a man. Her mother's desires for Ashley rested on the premise that women should cultivate and project a feminine familial/sexual self to attract and keep men. This type of self is embodied in the popular image of the "all-American girl" that, according to Ashley, is most epitomized by girls who date athletic jocks. "Jocks' girlfriends ... all look alike. They're tall, thin, and sexy. They have the exact same hairstyles and wear the exact same clothes. They're cheerleaders and homecoming queens. They get the best jobs in the mall. See, they're the perfect picture of the all-American girl." For Ashley, the all-American girl image adopted by jocks' girlfriends and promoted by her mother was self-destructive. "If you really listen to my mom, it was like she was saying women should starve themselves, sleep with bums, and spend the rest of their lives popping Prozac. No way, no way, not for me." Ashley, in self-defense, refused to fall in line with her mother's prescriptions. Battle lines were drawn, tempers mounted, and relations finally exploded when Ashley revealed to her mother that she was a lesbian. Two days after she came out, Ashley came home to an empty apartment. Her mother had packed up and moved away. Completely abandoned at the age of 17, Ashley sank into a deep, self-devouring depression.

Then Paul told his story. He had been raised in a family of strict Southern Baptists and had been close to his parents, especially to his mother. Paul, as a young boy, had homosexual inklings but he suppressed them as "utterly sinful. Baptists, like when you're a Baptist, being gay is utterly sinful. It's the work of the devil and you're going to hell and all of that. If you're not straight, you're evil, as bad as you can get."

But his emergent true self as a gay man could not be denied. "It had to come out," Paul explained. "So I decided I had to tell my mother and when I did she completely freaked out. She got mad and told me, 'You can stay if you're not gay.' She was saying she couldn't deal with me, with me being gay so she was like get out of here if you can't be straight. Like go to hell or something." Paul left and moved in with friends who became his "new family."

Naomi, another member of the clique, also left home. She moved in with a male cousin for reasons she never made clear. Unlike her friends who felt some certainty about their true selves, she was entangled in familial/sexual self-contradictions dispersed through discursive extremes of macho-male aggression and docile-woman submission. Naomi's espoused ambition was to join the Marines. She would come to school wearing camouflage pants and U.S. Marine t-shirts. I watched as she approached boys in the hallway in her Marine garb and attempt to seduce them as if she were the predator and they the prey. On the public stage of corridor life, she looked, talked, and performed like a woman who rejected any and all conventional prescriptions for women. Yet Naomi, in our private conversations, showed me love poetry she had written about being carried off by male suitors into "rainbow flower gardens with sparkling blue lakes." The poems, many of them addressed to her cousin, were a far cry from the soldier-girl conqueror who patrolled the hallways with such masculine self-assurance. They were the cries of a much less self-assured girl who retreated into the currents of feminine romance after breaking away from the warring torrents within her family world.

Naomi and other graduating seniors struggled with their identity and integration work with or against public cultural currents and the more directly felt prescriptive currents of their local family worlds. Although much of this work was accomplished at home, it also was carried out in high schools, where seniors were offered a variety of educational programs for the sake of their families in particular and the American family in general.

EDUCATION FOR FAMILIES' SAKE

The essential thrust within high schools with regard to student integration into the kinship domain is to provide educational experiences that support the family. Social scientists for many decades analyzed schooling as a process where children are weaned from their families. Parsons (1959) stated as a matter of social fact how American high schools typically socialize students to transcend their familial identification so that they can identify with socioeconomic roles within the larger society. "The old familial identification is broken up," he wrote, "and a new identification is gradually built up" (p. 310). Anthropologists also viewed schools as being somewhat incompatible with family life. Many of them, in response to the deficit theories that prevailed in the 1960s, focused their attention on the deleterious effects of home/school cultural discontinuities, especially on students' academic achievement.[13] Their basic contention was that many families and schools are divided by cultural chasms that students must cross in order to succeed. Those who experience conflict in their crossings have to make a difficult choice. They must either give up their family affiliation to do well in school or reject schooling in order to remain in the family.

Although home/school cultural conflict certainly does occur, high schools are not and never were purposefully established to separate children from their families. Developers of secondary school curricula as early as 1901 were instituting programs of study that were expressly designed to prepare adolescents for existing adult roles, including roles in the family (Kliebard, 1987). It was initially assumed that the curricular needs of boys were different from those of girls. Boys, as future breadwinners, were required to take vocational classes, whereas girls took classes in home economics where they learned the basics of conventional homemaking skills. As family life has changed, so, too, has the curriculum. Contemporary high schools now offer an array of coeducational classes on cooking and sewing, consumer education, family and independent living, child development and care, and sex education. Programs have been established to prevent teenage pregnancy and, when that fails, provide parenting classes, day care, or other support services for students with children. Schools also have expanded their counseling programs to assist students with whatever family problems they may be experiencing. The issue for schools has not been how to wean adolescents from their families but, rather, how to make sure students adapt to the real and perceived circumstances of family life. I found that high schools in their curricular and other approaches to education for family's sake were generally geared toward transmitting dominant family traditions in a manner that reinforces the integrity of local families.

Curriculum of Socially Efficient Family Management

All three high schools offered required and elective classes on family living and related topics such as sex education. Much of the content of these classes included standard curricular fare meant to teach students how to handle ordinary domestic tasks, parental roles, and sexual activity in socially efficient ways. Although such a curriculum was common in every school, what and how lessons were taught varied significantly as teachers made adjustments based on what they perceived to be the family needs of their particular student populations.

Teachers at Ridgewood High believed that the majority of their students were destined for middle-class occupations and family-life styles. They also felt they were serving kids from mostly White, affluent families that were quite capable of, indeed, insistent on, taking care of their own affairs. As one teacher told me, "We know better than to tell these parents how to raise their children." In keeping with their perceptions, teachers taught family skills in a way that augmented middle-class economic mobility and did so without actually telling students whether or how they ought to assume domestic roles or responsibilities. Classes were taught as if domestic roles and responsibilities for middle-class students were optional rather than obligatory, entertaining rather than involving a lot of unpleasant work.

There was a class on creative cooking where, according to a course catalog, students could learn about meal planning and food preparation as a "leisure time activity." Cultures and Cuisines was another class where students could experience "the excitement of gourmet cooking and the preparation of festive and holiday meals." Students could enroll in a singles living class where they learned how to choose a career and become independent consumers who could furnish an apartment, build a budget, manage money, and select and prepare food. They also could take classes on fashion expression and design or contemporary clothing construction, where they learned how to sew clothes that satisfied "individual needs" or functioned as "a form of self expression." In the sole class on parenting/child development, students were taught how to "think through the responsibilities and stress of parenthood" and where to get outside help if they needed it. Cooking was thus taught as a leisure-time hobby rather than an inescapable household chore. Sewing was a self-distinguishing fashion statement, whereas parenting was something to be avoided or handled in a manner that reduced the stresses of child care.

Stuart took the creative cooking class. I observed his teacher, a stout White woman, on one occasion as she showed the class how to make a "fluffy omelet." Students gathered around a stove and watched as she cooked a large omelet in a lively, humorous demonstration. Her performance resembled those on televised cooking shows where chefs are just as bent on entertaining their audiences as they are on following recipes. When she was done with the omelet, she cut it up into pieces and passed them out to students to eat. Stuart told me the class was fun but "kind of dumb."

The teacher also taught the course on parenting/child development. Although I did not observe the class, the teacher allowed me to examine her curricular materials as she explained her instructional approach to me. Much of the content she covered was based on a textbook that had chapters on the negative consequences of teenage pregnancy, the development of children from conception to age seven, and parenting. The teacher also taught a unit on sex and birth control where, she told me, "we cover contraceptive devices but advise abstinence." She said that parents in the community were conservative and would raise "holy hell" if she appeared to be "pushing condoms on their kids."

The approach teachers took at Central City High was a virtual antithesis of the one at Ridgewood High. Every student in the school was required to take a health class covering marriage and family, nutrition, human sexuality, drug, alcohol, and tobacco abuse, and mental and physical health. They could sign up for electives in parenting, family relations, nutrition/wellness, and resource management. Pregnant teens were strongly encouraged to enroll in GRADS (Graduation, Reality, and Dual-role Skills), a program designed to:

Give you information about your pregnancy
Ready you for raising a healthy, happy child
Assist you with staying in school
Deal with making important personal decisions
Start you thinking about your future as a working parent

The curricular tack taken in these classes and programs was set mostly by White teachers and staff bent on addressing what they perceived to be vexing social problems in the impoverished, predominantly Black neighborhoods that surrounded the school. Among the problems they perceived were high teenage pregnancy rates, the preponderance of single-female-headed households, and the constant threat of sexually transmitted diseases. Rather than adopt the kind of indirect, hands-off approach prevalent at Ridgewood High, Central City High teachers provided direct, interventionist instruction meant to solve problems that were destroying students and their families.

Teachers taught blunt, up-front lessons about the risks of promiscuous sex, the poverty and other negative consequences associated with single parenting, and the dangers of AIDS and other diseases. Among them was the teacher who taught the required health class. I was accidently exposed to the health curriculum while sitting with a group of girls in a Spanish class. One of the girls knocked a folder on the floor and several papers spilled out with graphic drawings of male and female genitalia. There was a six-inch drawing of an erect penis with herpes, a vagina with a penis penetrating it, and other pictures that struck me as obscene. I thought the girl might have brought the pictures to school to amuse her friends, but it turns out that she had gotten them from the health teacher who used them to illustrate the hazards of unprotected, out-of-control sex. The pictures and the curricular messages accompanying them were loud and clear: If you do not curb your out-of-control sexual desires and activities, then you will get pregnant, catch deadly diseases, and otherwise suffer terrible consequences.

The girls in the group did not appear to be put off by, or even aware of, messages that were positioning them as sexually promiscuous and irresponsible or as people with pathological family-life styles. They felt their teachers were helping them make informed decisions, as the girl with the folder explained, "by telling us like it is, like, you better know what can happen to you if you have sex." As we were talking, another girl pulled up her shirt sleeve and showed me five Norplant birth control sticks that had been inserted into her arm. She had learned about this form of birth control in class and liked it "because I can have sex for 5 years and not worry about having a baby until I'm like 20, you know, old enough to be a mother."

The school that offered the most extensive curricular offerings on family life was Jefferson High. As was the case at Central City High, students were required to take a health class that covered sex education, sexually transmitted disease, and related topics. They could take electives in home economics on work and family life, child development, independent living, clothing and textiles, food and nutrition. Or they could enroll in career oriented vocational education classes on clothing and interior production and services, vocational homemaking, child care, and food service. Students could thus learn how to efficiently manage domestic work in the home as well as how to do paid domestic work in the economic service sector.

Although their school offered several classes, none of the seniors I spoke with took electives in home economics nor did they have any interest in signing up for vocational education. They regarded the kinds of domestic work taught in the vocational education classes as demeaning or, in Lona's words, "crappy jobs where you take care of other people's dirt and brats." There was an obvious disdain for employment in food, clothing, cleaning, and child-care services where jobs are low paying, low status, and stuck on the lowest rungs of the economic ladder. And students clearly resented messages that encouraged them to seek these kinds of jobs. Messages about opportunities in such areas, in students' opinion, were discursively equivalent to servitude.

Seniors did take the required health class. When I asked them about what they learned, most provided cynical commentaries on a "boring" curriculum that struck them as disconnected from reality. Much of the time, the health teacher had students read textbook passages and fill out worksheets on material about good nutrition, the nature and avoidance of sexually transmitted disease, birth control, and other topics. Adam said that on the few occasions when there was a lecture, the teacher would talk about "not doing drugs, sex, and everything else kids do around here." Lona recalled a unit on AIDS that made her think twice about having sex with gays and other people with whom she was not inclined to have sex in the first place. David said that as far as he could tell, the purpose of the health class was to "stop kids from acting like adults." In these and other remarks, seniors poked fun at what they perceived to be an uninteresting, rather naive curricular approach to the realities in their schools, their families, and American society.

DYSFUNCTIONAL FAMILY TREATMENTS

High schools also have greatly expanded their support services for students. Guidance counselors, school psychologists, nurses, and other staff were employed in all of the research sites to assist students with an array of nonacademic issues, including issues with their families. At Central City High, CASE advisors were the ones who provided students with the most direct assistance with their families. They were originally hired to work for the Career and Academic Success Education (CASE) school-to-work program. Although their main duty was to facilitate students' job internship placements, most of them defined their roles in ways they felt subverted their officially stated responsibilities. As a Black male CASE advisor explained, they were more interested in ensuring the "overall success of the child" than making sure that students showed up for internships involving minimum-wage jobs. "The way we have taken hold of this job, we are changing the direction because we want to see kids succeed mentally, physically, psychologically, and not get stuck in dead-end jobs. A lot of us could care less about their internships."

His colleague, a Black woman who was once a social worker, went on to explain how CASE advisors ensure overall success by becoming liaisons between students and their classroom teachers, workplace employers, social services, and parents. "We're the overall liaison person," she said. "We are the links between kids and teachers, employers, and everyone else they need to make things happen."

CASE advisors were especially keen on forging liaisons with parents. I was told during a group interview about how they would go into homes to see what was really happening to kids. "When we do that," the former social worker said, "we can see that the kid has no food to eat, has to go out and hustle on the street to take care of his mom 'cause she can't take care of the family."

> I see they have little kids, little brothers and sisters they have to take care of. So the student is not functioning in the classroom because he's lucky just to be able to get up enough strength to get to school. To me, our program is a last ditch effort for some of these kids because I think the family structure has diminished so low in the past 5 or 10 years that things are dramatically different for the lives of these kids. Something has to happen. Something has to take the place of that family that is no longer able to get them to survive.

CASE advisors claimed to have neutral positions toward students and their families, yet they frequently used words like "dysfunctional" or "not functioning" when they described what these families were like. Although most of them regarded themselves as liberal-minded college graduates who blamed the plight of Black people on society rather than on the people themselves, all of them made a concerted point of working within society's educational institutions and social services. The approaches they adopted attempted to salvage the Black family through compensatory interventions within established systems rather than by changing society through radical reform.

CASE advisors salvaged families through what they referred to as "treatments." They talked about how they would infiltrate students' families and become parental role models or surrogates. "There are times," one of them explained, "when you are called upon to be a surrogate parent so that you're like part of the family." Once they were part of the family, they could administer their treatments. "What I think makes us unique is that, um, we're family once we've established relationships. I mean, we're still a CASE advisor and support them in that role. But once we have the relationships, then it's up to us to make sure they receive the particular treatment that they need."

A White female CASE advisor ran through the list of treatments she provided parents:

> I've had parents where I speak to them every week, twice a week, three times a week. You know, it just depends on the particular relationship involving the need. There are often times when, you know, a student is not successful because of some trauma or crisis the parent is going through. So I address the crisis by making sure parents' needs are met. Parents need everything from medical care, GED programs, getting them hooked up with social services, getting them back into school, getting them substance abuse treatment, and getting them to work.

Whereas she and others talked at length about the nature and effectiveness of their treatments, most seniors told me that CASE advisors actually played little or no direct role in their lives, much less their family life. A few students credited CASE advisors who had come to the rescue when they became pregnant or got into trouble with the law. But most of them limited their interactions with advisors to short, weekly meetings where they discussed internships and school-related matters such as whether or not they were showing up to class. In some instances, relations between students and CASE advisors had run completely afoul. A boy told me how his advisor abandoned him when he dropped out of the CASE program. "I was nothing but a worthless piece of crap after that." Other students told me how they stopped seeing their advisors because they weren't getting much assistance. So although it occasionally happened that CASE advisors accomplished positive interventions with their family treatments, it was more often the case that they neither became an integral part of students' families nor were necessarily successful in their treatments. Their forging of family connections was hopeful in intent but limited in practice.

Therapy for Better Family Functioning

The strategy among support staff at Ridgewood High was not to infiltrate dysfunctional families in order to salvage them, but to provide therapy for mostly middle-class students so they could function better in school, their families, and other middle-class domains. The staff who offered the most therapy were counselors who facilitated weekly group sessions for students who were recovering from substance abuse, pregnancies, depression or, in the case of Cassandra and Peter, family losses and problematic relationships.

Cassandra had been a member of the Grieving Group for nearly 2 years after the death of her father. She was one of six girls who attended on a regular basis. There were a few boys in the group who never showed up. As was the case with all of the groups, the Grieving Group was facilitated by a White female counselor and one or two White female university interns.

They would sit on chairs in a small room next to the guidance counselor offices while students sat in a semicircle on the floor. Sessions usually began with an activity or lecture on a topic that was somehow related to the students' problem. One of the most intense sessions that I observed started when the counselor held up a chart with four theories on the stages of death. She asked the girls to look at the chart and talk about whether they had gone through any of the stages. Cassandra immediately spoke up and said that the theory by Kubler Ross was closest to what she had experienced when her father died. She had become depressed and was in denial until she found out that she was pregnant with "new life. When my dad died it was a shock, such a terrible loss. I got very, very depressed. But then I found out I was pregnant and I felt like someone new was coming into my life. I miss my dad, but I knew I would love that new life. I knew I would love that baby. The baby, my son, looks like my dad. He looks like my dad."

A White girl sitting near Cassandra talked about how she had read a story about someone dying only to be replaced by a new baby who resembled the person who had passed away. Another girl said that it seems like when someone dies, somebody finds out they are pregnant. Cassandra told the group about how her father and mother had been separated for 11 years. Even though her dad had moved to South Carolina, he had always driven to the city once a week to see her. When her dad was dying of cancer in the hospital, he would say funny things like, "I was so happy when I walked you down the aisle at your wedding" and "I'm so proud that all of you graduated from college." She said his comments were funny because none of what he said had happened yet. A girl said, "He was telling you what he hoped for you. He was telling you his dreams." In a voice quivering with emotion, Cassandra said the hardest part was knowing that her dad would not be at her graduation or wedding. Then she leaned over, put her head on the shoulder of the girl next to her, and began to cry. A girl across the room spoke in a sympathetic voice about how she had been at a wedding of someone who's father had just died and the priest told the attendees that "I can see him here. He's here with you." Then she turned to Cassandra and said, "He'll be there for you, too."

Cassandra quickly regained her composure after the session was over. She said it was a good thing for her and the other girls to "get it out of our system once a week so we can go on with our lives."

Peter was a member of the Mixed Relationship Group. He told me that students who joined the group had trouble "getting along with just about everyone." When I asked about the goals of the group, he said that counselors tried to help members "to get people to put up with us and us with them." One way they did this was by encouraging group members to be more open-minded about diversity. Peter said they were expected to be "politically correct," that is, to go along with liminal liberal/radical ideologies where people are supposed to "watch their language so that they don't say anything bad about Blacks, girls, criminals, morons, queers, weirdos, you name it."

Homosexuals were among the people about which nothing bad could be said. Peter said he knew a lot of students at Ridgewood High who considered gays, lesbians, bisexuals, and transsexuals as "sick." But to openly state such opinions in the discursive climate of the Mixed Relationship Group was to reveal one's inability to function in social relations in tolerable or tolerant ways. When the topic of homosexuality came up in one of the sessions, members were very careful not to use language that could be construed as intolerant. Instead, they adopted a communication style that was inundated with innuendoes, cloaked humor, and ambiguously phrased personal opinion.

Students at the beginning of the session were instructed to fill out a form entitled *Index of Attitudes Towards Homosexuals: Homophobic Scale.* After that, the counselor and an intern took turns asking students questions about their responses. The counselor began with the question, "How would you feel about working with a gay person?" To which Peter responded, "In the military, a gay person would be ganged up on by other guys. Being gay is more divisive than race." The intern said there wasn't much the military could do anymore to keep gays out. Realizing that his remark might somehow be misconstrued as politically incorrect, Peter said, "I wouldn't gang up on them." The next question was, "If you were in a bar, would it be worse to be approached sexually by a homosexual or by a repulsive person?" A girl said it would be easier to reject a gay person because all she would have to say is that she's straight. "That's easier then telling someone he's ugly." The intern laughed and said, "You're right." Another girl said she wouldn't go into gay bars. The girl next to her said, "You can't always tell if a bar is for gays or not." The girl who said she wouldn't go to gay bars said, "You can tell pretty fast once you're inside." Students started to laugh but stopped short when the counselor told them in a serious tone of voice, "You can't always tell if people are gay or lesbian." The counselor then asked, "Just how easy is it to tell if someone is gay?" A girl said her mother had a male friend who definitely acted feminine and talked with a lisp. She began to talk with a lisp and I watched as several students stifled their laughter. The next question was, "Do you know any gay people in this school? Is this school safe for gays?" A girl said that although some students would accept homosexuals, most would not. Other members of the group went along with the remark without stating whether or not they would be among the accepting ones. The session ended when a girl talked about how she knew someone who went to New York and some gay guy rubbed up against him in a bar and then followed him out in the street. "Gays are flamboyant in big cities like that," she said, "but it's not a good idea around here." Students nodded in quiet agreement.

POPULARITY OF POPULAR SEX

The traditions, salvation, and functioning of family life so prevalent in classroom curricular scripts and support services were crossed up by the allure of popular culture. Momentous improvements in birth control technologies and a steady loosening of censorship in public media have opened up markets and attitudes for sexual relations that are noncommittal, nonprocreative and, above all else, carnally pleasurable. The public repression of sex has been revolutionized, indeed, transformed by discourses that are shearing away social inhibitions. Bodies once sexually contained are now pulsating with sexual desire. Young women who veiled their docile bodies in modest attire are now exposing themselves as half-clad, brazenly seductive figures. Straight men who used to appear as upright citizens honoring, indeed, protecting feminine chasteness are now parading their virility in order to seduce women into having sex with them. Even gays, lesbians, bisexuals, and transsexuals are advertising their sexual desirability in unabashed fashion.

Sex has become a popular game where the goal is to find a partner who will engage in casual, consensual lovemaking—lovemaking that ends when the game is over. The language of the game brims with sport metaphors that render sexual acts into mutually entertaining, inconsequential play. Participants are "play boys," "play girls," or simply "playas" who "play the field." Sexual advances are accomplished by "hitting on," "bouncing," or "hooking up with" someone. A "loser" is someone who can't or doesn't know how to "score" a partner.

Seniors used this language in their accounts of how they and other adolescents play the game. I spoke with a boy at Central City High who estimated that around 89% of kids in his school have sex before they graduate. When I asked Cassandra at Ridgewood High if her peers were having sex, she responded by saying, "Yeah. Yes, I think so. Probably. Probably most of them have done it at least once. They, kids are like curious to see what sex is like 'cause in movies, in music it's like go ahead and do it 'cause it feels good and there's nothing bad about it. Have a good time and don't worry 'cause nothing bad is going to happen."

"In this country," Peter said, "everyone is having sex with everyone else" and he felt kids in his school were no different. "A lot of kids have sex, but they keep it under the covers so to speak. Some guys like me don't play the field in their schools because other guys might step in and because if something goes wrong you can walk away without anyone knowing about it. My brother taught me not to date girls where people know who you are and can see what you're doing. You have more fun that way."

Whereas the game was under the covers at Ridgewood High, it was out in the open at Central City High. One morning when Nay and I were in the secretaries' office, a girl wearing a hip-high skirt bent over and exposed her backside. Nay yelled, "Stand up, girl. You're showing something that is goin' to get you something bigger than you can handle." The girl stood up, laughed and said, "I ain't all bare down there." Nay then turned to me and said, "When the weather is hot, the girls put on those short skirts. They get the boys hot, you know, like cookin'."

And boys were cookin' especially in corridors where they would approach attractive girls and sexually come on to them. I saw a boy press his entire body up against a girl as he caressed her breasts and told her how "beautiful" and "sexy" she was. He did it in front of every passerby, including an administrator who tapped him on the shoulder and told him to "cool it." The boy laughed, backed away, and heated up again after the administrator was gone.

It was not unusual for girls to instigate the play. David at Jefferson High told me about a girl who tried to hook up with his friend, Cory. "There's this girl in our psychology class who is in love with Cory. She writes these sexy notes to him with nude drawings and stuff. He doesn't like her but he sort of enjoys the notes."

There could be much playfulness in the execution of plays. I was in the hallway with Lona and her friends when Naomi told us about how a boy she was pursuing was threatening to get a "restraining order." She wondered if he could actually do something like that. "I don't think so," Ashley said, "although there should be restraints, especially on this guy I know who has two girlfriends." "I know the guy," Lona said. "An order like that would do him good 'cause he's probably going to get something from those girls that will make his dick fall off." Dee Dee laughed and said, "Boys like that are stupid and girls are evil." Stevie, her boyfriend, responded, "I'm not stupid." Dee Dee made a face and Stevie pushed her. A girl asked if what they were engaging in was foreplay. Dee Dee said, "No, it's harassment." Lona said, "It's foreplay for Stevie and harassment for Dee Dee." Suddenly, Naomi suddenly spotted the boy she was after. She yelled at him, "Come here, my pretty!" He gave her a dirty look and walked away. "Screw him," she said in feigned frustration. "I even sent him suckers for Valentine's Day."

Such bravado and exaggerated accounts of sexual exploits were all part of the talk about the pleasures of the game. But plays were not without their painful consequences, as consensual lovemaking often led to intense gender antagonisms.

GENDER ANTAGONISMS

Ortner (1991), in her readings, discovered more or less accidently that American gender relations carry a burden of antagonistic class meaning. Gender antagonisms in class discourses are "submerged within, and spoken through, sexual discourse, taking 'sex' here in the double English sense of pertaining to both gender and the erotic" (pp. 171–172). Although the general point holds for both working and middle classes, it works differently in each case. Women in a working-class culture tend to symbolically align themselves with respectable, middle-class, family-life styles. Antagonisms often arise as they exert a middle-class pull on men in their efforts to raise their own and their children's socioeconomic status. The pressure causes men to feel inadequate, and many of them respond by dominating or, as is more often the case, leaving the women.

The issue in middle-class culture is fear of falling or "the terror of downward mobility." Parents exert tremendous controls on their children's behavior so that future generations do not fall downward into lower socioeconomic strata. Adolescents may resist these controls through symbolic representations of working-class affiliation. The working classes in such representations are cast as the bearer of an exaggerated sexuality against which middle-class respectability is defined. Antagonisms arise as girls who appear to follow variants of working-class lifestyles are treated as "sluts" or as a "smorgasbord of sexual-cum-class possibilities" for boys (p. 179). Or when boys are chased away as undesirable mates for girls.

Gender antagonisms entangled in social class/sexual discourses were evident at the high school sites. But I also found that they were being stirred up by cultural undertows that produced unwanted, sometimes violent acts of sexual predation and harassment. Antagonisms affected by socioeconomic pressures did not bode well for teenagers, especially those who were parents.

Teenage Parent Power

Although I was not able to obtain actual figures, I was told by several seniors at Jefferson and Central City High that pregnancy rates were high in their schools. Pregnancies also occurred at Ridgewood High. For pregnant teenagers who decided to have and keep their babies, antagonisms were not uncommon as they attempted to accrue parent power.

The discursive dynamics of gender antagonisms actually did vary somewhat between social classes. Wilson (1996), in his comprehensive study of the new urban poor, described the devastating effects that male joblessness has had on young parents in inner-city neighborhoods. Women no longer regard men as reliable sources of income or as fit fathers for their children. Men are being displaced as heads of households as women look elsewhere for financial and domestic security. They are losing power over the family as women are gaining it. Seniors at Central City High and Jefferson High were quite cognizant of how gender antagonisms in their working-class and low-income neighborhoods were, as one girl explained them, "basically about control."

> There can be a commitment there. There might be a man who doesn't even want another woman but he just wants to control the woman he has. Like in the household I grew up in, my mom was with this man who wasn't even my father. As time progressed, he got more and more aggressive and wanted to be in control. That's when the fighting started and like it never stopped. That's the way it is in my home and I see it going on in this school. I've never understood it, but there it is.

David talked about how girls in his school become "powerful" when they have babies and how they consolidate their positions by driving fathers away.

> Their attitude is almost like, "I can do whatever I want to. I can choose to be your mother. It's like powerful. I have my kid and your future in my hands. I can do whatever I want with it." When they get pregnant, they look in the mirror and see what they've become and like try to drive men away. They don't need the males, the young males anymore.

According to Monica, boys in the low-income neighborhood surrounding Central City High usually left the mothers of their children on their own volition. "This is how it goes," she explained.

> Girls have babies to keep boys, but babies run the boys off. Boys say to me, "I used to love her but now I hate her 'cause she made me get her pregnant." Instead of staying, he leaves the girl. When the baby is born, the daddy wants to see him but the mama bitches at him every time he comes around. She's mad at him 'cause he left her or is with another woman or something. The baby ends up growing up without a daddy and not much of a chance in hell.

Whether they drove men away or fought with them, many of the single teenage mothers at Central City High and Jefferson High had severed or limited ties with the fathers of their children. When Lona's friend Dee Dee got pregnant, her boyfriend immediately broke up with her. She was more than happy to raise her child by herself and had no desire for a relationship with another man. Although she changed her mind about relations with men when she met Stevie, she did not want him or any other unrelated man to have anything to do with her baby. "She's my baby," she said. "Not theirs."

Girls also got pregnant at Ridgewood High. A student said that she personally knew "about 10 girls who have gotten pregnant. One of them got pregnant in her senior year. She had the baby, then it died. Now she's out of school but is pregnant again. They teach us about birth control in sex education. They might as well since most of us have sex anyway. They can't stop us from having sex or babies."

Cassandra got pregnant when she was 15. Shortly after she gave birth, the father of the child committed a crime and was sentenced to a juvenile detention center. Although she wanted her son to have a father, she did not want him exposed to a man who embodied a whole host of undesirable traits associated with middle-class representations of street-hustling, criminally inclined, and otherwise lower-class young Black men. Such a person, in Cassandra's estimation, could not possibly help her to mold her son into a respectable, middle-class man. She felt that her mother was the only person who could assist her with child rearing. "My mom was behind me all the way when I got pregnant. She's the only one who can tell me what to do, like how to raise my son so that he doesn't turn out like his dad. She raised me up when I was, you know, like messin' up so I know she can help me with my son."

While Cassandra, with the help of her mother, hoped to bring up her son as a respectable, middle-class man, she also tried to shore up her own tarnished image as a respectable, middle-class woman. In the judgment of those who adhered to middle-class codes of propriety, she was a fallen woman who had slept with a convicted criminal, given birth to an illegitimate child, and lived in iniquity as a single mother. Having spiraled downward into the symbolic depths of lower-class life, she did everything she could to redeem herself and her middle-class standing. She became a staunch Christian who condemned the Godlessness of people who deviated from conventional, middle-class family values. She took full advantage of counseling sessions and other programs established to help students function better in middle-class society. She dressed, spoke, and behaved like a preppie with professional aspirations. And she otherwise sought redemption without her father, who had passed away, the father of her son, who was locked away, and other male relatives.

Sexual Politics

Among the discourses that streamed through students' youth culture were those revolving around notions of respect. As discussed in more detail in chapter 6, gaining respect was vital for asserting and challenging political dominance in everyday peer relations. Discourses of respect very much affected relations between adolescent males. But they also generated hostile antagonisms between boys and girls.

I heard numerous stories about how boys constantly subjected girls to unwanted predatory advances, verbal and physical harassment, and other forms of sexual domination. I also listened as girls told me how they would fight back. Adams (1999), in a study she conducted, found that teenage girls who fight boys are often engaged in a form of sexual politics where they are negotiating contradictory discourses that position them, on one hand, as passive docile bodies that ought to be treated with respect and, on the other hand, as active agents with the power to control who will or will not have authority over their bodies. Girls, in their fights, tried to position boys into more respectable relations with them while simultaneously positioning themselves as just as tough and aggressive as boys.

At Jefferson High, Adam's girlfriend, Mary, her friends, and many other White girls were routinely harassed by Black boys who formed a gauntlet in the hallway leading to the lunchroom. As the girls walked by, the boys would touch, grope, pinch, and punch them, and call them sexually derogatory names like "ho," "bitch," and "White ass." One of the girls told me how a boy splattered red ink all over her friend's white sweater. The girls decided to call attention to the problem by publishing a story about it in the school newspaper. They hoped administrators would read the story and use their disciplinary authority to force the boys into more respectable relations with them. But rather than crack down on the harassment, the principal ordered all subsequent editions of the newspaper to be approved by him before they went to press. The girls concluded that the principal was more concerned about censoring bad press than stopping the bad things the boys were doing. They were, in effect, being left alone to defend themselves.

And defend themselves they did. Lona and the girls in her clique were cases in point. One of them told me about a boy who sat next to her in class. He had gotten into a "physical molestation thing" where he would fondle her breasts and buttocks. She asked him to stop. When he kept doing it, she yelled, "Get the fuck off me" in a voice loud enough for the teacher to hear. The teacher ignored her so she decided to take matters into her own hands. When the boy leaned over to touch her, she kicked him in the face.

Amber, a CASE advisor at Central City High, said that girls were subjected to some of the worst forms of sexual violence. She blamed the ways boys treated girls on gangsta rap music where women were positioned in lyrics as "sex toys for men to play with as they pleased. A lot of the lyrics are about explicit violence and sex, raping women, beating them into submission. The language is crude, like the f-word is used all the time. The lyrics influence how kids make love. I mean, they don't make love, they make girls, force girls to have sex through violence, not love."

Girls at Ridgewood High were subjected to sexual harassment. According to Peter, hassling girls about sex was something that happens in high schools, at colleges, and "everywhere else." When I asked a group of White students if sexual harassment was commonplace in their school, the students glanced at each other, not knowing exactly what to say. Finally a boy said, "Yeah, kids kinda do that a lot." I asked the girls what, if anything, they did about it. One of them shrugged her shoulders and said, "Not too much. You kind of put up with it." Another girl said, "Some of us ignore it, but there are some who dish it right back." She then told us about how she saw a girl grab a boy in the crotch. "He was walking down the hallway and she suddenly grabs him down there. That was pretty gross."

Girls definitely could be as sexually aggressive as boys. Naomi, the member of Lona's clique who came to school dressed like a Marine, would approach boys in the hallway and attempt to seduce or harass them. I watched one morning as other members of the clique attempted to reposition her into more respectable gender relations. They surrounded her and grilled her with statements like, "You don't like being harassed, what makes you think they do?" "Your tail end is gonna get knocked up. Those guys are gonna stick it to you." And "It's bad enough that guys are like that, why do you want to be like that?"

Naomi was effectively restrained by the discursive tongue lashing. She stopped preying on boys and immersed herself more deeply into a clique subculture that engendered more family-like linkages, at least among friends.

FAMILY AMONG FRIENDS

Seniors, as they came of age in the kinship domain, were navigating discourses in classrooms and corridors that connected them to, or disconnected them from, crosscurrents flowing through American family life. Navigations were difficult, indeed, treacherous at times. I found that many seniors sought refuge in the safe social spaces of their friendship cliques. Within these spaces, they could do their identity and integration work in a manner that shielded them from the judgment and interference of parents, teachers, other adults, and other peers. They could construct subcultural currents that allowed them to preserve, modify, experiment with, or invent discursive possibilities.

The subculture that was spun in Adam's clique reinforced dominant, conventional family arrangements in a manner that preserved the intergenerational continuity of members' own nuclear families. Adam and his girlfriend, Mary, came from, and hoped to remain connected to, intact families headed by parents who had been married for several years. They and other members of the clique were heterosexuals who were quite faithful in their relational commitments to boyfriends or girlfriends. Adam and Mary became engaged at the end of their senior year in high school. Years later when I talked to Adam on the phone, they were still engaged. He told me that they were postponing the wedding until Mary finished college and they could afford to set up their own nuclear family household.

Christina and her friends built a bordered subcultural enclave within their school. Inside their enclave, they remained closely connected to the norms, values, and beliefs that constituted their families' traditional, ethnic cultures. They symbolically disconnected themselves from what they regarded as the corrupting influences of American family traditions and other crosscurrents. In their strong identifications with their family heritages, the girls were poised to accept the marriage arrangements, domestic roles, and family responsibilities that women in their traditions had adopted for many generations.

Perhaps the most intriguing peer clique was the one formed by Lona and her friends. Most members of the clique had undergone painful or, in some cases, violent breakages with their families. Much of the conflict that led to the breakages was caused by identity work where members resisted or openly rejected local family pressures in order to assert what they felt were their true sexual selves. Conflicts also arose over gender roles and other prescriptions for family-life styles. Members, in their resistance and/or attempts to realize their own true selves and desirable styles of life, were evicted from, abandoned by, or isolated within their families. They lived as outcasts until they finally found a home in Lona's clique.

Lona, in her interactions with clique members, saw herself as a natural-born counselor with a God-given talent for analyzing and solving adolescent problems. She would spend hours counseling her friends on the phone, in hallways, in class, and other places. She told me how she felt like a psychiatrist. But in many respects, she was a cultural therapist who used dialogue to raise her friends' awareness of the psychocultural components of their ensuring selves and how their selves were in conflict with powerful cultural currents.

Her interactions with Ashley provide a good example of how therapeutic the dialogues could be. After her mother moved out of their apartment, Ashley quit her job, lost interest in school, and sank into deep depression. "She was like a bum," Lona said. "Then I went to work. I'd constantly talk to her, like we'd go back and forth. She'd say, 'I don't want to wear makeup.' I'd say, 'Fine, don't wear it.' She'd say, 'I don't want to go out with creeps.' I'd say, 'Okay, go out with your dog.' But the biggest issue was her being a lesbian. I kept asking, 'Are you sure you're a lesbian, or are you just going through a phase?' We talked and talked until she was absolutely sure."

As they talked and talked, Lona made Ashley think about the family-life style ramifications of being a lesbian. Ashley said Lona "brought up stuff like ... having kids and everything. She got me thinking about the reality of being a lesbian woman. She was like 'be real but get real.' So I thought a lot about that."

Lona, in an effort to build linkages, also encouraged Ashley to think about how to express a true-self-affirming identity in relation to other people's cultural commitments (Hemmings, 2000b). A subcultural ethic of relative difference emerged in the clique that was premised on two essential principles. The first was that every individual is different and therefore should not be expected to conform to the same cultural expectations. Individuals have the right to make adaptations that reflect their true, enduring selves. The second principle was that individual differences should be made relative to the differences of others. As individuals express their identities, they should think about the social consequences of their choices. They should, in other words, express their true selves in ethical relation to others.

Jennifer described how the first principle operated among her friends. "We are who we are," she said. "The head bangers, jocks, or whatever are all trying to be like each other. We're not like that, you know, like sheep who follow what everyone is doing."

Beth, Ashley's partner, said that clique members did not pressure each other to be the same. Everyone had his or her own voice. "You don't have your own voice in other groups. It's like everyone else speaks for you. But if you're like us, you're being yourself. You have your own thoughts, your own opinions, and you do what you want to do."

The first principle gave clique members the liberty to construct familial/sexual identities that worked for them. Ashley and Paul were able to come out as lesbian and gay. Dee Dee could openly display her identity as a mother. Other members were not as certain about their selves. Carole, who was pregnant, wrestled with the impending realities and negative images of being a poor Black single mother. She did not want to come off as a "stereotype of the Black welfare queen" but was not sure how to get around it. Naomi swung wildly between her masculinist obsession with becoming a U.S. Marine and her feminine romantic fantasies of being carried away by male protectors like her cousin. These girls' identity work was fraught with contradictions, yet their navigations were patiently tolerated by friends who recognized their right to find their own path to true selfhood.

The second principle was most apparent in group conversations. Lona said that she and her friends talked about "anything and everything." They discussed sex and sexuality, religion, politics, television shows, and other issues. Lona usually was the chief facilitator. She would initiate interesting conversations and debates and keep them going. When arguments became too heated, she would calm down combatants with humor or conciliatory remarks. She comforted friends who became upset and put the kibosh on those who were becoming meanspirited. It was during these discussions that the second principle came into play. Clique members not only honored everyone's right to express themselves, but also made a point of considering the social consequences of their own and other people's stances.

The principle surfaced when clique members peppered Naomi with questions about the consequences of sexual predation and harassment. It also was evident in a discussion the group had about the article that appeared in the school newspaper about the gauntlet of Black boys who harassed the White girls in the tunnel leading to the lunchroom. They analyzed the sexual politics in the tunnel as being somehow interwoven with racial politics.

> **Jennifer:** Black boys got this street image thing they have to put out. Like they have to dress sharp and be tough to survive on the street and all that. But why do they have to pick on White girls? What's the point?
>
> **Ashley:** They erroneously believe they have to do things like that because a lot of White kids in this school are prejudiced.
>
> **Carole:** Yeah, it's a two-way thing. Whites call Blacks niggers, and Black call Whites honkies. Both sides rub up against each other, and both come off looking real bad.
>
> **Lona:** Blacks and Whites need to show more respect. They have to do what they have to do, but they should show more respect.
>
> **Ashley [looking at Lona]:** They need to be more like you.
>
> **Jennifer:** Lona is an alien in a Black body.
>
> **Lona:** No. I'm a beautiful Black girl in a fat body. [Laughter] I don't call Whites honky, and they shouldn't call me fatty.

Although members understood the survival reasons for the boys' behaviors, they deplored the consequences of "erroneous" actions that incited gender antagonisms and interracial animosities. Identity expressions and adaptations that were openly sexist and racist made everyone look bad. Although Lona made humorous remarks at the end of the exchange, she was dead serious in her conviction that although people have the right to be different, they should not be disrespectful or, for that matter, hostile in ways that are socially destructive.

The principles of the ethic of relative difference made it possible for Lona and her friends to forge the social and cultural linkages they needed to work out their true selves and to consider adaptations that would enable them and others to live a good life. But forging linkages within the safe social spaces of their cliques did not necessarily mean that members were able to build bridges that reconnected them to their families or, for that matter, with pe ›ple in other community domains. As my fieldwork progressed, I was to learn that one of the most important of these domains was that of reiigion.

5

Religious Domain: Freedom of/From Religion

I did not originally intend to conduct in-depth explorations of how graduating seniors came of age in the religious domain. I included a few interview questions about the role of organized churches in community life but otherwise had not identified religion as a main area of inquiry or even feasible in a study involving public schools. Federal courts have effectively purged public schools of explicit religious curricula and practices.[14] Despite the ban, traces of religion do remain, as it is difficult to cover material in social studies, literature, and other subject areas without some familiarity with Judeo-Christianity. There also are occasional disputes over curricular material, school holidays, and other matters with religious overtones or that rub against religious beliefs. But although there are vestiges of religion in schools and lingering debates, I did not think it would be possible to collect much data on how religious cultural processes unfolded in the particular schools I had chosen for my research.

But I changed my mind and research design[15] when it became clear that religion loomed large in the lives of graduating seniors. So large, in fact, that I felt compelled to delve more deeply into navigations of religious theological crosscurrents. Seniors were thoughtful and very serious about their religious identity and integration work as they sorted out their beliefs in God and the supernatural; held fast to, or broke away from, affiliations with organized religions; indulged in religious critical consciousness; wrestled with morality; and sought spirituality. Much of this work was carried out in communities and families, but it also took place in public high schools where students engaged in some of their most intense work as they sought freedom of, and from, religion.

THEOLOGICAL DISCOURSE

Historically, Western European and American thinkers in the humanities and social sciences had much to say about religion. The study of religion as a significant cultural force has evolved from Hegel's 19th-century vision of history as a divine, cosmic progression toward human harmony to contemporary scholarship rooted in Marxism that examines how religion is an extension of the structures of socioeconomic inequality and has been used to reinforce the policies of Western expansionism. Marching through the procession are anthropologists like E.E. Evans-Pritchard, Bronislaw Malinowski, Lucien Levy-Bruhl, and Claude Levi-Strauss, who did ethnographic studies of the religions of "primitive" non-Western tribal groups. They made generalizations about the rational or irrational features of religious systems, often with the assumption that the primitive ones they documented were static and unsophisticated in comparison to those of the more civilized West (Lambeck, 2002; Morris, 1987).

It was not until scholars like Clifford Geertz (1973) arrived on the scene that anthropologists began to pay more attention to how people actively construct and enact religion at the emic level of their own lived experience. Geertz is widely regarded as a major figure in interpretive anthropology, which conceives of religion as webs of meaning spun by adherents with reference to their complex, ever-changing historical circumstances. These webs serve as guides for action so long as adherents find them to be comprehensive, comprehensible, and fairly effective in handling the perennial problems of life, death, and the after-life. When such assurances break down, liminal religions inevitably rise up.

As I searched through the literature for more contemporary perspectives, I ran across a book chapter by Taylor (2000) on theology's contributions to anthropology. The chapter is insightful because it offers a working definition of a theological discourse for anthropological inquiries into religion. The definition is fundamentally a "discourse (-*logos*) about whatever in cultural beliefs and practices is taken as mystery or sacral presence of some sort (*theos-*)" (p. 36). The discourse seeks to identify, comment on, or articulate the importance of what people hold as mysterious and sacral in at least three senses. First, it acknowledges supernatural beings and supernaturalistic beliefs as major referents in religion. Second, the discourse recognizes that in all webs of meaning, there is a critical consciousness built into adherents' own systems of belief. People may be "true believers" who avoid or discourage critique or "truth seekers" who are informed by various theories, mythologies, and other narratives as they ponder indigenous religions or those of other cultures. The discourse in the third sense recognizes the spiritual dimension, which is often hidden yet significant in all realms of culture. The spiritual dimension can be discerned not just in religious institutions and bodies, but also at the "heart of artistic expression in painting, music and popular culture, certain philosophical styles, ... the sports industry, experiences of nature, amid the experiences of pain and of ecstasy" (p. 38). Adding to Taylor's working definition is a fourth sense that emphasizes systems of moral values, norms, and ethical codes (Adams, 2000). Morality in every society is closely associated—indeed, inextricably intertwined—with religion.

Inherent in all of these senses of theological discourse are notions of power. Beliefs in God and the supernatural are permeated with symbolic representations of supreme authority and conceptions of power over nature, society, and individual destiny. Critical consciousness is the intellectual power to contemplate, generate, and question truth. Power over human psychological and material experience is the basic urge in spirituality, whereas morality has to do with exercising control over and within human social relations. Theological discourses empower or disempower people in ways that extend well beyond strictly religious realms. That is why they are so controversial in secular settings like public schools. But that did not stop graduating seniors from considering them within the contexts of their schools as they came of age in the U.S. religious domain.

THE RELIGIOUS SELF

When asked about their religious identities, people in the United States usually respond by discussing their identification with religious institutions and widely recognized classifications. They may refer to themselves as Catholic, Jewish, Lutherans, or as persons who identify with other organized religions. Or they may talk about having unconventional identifications with mysticism or the occult or indicate a lack of identification by describing themselves as agnostic or atheist. Identities also are discussed in terms of the extent to which a person is committed to particular sets of doctrinal beliefs and moral strictures. And they may be addressed as a key aspect of people's ethnic or racial identities.

An important distinction also is made between having a religious identity and adopting religious practices. All religions have disciplinary practices intended to lock adherents into particular courses or paths of thought, feeling, and action. Practices include the daily discipline of prayer, meditation, or scripture reading and ceremonial rites that mark significant religious events and life passages. There are practices that discipline the body through modest dress codes and by placing constraints on sexual activity, diet, and the use of intoxicants. Marriage, work, and other areas of life also are regulated by practices supported by the moral authority of sacred scriptures and religious leaders.

Adopting such practices is the most obvious outward sign that an individual has made a commitment to, or is being effectively controlled by,
a religious system. As was evident among graduating seniors, religious
identification and the adoption of a religion's disciplinary practices did
not necessarily go hand in hand. But sometimes they did, as was the case
with Cassandra who was a self-proclaimed true believer and religious
practitioner. A devout member of a Black Pentecostal church, she spoke
of having been called by God to center her self and her whole life around
the Christian faith:

> After my dad died and my baby came, I was called by God to go to church
> and be a better person than I was. I didn't hear any voices or anything but I
> felt deep in my heart, in my soul, I felt Him. I felt God there and knew then
> and there that I believe in God. I believe in our Lord Jesus Christ. I believe
> in everything the Bible says. I am a Christian and I base my whole life
> around that 'cause all I do is pray. When you pray, God blesses you. You
> gotta do right, too. You can't do bad things and keep askin' God for forgive-
> ness. You can't do that.

Monica also was a true believer who described herself as a "plain Christian who don't wear the faith on my sleeve." She attended a Black Baptist
Church until she left to join a White Methodist one where, she said, "I can
be more myself as I give praise to God."

Christina sustained ethnic and religious connections in her identification as a Mexican-American Roman Catholic. She belonged to a Hispanic
Catholic church located at the hub of the social and cultural life of the local Spanish-speaking community. Even though she professed a strong
commitment to Catholicism, she had yet to embrace what she referred to
as the "Catholic lifestyle."

Peter sought to reconnect himself to his ancient religious ethnic heritage. He had been raised in a Chinese Christian church but felt like a foreigner in an institution that had been imposed on China by Western
European colonizers. He was a truth seeker searching for an alternative
identity and path that were more in line with what he described as the
"philosophical way of Taoism and Confucianism."

Stuart said he was "definitely Jewish" although he did not adopt many
of the distinctively Talmudic practices of Judaism nor did he regard himself as someone with deep, inner faith. He was suspicious of religious zeal-
ots, especially Christians who embraced religion as a "psychological
crutch." At the same time, he had enormous respect for his grandparents,
who were quite devout in their religious observances.

Lona had a self-consciously unsettled religious identity. She had been a
practicing Roman Catholic until the death of her grandmother. "When
my grandmother died, God and religion were taken away from me. I

stopped going to church and went to hell." She eventually began a spiritual quest where she hoped to reconcile with her hellish past as she explored more "paranormal" realms of religious experience.

Michael was noncommittal about religion although he went to church every week. Nay and I had a brief exchange about her commitments that began when I asked if she attended a church.

> **AH:** Do you go to church?
>
> **Nay:** Uh huh.
>
> **AH:** Is it important to you?
>
> **Nay:** Yeah, it's important. Some people need a little bit of God in their lives.
>
> **AH:** Do you believe in God?
>
> **Nay:** Uh huh.
>
> **AH:** Would you describe yourself as a religious person?
>
> **Nay:** Uh huh. I go to church.
>
> **AH:** Because you need a little bit of God in your life?
>
> **Nay:** Uh huh. A lot of God sometimes.

I had an even briefer conversation with Adam, who seemed to be indifferent about religious matters. When I asked if religion was important to him, he said, "I don't know. Not really too much. I don't see it that much but like my church, there's a lot of helping in my church and that's about it. I guess I don't think about it too much. It's there, I mean, religion is there but I don't think about it a lot."

When I asked David the question, he exclaimed "No, No! I'm agnostic. What I have to say about religion is not that good. I dislike hypocrisy. Some churches, I don't want to go to extremes here, but some churches their main goal is like a business, to make money. They don't really care that much about people or God."

These and other seniors' remarks could not be fully understood apart from how identity and integration work was carried out within the layers of religious crosscurrents. Among the most powerful of these currents were those that upheld the dominant theological mainlines of Christianity and Judaism.

HOLDING THE MAINLINES

Protestant (S)elect

Since the ratification of the United States Constitution, the official position of the federal government has been, in Thomas Jefferson's words, to erect a "wall of separation between church and state" and to protect the free exercise of religion. A public rhetoric arose that stressed personal freedom in religious expression and tolerance of religious diversity. But the rhetoric was and continues to be circumscribed by the dominant hold that the mainlines of Christianity have had on mainstream American culture. The most dominant mainline is Protestantism.

There are dozens of denominational Protestant churches that differ in the details of their doctrines and many of their practices. But all of them are based on a monotheistic belief system that revolves around the Biblical life and teachings of Jesus Christ. The churches endorse conservative moral values and a worldly asceticism that discourages indulgence in bodily pleasures. Protestant churches also are organizationally similar. They are administered by ministers chosen with some input from parishioners. Ministries may be exclusively male or, as has been increasingly the case in recent years, open to women.

Protestant churches also have an overriding theological ethos or what Weber (1958) referred to as an "ethic" in his classic study, *The Protestant Ethic and the Spirit of Capitalism.* Although Weber focused mainly on how the Protestant attitude of mind made modern capitalism possible, he also offered insights on the profound impact that the ethic has had on the lifestyles of high-status groups in Europe and the United States. One of the distinctive elements of the ethic is the doctrine that each person enters the world with a calling or task set by God. Even more distinctive is the Calvinistic doctrine of predestination or the conviction that only an elect few are chosen by God to receive eternal grace. Although this doctrine is not officially recognized in every denomination, it has contributed to a pervasive anxiety prompting generations of Protestants to look and behave as if they are worthy enough to be selected as one of the elect. This adaptation is succinctly encapsulated in the adage, "God helps those who help themselves."

Helping oneself in cultural terms is accomplished through belief in, and adherence to, the Biblical word of God and Jesus Christ, consistent displays of good moral behavior, and diligent hard work in whatever one's calling happens to be. The essential idea is for people to do their best to express and hopefully attain individual salvation or at least some modicum of disciplined control over their destinies. If people make mistakes or become undisciplined, they may seek redemption by admitting their wrongdoing, undergoing a period of atonement, and getting back on the Protestant track.

Whether or not God's grace is bestowed on an elect few, there is little doubt that this theological ethic has contributed to the accumulation of wealth, prestige, and power among White, Anglo-Saxon, Protestant Americans. This group constitutes a kind of Christian aristocracy from which individuals are called to assume leadership roles in secular institutions as well as religious ones. Since the establishment of the United States government in the late 18th century, Protestants, especially White male Protestants, have occupied the most elite positions of authority in government, major corporations, public schools and universities, and other organizations. The power inherent in the Protestant theological ethic is so potent that many other religious and nonreligious groups have absorbed it into their own cultural systems.

There are discursive strands streaming through this ethic, two of which surfaced during an interview I conducted with members of the Young Life Club formed by Christian students at Ridgewood High. Participants included five Protestants and two Roman Catholics, all of whom were White and growing up in middle-class families. We engaged in a rather lengthy discussion on religion, where it became evident that religious freedom was an especially prominent theological strand among the Protestants. These members of the club insisted that religion is a matter of conscience and free choice and that people, as they consider different religions, should exercise critical consciousness. Having an open mind, one of them explained, was the best gift he had ever been given. "My parents have like given me an incredible amount of freedom of mind, like, incredible freedom to think what I want, come up with what I want. They respect me for that. I think that's the best gift they ever could have given me. Instead of like pressuring me, and saying like this is what you have to believe, this is what you should believe, this is the only way. That's like giving me an open mind, total freedom of making choices, and finding out what I want to believe in religion and other stuff is like the best gift."

But another strand also emerged that disposes Protestants toward religious enforcement. Adherents in many Protestant denominations venture forth, or are sent out, to proselytize in an effort to integrate more people into the theological folds of their churches. Pressure is put on potential converts to accept what are presented to them as the only right or true religious beliefs. Those who come around to the faith are initiated into what is held up to them as a select, potentially elect group. They are then called on to enforce the faith against anyone or any movement that disagrees with it. Critical consciousness is curbed and religious intolerance may be exhibited as deviant members are reined in or, in the most extreme cases, expelled.

This strand made its appearance during the interview when a Protestant boy stared intently into the eyes of a Protestant girl and spoke in a forceful, confident tone of voice about how she had made the "right choice" in her religion. I found out later that he had played an instrumental role in converting the girl and getting her to join his church. After he made the remark, the girl smiled at him and said, "Yes, I made the right choice." She then proceeded to talk about how they and other members of the Young Life Club were a "select group" in relation to other people. "We're not like most other kids or maybe people. We're like a select group that has this incredible faith that sets us off and we know how to live our lives in God, in God's way."

Although these strands seem to diverge, they actually complement one another in how they recruit and keep people within Protestant mainlines. Religious freedom where individual choice is extolled binds people to a religion much more firmly then does coercion or the threat of persecution. Religious enforcement also forges strong bonds, especially when it is undertaken by people who are convinced they really are members of a (s)elect group. These strands were certainly operating in tangent in Cassandra's positionings as a true-believing member of a Black Pentecostal Christian church. She spoke of having been "called by God" to embrace the church's theological guidance in her efforts to live a more spiritual, better way of life. She also talked about how much she wanted to be among the "special people sittin' there, right there ... next to God and Jesus Christ Our Lord" when the world came to an end. And she condemned people who did not abide by the moral strictures and other beliefs associated with her Protestant faith.

Among the Protestant seniors who could not abide was Paul, Lona's gay friend. Paul was a practicing Baptist when he came out to relatives who also adhered to the faith. Lona explained what happened as "true" religious beliefs were pitted against Paul's "true" sexual/familial self:

> Paul's family is very religious and he was religious. Then this gay thing came up. That's why he got kicked out of his house 'cause his mother found out and it was against the Bible and what Baptists believe. His mother can't accept the way he is because of her religion 'cause I think she loves him but the Bible says he's a sinner and has to change his ways. He went to live with his friends and then he lived with his father down the street but his father kicked him out 'cause they were like, you know, struggling with the gay thing. Everywhere he went in his family he kept running into religion. He gets kicked out even though, and this is weird, he sees himself as a Baptist like he still wants to belong to that church.

Despite his expulsion, Paul clung to his Baptist identity and prayed that the day would come when he would be accepted as a fully integrated s(elect) member of the church and, for that matter, his family. Until then, he would be suspended within the strands of a Protestant theology that has deep roots in the United States and might have dominated much more of the religious seascape were it not for Roman Catholicism and other religious mainlines.

Catholic Compliance

The latest census data indicate that Catholics constitute 23% of the total Christian population, making them the largest denomination in the United States. In the county where the three high schools were located, 51% of people identified themselves as Catholic in a survey conducted by a private church growth research center. Catholics were a significant population not only in terms of their numbers, but also in their local influence, particularly in the realm of education. The regional Catholic archdiocese ran one of the largest private parochial school systems in the state. There were 15 elementary parish and city-wide schools, twelve coeducational and same-sex high schools, and two Catholic colleges.

A good share of the graduating seniors in my study were or had been Catholic. Many had attended Catholic elementary schools before their enrollment in public secondary schools. Although some were committed adherents, others had become quite alienated. Their religious experiences in either case were shaped by theological impositions intended to hold them in obedient compliance to Catholic theology.

The Roman Catholic church is the oldest formally established Christian church. It has been administered for hundreds of years by a hierarchically organized male clergy headed by a patriarchal Pope. The traditional role of lay parishioners is that of the faithful follower who obeys the teachings and decrees of higher religious officials. Parishioners do not participate in the formulation of official Catholic beliefs or modes of Catholic spirituality. Nor do they have much say over the substance of Catholic morality. They are to abide by church teachings, often under threat of eternal perdition. Among these teachings are those meant to govern social relations. Heterosexual marriage is regarded as the only acceptable relationship for the expression of sexual intimacies. Divorce is forbidden. Out-of-wedlock births are sinful. Artificial birth control and abortion are ruled out as violating the sanctity of life.

I found that Catholic students were profoundly affected by pressures to comply with these religious and social tenets. When the Young Life Club was discussing freedom of religion, one of the Catholic members talked about how "there were no questions to be asked" in her church. "I go to St. Paul which is like a small community and I still get the same feeling that I had when we lived in Michigan and went to another Catholic church. Everyone knew there were no questions to be asked. You just believed what you were told to believe."

Most of Lona's Catholic friends did ask a lot of questions as they experienced and eventually resisted church pressures as personally oppressive. Jennifer likened the church to a "big Xerox machine" where everyone was expected to come out looking like the exact same "perfect holy person."

She had attended Catholic schools where priests and nuns fed all of the children into the machine. She was the only one who did not end up "showing the image."

> I went to Catholic schools for 9 years and at my school I was the only person that did not truly believe where I was. I did not truly believe in the faith. I wasn't, you know, anything that they were about. It's like they took one person and Xeroxed them off and threw them into a classroom with 16 of the same people. I would sit there in school and see copies of the exact same kids and I felt like someone looking in a mirror who wasn't showing the image.

What bothered her most were the severe restrictions placed on her religious freedom, specifically her freedom as an American to construct her own religious identity and consider other religious faiths. "We all were supposed to be 100% Catholic like nothing else but mindless Catholics. It used to be you didn't go to other people's churches or you'd go to hell or something. Like they were afraid we might think for ourselves or become one of them heathens. God forbid that we should have a mind that thinks for itself."

Another former Catholic in Lona's group was adamant that clergy had no right to have absolute authority over people's lives. "I don't think any church should have absolute authority over our lives. I mean a priest or pastor isn't in a higher position then we are. Everybody is equal. We're all human. I mean that's my beliefs. That's my viewpoint. I don't think that just because he is like the head of my church that he like has more authority than me."

At the other extreme were students who regarded Catholic theology and church authorities as giving them a better, more enlightened direction in life. In marked contrast to Lona's friends, they interpreted and integrated themselves into Catholicism as a religious system that would ultimately liberate them from oppression. The other Catholic in the Young Life Club explained it this way:

> The way I see it, I mean if you believe in God, God probably wants you to be a certain way. If you let people decide what that way is, then it gets confusing and things can get very bad. How does the saying go? It's something like you are led into evil but what it means is that you go to hell. I'm not saying the Catholic church should have a monopoly on religion but it's been around two thousand years and has shown millions of people how to live with God that's good. I know for myself that being a Catholic has given me a good direction that isn't confusing or whatever you feel like doing. It has helped me to, like, see the light, like, feel the light of God in myself.

People, the boy seemed to be saying, with too much power over their choices become confused and are likely to end up in the evil domain of hell. The reverse happens when people allow the centuries-old Catholic church to assert its tried-and-true power over them. People can go in one direction or the other but not both.

But there were some members of the clique who were in between discursive states. Lona, in her religious identity and integration work, was both inside and outside of the strongholds of mainline Catholicism. Her late grandmother had been a true- believing Catholic who had experienced miraculous visions of angels. The two of them had gone to church and prayed together. "I didn't see any angels," Lona said, "but I was sort of an angel in those days like I believed in God and didn't do anything real bad." When her grandmother died, so, too, did her Catholic faith. Lona said she "went to hell" as she lost her virginity, began to lie a lot, and "committed a million other sins." And then one day she looked inside herself and "hated what I saw." It was at that point that Lona began what she described as her "spiritual quest." In her quest, she tried to let go of Catholicism but Catholicism would not let go of her. "Like it or not," she said, "being Catholic will always be part of me even though I don't want to be a Catholic." She would always be in and out of compliance.

Jewish Adaptations

Jews comprise 2.2% of the total U.S. population and less than 1.5% of residents in the school districts where my study was conducted. Although they represent a small minority, Jewish people have exerted considerable influence on European theology. Jewish scripture, history, and commentary are the foundations of Christianity. Like Christians, Jews believe there is only one God and that a savior king will come and establish God's kingdom on earth. Unlike Christians, they believe the savior has yet to arrive. The staunchest adherents of Judaism are those who follow Talmudic laws and ritual practices that are meant not only to structure life within Jewish communities, but also to set Jews off from other people.

For centuries, Jews have settled in countries where other religions are established by governments or where they do not represent the majority faith. As guests in host countries, the threat of forced conversion or voluntary assimilation into another religious system is ever present. An even worse threat is anti-Semitism, which over the course of history has incited pogroms, the Nazi holocaust, and other horrendous acts of Jewish genocide.

Jews, in response to their precarious positionings, have made adaptations to preserve their identities, lifestyles, and in some cases, their physical existence. Chassidim and other orthodox Jews strive to hold on to Judaism's mainlines by isolating themselves in bounded communities where members are stringent in their practice of Talmudic law and custom. Many Jews belong to conservative or reformed synagogues where social distancing and religious observances are not as strictly enforced.

Others have undergone various degrees of assimilation into the non-Jewish cultures of their host countries. They retain a distinctive Jewish identity but have given up most distinctively Jewish practices. Then there are those who reject all religions as irrational, intellectually untenable, or, as is espoused by Marx and his followers, opiates prescribed in heavy, hegemonic dosages by oppressive rulers and ruling classes.

Stuart's approach to Judaism's mainlines was an adaptively powerful mix. He had what he described as a definite sense of himself as a Jew. He attended synagogue on the high holidays and had gone through an elaborate Bar Mitzvah ceremony when he was thirteen. But although he enjoyed the ceremonial trappings of Judaism, he did not consider himself to be a religious person. He was, in fact, critical of "overly religious" people, especially Christians like the kids who belonged to the Young Life Club. Kids like that are "crazy emotional nut cases."

> There are kids here at this school who really get into religion because, like, take the Young Life group. A lot of them are crazy emotional nut cases who are into religion because there's a low point in their life. The group, um, their churches are like a family that says, 'Come here. We'll take care of you.' It's like a way out of what real life is. They're weak and can't make it themselves so they let other people tell them what to do.

Although he did not have an accurate read on Young Life Club members' own perceptions of themselves as a (s)elect group, Stuart had a historical sense of how Christians have deployed the power of their beliefs in order to control "weak" people and incite them to convert or persecute non-Christians. These groups, paraphrasing Stuart's words, promote religious systems that stir up emotions, distort reality, and cause people to follow the dictates of leaders who tell them exactly what to do.

Stuart's opinion of religious Jews was entirely different. He had enormous respect for Jews like his grandparents who were "extremely religious." "My grandparents are extremely religious and have the most respect. I can't go use a credit card anywhere because people say 'Oh, you know Dr. Lyon?' Substitute teachers, everybody here. So it's like he has so much respect and they're very religious."

To be a religious Jew in an overwhelmingly Christian city was impressive. Even more impressive was the number of Christians who openly respected his grandparents and their faith. Although Stuart was inspired by his grandparents, he did not adopt Talmudic practices or otherwise follow their example. What he did do was assimilate for all practical purpose into the Protestant-like world of his preppie classmates. Like other preppies, he saw himself as someone born with a special calling or what one boy described as a "distinguishing mark." He also adopted some of the same tactics of power that "crazy" Christians supposedly use to manipulate weak people. Stuart thus took hold of the Protestant ethic sans Protestant Christian beliefs as he competed for a chance to become a (s)elect member of affluent middle-class society.

LIMINAL RELIGIOUS MOVEMENTS

Secular Tide

There was a time when Christianity not only had a commanding hold on millions of individual Americans, but also on the public customs of American institutions. Government offices, private businesses, and other nonreligious organizations were closed on Sundays, the day reserved for most Christian church worship. It was common for public schools to recognize major Christian holidays by decorating buildings, staging religious musicals or other performances, and sponsoring parties for students. Ministers would begin official government proceedings with a prayer. Even the U.S. Pledge of Allegiance makes mention of a "nation under God" in keeping with Christian beliefs.

But a liminal tidal wave of secularism has swept many of these religious customs out of the realm of public conventions. A Young Life Club member described how Christianity, which had "partially institutionalized society," was fading away:

> Like on Sundays, when everything was closed, that's all gone. You hardly find a place that's not open on Sunday. Religion partially institutionalized society, kind of formed society or whatever. I think that's eroded away and getting worse. Like in fifty years, Sundays are going to be like a Monday or a Tuesday. People will be working on the weekends like they're starting to do right now. Even at Christmas time, you see Santa Claus in stores more than you see Jesus Christ. Jesus is like fading away.

The erosion of public Christian conventions has met with little resistance and has, in fact, been advanced in a fairly noncontroversial fashion through the federal court system. In 1947, the Supreme Court concluded that the religion establishment clause in the Constitution meant that neither a state nor the federal government could set up a church or pass laws that aid one religion, aid all religions, or prefer one religion over another (McCarthy, 1985). The Court in the 1960s added more criteria through a series of rulings that have effectively banned prayer, Bible readings, and other explicitly religious practices in public schools and other organizations receiving tax dollars. There are Protestant groups challenging these rulings, but the majority of Americans are quite comfortable with their consequences. "In this country," a senior explained, "the government doesn't govern what you believe so there aren't too many people who have a problem with not saying prayers in public schools or hanging the Ten Commandments on the wall."

Secularization also has removed religion from the language of national dialogue. Words like "God," quotes from the Bible, and other explicitly religious references have been expunged from the public speech of public officials. Religious groups are not as verbally aggressive in their national conversion campaigns nor are they as likely to openly censure other faiths. Even academics have backed away from examinations of religion in their publicly disseminated writings and college courses.

Another liminal thrust has been the explosion of religious expression outside of the mainlines of organized religion. Americans no longer view churches, synagogues, or other places of worship as the only acceptable contexts for expressing a faith. A girl at Central City High saw no reason why people of faith should ever have to go to such places. "I have a problem with people who think that you have to go to church to be a Christian or whatever it is that you are. I believe in God and I have faith. But I don't feel I'm atheist or whatever just because I don't attend church every Sunday."

Many other Americans apparently agree. Not only are people feeling less compunction to attend places of worship, they also are more apt to investigate religious alternatives. Among these alternatives are so-called new age religious movements.

Attractions of the New/Ancient Age

New-age religious movements infiltrated popular culture in the 1970s and have continued to swell as more Americans became attracted to them as reactions against, or supplements to, the mainlines of Western religions. A substantial portion of new age beliefs are actually drawn from ancient sources. They are drawn from Hinduism, Buddhism, Taoism, and other Eastern mystical traditions that have existed for thousands of years. They also are extracted from medieval Western European astrology, antiquated Anglo paganism, and Native American pantheism. Although these beliefs vary in specifics, they rest on a common foundation of theological views widely embraced by adherents. Among these views is that everything in existence is derived from a single wellspring of divine energy. Human beings possess this energy. They also have immortal souls that are reincarnated through several lifetimes until they reach a state of perfect bliss or are reabsorbed into the supreme spirit. Practices for reaching such a state include mental meditation, bodily exercises, and other methods for raising spiritual consciousness. There also are practices for dealing with the perennial challenges of material existence. Many adherents use Tarot cards, crystals, Ouija boards, herbs, and other quasimagical means for telling the future, healing the sick, communicating with the dead, and warding off evil.

Most new/ancient age beliefs and practices are disseminated through books, audio and video tapes, and other merchandise. People also may learn about them by signing up for courses, workshops, and retreats facilitated by independent teachers and guides. Popular cultural markets for the movement have multiplied across the United States as people, especially young adults, are captivated by the attractions of exotic religious alternatives that give them much more individualized control over their religious experiences. These alternatives offer freer, more unrestricted paths to truth and spiritual self-realization. They provide a range of practices from which people can pick and choose to meet their personal religious goals and desires. Another allure is the promise of heightened consciousness that transcends the less blissful states of ordinary human psychology. Adherents also are intrigued by the idea that they can tap into supernatural powers in efforts to control the forces of nature.

Lona was quite fascinated with what she described as the "paranormal experiences" of her family members. Her late grandmother had seen angels and her sister had "mysterious stuff happen to her." She was thinking about utilizing methods of channeling so that she could communicate with her late grandmother and other dead ancestors. "Someday I'm gonna write a book about the paranormal experiences in my family. Weird, I mean it sounds weird but it's like something that happens to us. Channeling, have you heard of that? That's where you communicate with the dead. I want to try it to, like, talk to my grandmother and other dead people. [Laughter] I'm not kidding. Can you imagine what they'd tell me?"

New/ancient age movements offer powerful attractions like communicating with the dead, but they are not without their detractors. Conservative Christians are critical of them and have even gone so far as to construe the movements as forms of occult devil worship. Cassandra certainly saw the devil in them. She described new/ancient age adherents (or what she called "misguided types") as under the evil spell of Satan and as destined for hell if they did not return to the way of "Jesus Christ our Lord."

Peter had an entirely different opinion about where the devil was located. When I asked about his religious beliefs, he transformed the Christian God into a horned devil. "God? Yes! See? I see Him right there. Can't you see him right down there at the base of the stairs? He's got horns. See the horns?" He then spoke about how he could not accept an image of God as an all-powerful, all-good patriarchal figure to whom all people were to bow down in obedience. This was one of the reasons why he chose the (alternative) paths of Taoism and Confucianism. Taoism was especially attractive because of how it might enable him to find his own inner truth. "The whole idea of Taoism is that truth is inside us and you can know it by concentrating on it. Tao means 'way.' It means 'the way' in Chinese, the way to truth."

Embracing Taoism and other ancient Chinese teachings also reconnected Peter to his ancient ancestral background. He felt like a foreigner in the Chinese Christian church to which his parents belonged. Christianity, he explained, was a foreign faith that had been forced on Chinese people by British colonizers. "Chinese people for thousands of years had Taoism and Confucianism. Along comes the British colonizers who try to convert everyone to Christianity. Christianity is as foreign as it gets in China. I'm like a foreigner in my parents' church like all the people in that church are foreigners. I go there to socialize and that's it." Peter, in his new/ancient age religious work, thus attempted to return to his ethnic roots as he discovered true beliefs within himself, escaped the colonization of Western Christianity, and acquired more personal control over his consciousness.

Whereas Peter essentially carved out his own inner religious space within the currents of liminal change, other seniors kept faith within church-centered communities that remained well within the borders of religious mainlines. This was especially the case for those who belonged to, or had crossed the borders of, ethnic and racial communities.

KEEPING FAITH WITH(IN) ETHNIC AND RACIAL COMMUNITIES

Ethnic Havens of Hope

In many ethnic communities, mainline churches and synagogues are the institutional cogs that connect members together. Organized religions in these communities forge social bonds and also provide a wealth of symbolic material for the construction of a secure cultural haven for members. These constructions not only are embroidered with rich ethnic traditions, but also are framed by members' historical circumstances as minorities in a predominantly European, White, English-speaking, Protestant nation. Religion within the cultural perimeters of these communities functions as a powerful adhesive that connects members together in a faith that has helped many of them to overcome hardships as they seek a good life and/or salvation in the United States. The faith they keep rests on discourses of hope.

Christina was a member of such a community. She and her family belonged to a Hispanic Catholic church that was the center of the social and cultural life of many first- and second-generation, Spanish-speaking immigrants from Mexico and other countries in Central and South America. Christina said that although parishioners came from different countries, they all shared a language and "something from each of our traditions."

> We all like share this language, the Spanish language. We have all different kinds of people from every, from different countries. We celebrate their church traditions and celebrate ours also. Like when the day comes up, like the Day of the Dead which only happens in Mexico, we celebrate that. When Columbians have their, you know, their marriages we do that. In a weird way we all connect 'cause of the language and also because we share something from each of our traditions.

Members of the church community gathered together for worship throughout the week. In their worship they kept faith through a rendition of Catholicism that combined mainline theology with Hispanic ethnic traditions. Parishioners convened on Sunday mornings where they would celebrate Mass in Spanish. Children attended catechism classes on Thursdays where they were taught Catholic theology and about how Catholicism was practiced throughout the Spanish-speaking world. Adults could participate in a Friday prayer group facilitated in Spanish by Christina's mother. Parishioners young and old also would join together on special religious holidays, including those celebrated in other countries such as the Mexican Day of the Dead.

Members went to the church for other reasons. The church was a place where immigrants could meet people and, more importantly, get help. A Hispanic Catholic Community Board had been established to aid people who were looking for jobs, needed housing and medical care, and wanted to learn English. The work of the Board rested on a moral orientation that occasionally transcended the laws of United States. Christina knew a great deal about what the Board did because her father was the president. "They help a lot of people," she explained, including people "who aren't supposed to be here."

> Like there might be a family that comes and they don't speak any English. My dad used to teach English but he doesn't anymore. He knows people, um, about classes where people can learn English and he like sets it up for them 'cause he still knows a lot about that. Sometimes people need help who aren't supposed to be here. Like illegal aliens come to our church. They don't get turned away 'cause that would be wrong, almost like a sin to turn people away, not help them just because they aren't legal.

The church's morality as it was put into practice by the Board was spurred by an ethic of good works where people are assisted in basic survival regardless of their social and legal status. The ethic is a long-standing one in the Catholic church, where for centuries parishes and various orders of monastics and nuns have set up shelters, hospitals, orphanages, and other facilities for people who are indigent, ill, or left for dead. Good works in the particular case of the Hispanic Catholic Church went well beyond provisions for survival. As a haven of hope for a better life, the church helped immigrants cross cultural and judicial borders in order to take advantage of economic and other opportunities in the United States. It provided access to social services that facilitated assimilation into American cultural currents while simultaneously sustaining immigrants' cultural identities and most cherished ethnic traditions.

Christina went to the Hispanic Catholic Church, where her Mexican cultural identity and heritage flourished. She also was sent to Ridgewood High School in order to become assimilated into middle-class socioeconomic strata. But crossings between church and school were anything but smooth as Christina felt most secure in the communal haven of the church and had trouble identifying with middle-class preppie classmates and their highly competitive pursuits. She could be herself in church because of the sense of community she experienced. That was less possible in a school where people were "cold." "Like in church I can just be me and everyone accepts that 'cause that's the way we are. It's not like that in school where everyone is a snob and it seems like no one cares about what you do. It's cold there. Cold in school. Warm in church."

The sense of community had another effect on Christina. In contrast to many of the other Catholics I interviewed, Christina did not appear to be grappling in a critically self-conscious way with Catholic theology. Although she sensed Catholicism's historical constraints on individual religious freedom, theological pressures did not appear to have taken hold of her, at least not at that juncture in her life. "The church has been going on like it has for a long time. I don't think they'll be changing. They've changed in some ways but mostly they've stayed the same about what, about lifestyles people should have. There are people who enjoy that lifestyle. They follow that way of living. I don't follow everything but probably eventually I will live that way but not right now."

Christina was not specific about which aspects of the Catholic lifestyle she was not practicing. Nor did she seem concerned about what it might mean if she were not acting in total compliance. Of utmost concern to her were the bonds that she enjoyed as a member of the Hispanic Catholic Church. They connected her in a "weird way" to a religious system without being utterly controlled by the system. Catholicism for Christina was a roof that shielded but did not consume her as she kept faith in the warmth of her community's church.

Harbors of Racial Upliftment

There is an adage in the United States that Sunday morning is the country's most segregated hour. Millions of practicing Christians congregate on those mornings in racially separated churches. Among them are Black people who have established independent churches, that is, churches independent of White ones.

The African-American religious experience is told through the story of these churches. Maffly-Kipp (2002) told of how enslaved Africans brought a variety of tribal religions with them to the United States. Preserving their native practices was difficult under the harsh circumstances of slavery. But African songs, rhythms, movements, and beliefs in the medicinal powers of roots and the world of spirits and ancestors survived well into the 19th century. These remnants of traditional worship were eventually combined with the Christianity introduced to slaves by Europeans.

After the slave trade ended in 1810, religion among Black slaves became more distinctively African-American. There was a period of revivalism prior to the Emancipation Proclamation when scores of slaves converted to Protestant evangelical Methodist and Baptist faiths. Among the beliefs promoted by these faiths was that all Christians including slaves were equal in the eyes of God. The styles of worship that evolved were similar or at least adaptable to African worship patterns as people joined together in spirited singing, clapping, dancing, and even spirit-possession.

Fearful that such independent forms of worship would incite rebellion, White slave owners required Black slave attendance at White-controlled churches. Slaves responded by organizing their own invisible "hush harbors" of worship. It was within these harbors that musical spirituals with their double meanings of religious salvation and freedom from slavery developed and began to flourish. Oral traditions also arose where preachers called on by God to speak His Word delivered chanted sermons as audiences vocally affirmed what preachers had to say.

The churches of Black slaves not only were harbors of independent religious worship, but also became undercover locations where Black people could express and enact their hopes for a better future. God's message for salvation was combined with political messages of liberation. As slave owners feared, these messages triggered acts of rebellion such as the one organized in 1831 by a self-styled Baptist preacher named Nat Turner that resulted in the deaths of dozens of White people. But not all rebellions were violent as slaves found more peaceful and, in many ways, more powerful means to challenge the oppression of White slave masters.

In the antebellum north, freed Blacks established independent denominational churches such as the African Methodist Episcopal Church (AME) and the African Methodist Episcopal Zion Church (AMEZ). These churches, along with others, began to multiply and spread throughout the Black community after slavery came to an end. Today, according to Lincoln and Mamiya (1990), there are seven major Black denominations including the AME, AMEZ, Christian Methodist Episcopal (CME), National Baptist Convention, USA, Incorporated (NBC), National Baptist Convention of America, Unincorporated (NBCA), Progressive National Baptist Convention (PNBC), and Church of God in Christ (COGIC). While these churches continue to evolve, they have retained the essential foundation of their historically distinctive religious systems. Adherents still keep faith in Black theological discourses of upliftment deeply entrenched in African-American Christian beliefs and grassroots political movements for liberation. But they also have absorbed many elements of the White middle-class Protestant ethic.

Cassandra, Nay, and Monica attended or used to attend Black churches. Cassandra belonged to a Black Pentecostal Christian church. Nay was a member of the Church of God in Christ, and Monica had gone to a Black church until she left to join a predominantly White one. The three girls' thoughts on how theological discourses were being implemented in contemporary Black churches were filtered through a spectrum of subjectivities. For Cassandra, the church was a genuine harbor for spiritual and social upliftment. Its beliefs and practices of worship lifted her up to higher planes of spirituality where she could almost touch the hands of God and Jesus. "In our church we sing gospel and other songs. The minister tells us about the Bible, how we need to love each other, forgive each other, and do onto others as they do onto you. It makes me feel spiritual, like it carries me right up to where I feel I could almost touch the hand of God and our Lord Jesus Christ. Sometimes when the service is over it takes me a long time to come down (laughter) like come back down to earth."

The church also helped Black people to help themselves through faith-based programs designed to empower them through education, job-search training, and other avenues to socioeconomic upliftment. The programs picked people "right up off the floor." "My church has programs, like, say you're a mother on welfare. They will pick that woman right up off the floor and teach her how to get a job. I mean sometimes they literally pick 'em up off the floor 'cause they been beaten down so far."

Nay was more neutral and characteristically vague in her thoughts on the Black church. She described herself as a religious person who went to church to get a "little bit of God." What the church did for her beyond that depended on what she wanted that day.

Nay: The church isn't the same for everyone, like what they get out of it. Depends on who you are, what you want.

AH: What do you want out of church?

Nay: What I feel like I want that day.

Monica represented the other pole of the spectrum with her rather scathing critique of Black churches. She had attended a Black Baptist church but disliked it because of how it placed more emphasis on outward styles of worship than on the substance of Christian beliefs. "Black churches sing loud and I didn't like that. I was like why be so loud? Why not talk in a more normal tone of voice about what you should believe? I still like some of it, like the revivalist stuff. If I go now it's because of that. But I don't go very much 'cause I can't stand how they got to sing, sing so loud." What bothered her even more was how members of the congregation would flaunt their socioeconomic status through their clothing and other signs of material success. "The Black church is like, like the women say "God, do you see what that girl got on? Do you see her?" I mean they worry more about what you got on instead of how you are doing. They get all dressed up and put you down." People were made to feel even lower if they did not have any money to put in the church collection. "It used to be if you didn't have any money you could still go to church. Now if you don't have no money to put in then don't bother coming 'cause they make you feel so low. A lot of Black churches have a net so they can see how much you put in there. You put your hand in there and you got nothing everybody knows it. So you don't bother going anymore."

Monica decided to leave the church because she felt it had abandoned the historical foundation of Black faith. Rather than keep faith in the belief that everyone is equal in the eyes of God, Black church leaders and parishioners were exacerbating inequalities through excessive displays of material and social success. People, in her estimation, were being judged more by their clothes and money than their beliefs and Godly acts. So she joined the White church where styles of worship were toned down and people appeared to be less socially judgmental.

But there were contortions in Monica's position, as she herself coveted the status supposedly flaunted in the Black church. In a stark inversion of the historical Black experience, she joined a White-controlled church inhabited by representatives of the upper echelons of White society. The minister and parishioners eased her religious and social upliftment through unadorned forms of worship and by acting as if they really did accept lower-class Black people like her into their fold. Monica, in the congenial comfort of liberal White church relations, was made to feel even more equal in the eyes of God. More equal, that is, to the Protestant White (s)elect.

LOCALIZED FAMILY/RELIGIOUS FAITH

Graduating seniors also navigated religious currents within the worlds of their families. Adolescents experience some of the most directly felt pressures as theologies of all kinds are translated by parents and other adult relatives into localized religious systems. These systems often constitute the front lines of conflict over religious freedom as adolescents put up strong defenses, wage fierce fights, or back off in defeat in their head-on encounters with localized family/religious faiths.

Many but certainly not all families practice religious rituals such as saying prayers at meals or at bedtime, reading scriptures, or requiring regular attendance at church, synagogue, or temple services. On religious holidays, families may decorate their homes with religious themes, exchange gifts, go to special services, sing special songs, or otherwise engage in ritual observances. Rites of passage marking births, puberty, marriages, and funerals also are frequently recognized through formal religious ceremonies.

The extent to which teenagers resist or accommodate to religious rituals depends on their relations with family members, their attitudes toward the family's religion, and the extent to which they think their independence or integrity as a person is being impinged on. Among some graduating seniors, acts of resistance were not so much about rituals per se as they were about challenging the overall authority of parents and churches. Such was the case with Lona, who did not like being told what to do, especially when it came to religion. "My sister was confirmed and she wanted me to be her sponsor but I told her I don't wanna do it, I don't want to have anything to do with the church. What it is, I think it's that there's still like that rebellion sense, you know, against the church and my parents 'cause that's what they want me to do and I don't want to do it because *they* want me to do it."

Resistence often extended well beyond refusal to participate in religious rituals. Seniors also talked about how their families would enforce adherence to localized morality through appeals to the higher moral authority of God and written scriptures. Morality could be very restrictive, especially for girls, who often bear the brunt of family/religious constraints on their sexual and domestic behavior. Beth, one of Lona's friends, told a story about a girl she knew who was "tortured" by the family/religious morality laid down by an excessively zealous mother and a tyrannically patriarchal father:

> This one friend, she was Catholic and it saddened me to see her in the type of environment she had at home. I mean, her father and her mother were extremely strict, like tortured her in how they were totally Catholic in everything. They had lots of kids and they all looked alike. They all had long hair because they think it's a sin to cut their hair. I mean, like her mother

was real religious and had real long hair. Her father would beat up her mom and the children 'cause he was like God almighty in the house. He was really strict and she was afraid to do anything. I just felt so sorry for her.

Even though many of them had experienced family/religious morality as unjust or overly punishing, there were a few members of the clique who were troubled by the possibility that there might actually be a higher moral authority. Lona was one of them. She agreed with her friends that it was wrong to place severe constraints on individual freedom, especially freedom of choice in intimate relations. "'Cause, you know, if you're in a relationship with, if it's like two guys or with two girls or you're not married and you're happy with that person and you're completely sure about it then you should go ahead with it. It's nobody else's business what goes on behind closed doors." But there was a lingering issue in Lona's mind about the authority of the Bible. "I was thinking the other night about, you know, the issue with what the Bible says. The Bible might be right. What if it is? There's no way of knowing, but what if it is?"

Lona, who had no qualms about defying adults, was subdued by abstract, scripture-based maxims and uncertainty about the consequences of violating those maxims. She was burdened by guilt, shame, humiliation, and other emotions that placed internal, surveillance-like constraints on her actions. These emotions are often more effective at controlling behavior than the threat of actual reprisal or punishment. As many Catholics, Jews, and other people will attest, the discourse of guilt is commonplace in their religious experiences.

Other seniors were subjected to even stricter restrictions. But rather than feel oppressed, they thought they were being taken to loftier, more virtuous planes of Godliness and goodness. There was a Pakistani girl in Christina's clique who was growing up in an Islamic family. Unmarried adolescent girls in her household were not allowed to go on unsupervised dates with boys. They knew they would be punished and vilified if they ever engaged in premarital sex or gave birth to an out-of-wedlock child. When it was time for them to get married, their choice of husbands would be arranged by their parents and those of another acceptable Islamic family. Instead of putting up a resistance, the Pakistani girl accommodated to the rules as protecting her purity as a good Muslim woman. As Christina explained, "She sees the rules as keeping her pure, um, like a beautiful, pure Muslim woman. Her parents tell her that so she doesn't think she's being treated unfairly or being abused or something. It must work because sometimes she comes off as being more pure, um, better than American girls who screw around all the time. Maybe she is better."

Better or not, Christina's Pakistani friend did have an aura of virtue. I had a brief conversation with her about what it was like to be a Muslim woman in the United States. She said it was difficult at times because "Americans think that Muslims treat women terrible, like all they do is make us wear these awful veils." The purpose of the veil or *hijab* was to prevent women from being viewed as sex objects. Women viewed as sex objects are asking for trouble, which is why, she said, "so many American girls have so many awful things happen to them." Then she smiled, crossed her arms, leaned back in her chair, and said "I will *not* be like them."

SACRILEGE OF THE SACRED

David was a self-proclaimed agnostic. "I'm a cynical person," he said, "when it comes to religion." There are a number of reasons for agnosticism or the more extreme positions of atheism. Some people choose such positions because they are under the sway of scientific discourses that promote skepticism in the absence of empirical evidence supporting the existence of God, supernatural phenomena, and the validity of religious claims. There also are skeptics with critical social consciousness about how religion has been used to subjugate women, justify slavery, incite war, and otherwise oppress people. Then there are those who are simply indifferent about religious matters.

But none of these reasons were cited by David or other seniors who disavowed religion or set off to look for more genuine evidence of religious commitments. What rankled these teenagers most were the sacrilegious undertows that destroyed the theological integrity of organized religions. All of them felt that religious leaders and parishioners, regardless of their faith, should be paragons of moral virtue, sincere in their reverence, and otherwise practice what is preached. But what many seniors observed instead was widespread hypocrisy, corruption, and scandal. It was David's cynical impression that many Christian churches were more interested in making money than in caring about people. They even carry out their shady business operations on television. "There are preachers on TV who promise everything like heaven on earth if you send money to them. Just call their 800 number. They take in millions of dollars from people who believe the lies they are telling. It's robbery and prosecutors are figuring that out 'cause some of them are in jail. All of them should go to jail."

The girl who saw no reason why anyone should ever go to a place of worship felt that people who do go are often the "biggest sinners." "There are people who go to church every Sunday and they are the biggest sinners. Like there's this one woman in my church who stole some clothes and she's sittin' there every Sunday wearing like she's an angel."

Another girl was so disturbed by church hypocrisy that she felt she might as well stay home:

There was something on the news about how churches preach all these good things and the faces of the people looked so pure. Then I see how these churches hold festivals where you gamble in the parking lot or whatever. What I'm saying is that it's an issue of trust. It's like why go to church to be amongst people who probably aren't really practicing what they are telling you to practice? I might as well sit home and teach it to myself. That's better than listening to a minister who tells me to live my life from the Bible when he's not even doing it himself.

Monica not only was critical of Black churches where people were overly concerned with social status, but also of the "sinful attitude" she had observed in a Baptist church.

I went to one church down here, some Southern Baptist church. It was funny. The preacher was having sex with a lady in the congregation and he was married and they were back there talking about it. I could hear them. I like turned around and thought, "Are we in church or what?" I mean these are older people. You could tell they had this sinful attitude that they've carried with them all their life. Their grandkids probably have that same attitude. "Well, gramma did it so I'm going to do it."

I was surprised at the number of seniors who described what amounted to the sacrilege of what their churches were supposed to hold sacred. Even more interesting was how they would venture forth to find other churches. A boy at Central City High had a different religion from his mother. "I had to leave her church because the preacher was smoking and stuff and I don't want to get told by someone who wasn't living a holy life." Monica left her Black church and found a White one that was more to her liking. These and other teenagers were looking for a place of worship where adult leaders and parishioners upheld the power of theology through the power of their example. They sought sanctuary in such places and sometimes within their schools.

FAITH IN SCHOOLS

Classroom Religious Voids

I observed dozens of classes in all three high schools, including those in subject matter areas with curricular references to religion. With two exceptions, I did not observe any teachers overtly cover or discuss religion in their classes. One was in an American government class at Ridgewood High where the teacher, during a discussion on the U.S. Constitution, explained how "religious rights are not absolute." The other exception was in Cassandra's world literature class where students interpreted Chinese, Indian, and other literature with religious themes. One example was during an unit on *Siddhartha* when students were asked to write an essay on whether the main character was true to, or uncertain about, his religious faith. There also was a discussion on religious differences that took place prior to a school dance where girls asked boys to accompany them. The teacher mentioned that such practices were forbidden in some religions. Christina's Pakistani friend then explained how Muslim girls would never ask a boy out and how "good Islamic men" do not ask girls out for casual dates. But such discussions were rare or nonexistent in other classes. There was a religious void in classrooms as teachers avoided lessons that could be interpreted as religious in substance or intent. I did not ask teachers why they did that, but I did sense an unspoken understanding that religion as an instructional topic was taboo.

Teachers also avoided substantive lessons on morality. Moral education is legal in public high schools as long as it does not endorse a particular religion. Secularized approaches have been initiated over the years with the purpose of molding students' "moral behavior and ... capacity to think about issues of right and wrong" (Purpel & Ryan, 1976, p. 5). Among them were initiatives aimed at the development of morally autonomous individuals who make behavioral choices on the basis of their own values or hierarchies of moral principles. Their heyday was in the 1970s when values clarification programs and Kohlberg's moral dilemmas gained some notoriety in K–12 educational circles (Kohlberg, 1975, 1976; Simon, Howe, & Kirschenbaum, 1972; Simon & Kirschenbaum, 1973). But they did not last, in part because parents and religious groups felt their values were being undermined by what struck them as an anything-goes approach to moral decision making.

Among the most popular approaches in the 1980s were those inspired by a feminist ethic of care. Teachers and students were encouraged to value their relationships and respond to one another's physical, emotional, and psychological needs through nurturing acts of caring (Noddings, 1984, 1992). The focus in more recent years has been on the formation of good, civic character. Sizer and Sizer (1999) have taken the lead in an effort that urges educators to pay more attention to how school size, structures, and routine practices promote or hinder moral behavior. They recommend that teachers be given the school-wide support necessary for forging moral contracts that engender mutual respect and responsibility through sincere expressions of civility and care.

Central City High had a formal school philosophy that reflected the language and spirit of contemporary trends in moral education. The philosophy, spelled out in a pamphlet distributed to students and parents, emphasized the school's commitment to establishing "a sense of community and care" through a team-teaching approach. Students as community members were to abide by behavioral norms of dependability, responsibility, and initiative and adopt communication skills emphasizing civil courtesies conveyed through phrases such as "please," "thank you," and "may I help you?" Ridgewood High did not have a stated philosophy, but students were well aware of middle-class proprieties that were virtually identical to the norms stated in the Central City High pamphlet. Students at Jefferson High had no idea if their school had a philosophy. Nor could I find any evidence that it did.

Whether philosophies with moral overtones were well articulated or not, the main concern of school authorities was the establishment of a normative order where they could wield effective disciplinary practices. The particular renditions of respect, responsibility, civility, and care they promoted were more conducive for controlling the organizational behavior of students than producing ethical, morally upright young men and women. Respect and responsibility, for them, was largely about getting students to obey rules and regulations. Expressions of civility were couched in languages of polite compliance and the meaning of care was mostly intended to curb disruptive actions and interactions.

Except for the constant reinforcement of such renditions, there was a moral vacuousness in classrooms as teachers rarely if ever purposefully engaged students in dialogues or activities that addressed weighty moral issues or what it really means to be a good person living in a good society. Unplanned discussions may have occurred. But teachers for the most part steered clear of any and all overt lessons on morality. This was not the case in corridors, where morality and other elements of religion were salient features of student cultural productions.

Corridor Netherworlds and Sanctuaries

Unlike classrooms, corridors were sites for religious identity and integration work. They were places where seniors could construct or deconstruct their religious commitments with little or no adult interference. They incorporated disparate theological material into their youth cultural or subcultural productions against the backdrop of the larger corridor scene.

Such was the case at Jefferson High, where Adam described corridors as "absolute hell." He and his friends traversed hallways, lunchrooms, and bathrooms as if they were God-forsaken netherworlds where inhabitants were, in effect, gods unto themselves. Some of his peers actually did appear to be assuming such positionings in their subcultural productions. Through processes of bricolage, they defied or elevated themselves above organized religion and other institutions while simultaneously maintaining symbolic connections with them. Among them were working-class skinheads who projected an intimidating image of supremist White (s)electness in their symbolic amalgamations of absolute power. They wore clothing, jewelry, or tattoos that combined Christian crucifixes and other religious symbols with Nazi swastikas as if they had taken over all of the discursively conceivable supernatural and earthly powers of good and evil. Other Jefferson High students also juxtaposed contradictory cultural material in fashions that were less threatening but just as provocative. I saw a girl leaning against a locker who looked like a witch dressed in black clothes with black lipstick, dyed black hair, and black eye shadow. Around her neck was a necklace with a large, ivory colored medallion. On the medallion was the image of the Virgin Mary, hands folded in prayer with her veiled head bowed in pious reverence.

Other subcultures were more reconstructive, like the one produced within the sanctuary of Lona's clique. Disconnected from their families, alienated from their churches, Lona and her friends carved out a safe social space where they found some solace and were able to express their identities as ex-Catholics, gay Baptists, or some other combination of psychocultural commitments. They also considered ways to reconcile theological discourses with personal expression as they settled into religious systems. Reconciliation did not mean political accommodation whereby one side surrenders or submits to another. Nor was it compromise where all sides incurred some losses. It was a settlement that worked to the benefit of everyone involved. One example was Lona's proposal for reconciliation with the Catholic church. If she ever did return to the church, she said, she would undergo a thorough cleansing to rid herself of the "dirty feeling" she had about her past. "I need to go to confession before I can get back into the church thing. I haven't been to confession since sixth grade. I don't feel I can go to church until I get rid of this dirty feeling I have about my past. I need a cleansing, like an exorcism or something."

The church for its part would have to "clean up its act" by lifting its uncompromising restrictions on critical consciousness, intimate relations, and other individual freedoms. Perhaps both parties could then produce new, mutually agreeable theological mainlines.

Ridgewood High corridors appeared on the surface to be good, orderly places. But below the facade were temptations that caused kids to transgress religious mainlines and middle-class propriety. Peter told of how his peers were superficially nice in public but "suspect" in private. Preppies, in Christina's estimation, were particularly suspect. They acted as if they were superior yet used drugs and indulged in other forbidden activities. When preppies got caught, their parents would blame druggies or other unsavory characters as devils responsible for corrupting their children. They would demand that administrators expel the devils and would then send their fallen children to rehab centers for redemption.

Seniors had various responses to the pressures encountered in corridors. Peter kept his own counsel as he retreated into the inner sanctum he had constructed out of ancient Chinese beliefs. Cassandra sought redemption in her church and in programs administered by school counselors. Stuart simply went about the business of amassing power through whatever tactics were most useful for him.

But some of the most interesting responses were those produced within peer groups surrounded by intentionally erected cultural boundaries. The Young Life Club had erected definite boundaries within which members could embrace and maintain similar religious commitments. Members of Christina's clique also established boundaries in order to protect their ethnic identities and lifestyles. The dynamics of subcultural productions within this clique were very much like those documented by Zine (2001) in her insightful research on the politics of religious identity among Muslim youths in Canadian high schools. Basing her analysis on prior ethnographic research, she explained how Muslim students negotiated the "continuity of their identity" in school contexts marked by competing peer pressures, racism, and Islamophobia (Barth, 1969; Berns McGowen, 1999; Gibson, 1988; Jacobson, 1998). The dominance of Western culture heightened Muslim students' sense of religiosity as well as their felt need to constantly mark the social and cultural boundaries of Islamic beliefs. Yet students also displayed ambivalence in their adaptations.

Such politics were evident in Christina's clique, where many of the girls had a heightened sense of their religiosity. The Pakistani girl spoke as if she were a young Muslim woman determined to stay on the Islamic Straight Path or *Siratal Mustaqeem* laid out in the Holy Qur'an. She exuded an aura of purity. Yet when she talked about Muslim *hijabs* as protecting a woman's sexual purity, I noticed that she did not have one on. What she usually wore to school were blue jeans and other less-modest styles of Western dress. Perhaps, as Chaudhry (2000) confessed in her reflexive tale, she was both "thrilled by the manner in which Muslims ... are enacting resistance to dominant [American] modes of thought" yet disturbed by Islamic practices that could be "oppressive in some ways" (p. 99). Or maybe Christina's Pakistani friend felt compelled to make some accommodations to protect herself against the social consequences of looking like someone who openly rejected Judeo-Christianity. Whatever the reason, there was a disconnect between what she expressed as her most deep-felt religious beliefs and her outward expression of religious practices.

Christina was cautiously ambivalent. Her eyes lit up when she described her experiences as a Roman Catholic Mexican-American basking in the warmth of the Hispanic Catholic church community. But she was not ready to adopt a totally Catholic lifestyle or, for that matter, a distinctively Chicano one. She anchored her ethnic religious self just short of adopting the practices that would have fostered complete integration into an Hispanic Catholic local world. It was as if she were putting off the last, final practical step until she was absolutely sure about whether she wanted to make, or could actually keep, a firm set of cultural commitments.

Christina's ambivalence was heightened, indeed, complicated at Ridgewood High where she was put off by the preppie scene. She identified with druggies, who were condemned by preppie parents as well as members of her own community as symbolic embodiments of the devil. Although she did not actually associate with druggies or use drugs on a regular basis, she was attracted to their image as kids who knew what they were doing as they led the preppies who imitated them into the depths of hell. Druggies could knock superior preppies down. But they also could lead kids away from the secure havens of families, churches, ethnic communities, and other worlds. That, perhaps, is why Christina could not bring herself to practice what druggies supposedly preached.

The imagined hell that preppie parents feared at Ridgewood High was something of a reality for many seniors at Central City High. The impression I got from seniors who agreed to be interviewed was that kids in their neighborhoods were pretty much on their own when it came to religion. When I asked a group of eight seniors about religion, they spoke about their own searches for good churches and were among the most critical of hypocritical church leaders and parishioners. A girl summed up the group sentiment when she said, "Religion and churches are supposed to be important because that's where you find a holy counselor. But you don't see a lot of them around here."

The group also described the perfidious corridor climate. A boy spoke about how he had been "honed in hell" in hallways where "kids get away with stuff they shouldn't do 'cause no one tells them how they supposed to behave." The group blamed the situation on the laxness in adult supervision but also on a society that no longer seemed to have an accepted moral order. As another girl explained, "I don't think people in this country establish values like they used to. People's values fluctuate so much. There aren't any set standards or set values."

In the absence of set standards and values, the teenagers in the group felt they had no choice but to be morally autonomous. Because there is no right or wrong, a boy reasoned, kids have to make up their own right and wrong. "Kids today have to make their own right and wrong. Like it's all in your mind. All the pressures are on you, you take it up here and think whether I'm going to do this or that. A person has to sit down with themselves and talk to themselves. I don't mean talk to himself about the weather and stuff. I mean question his own self, his own conscience, like ask 'why am I doing this?' Some of them don't ask the real questions that should be asked. They just do what they feel like doing."

But such free choice did necessarily free students from the hell they were experiencing in their neighborhoods, homes, and schools. "A lot of kids," the boy went on to say, "who just do what they feel like doing are the ones who are like making it hell, like hell for everyone but it's not all their fault 'cause they don't know any better. They just doing what they know."

Monica, in her escape from hell, searched for a church where she could be uplifted. Nay took it one day at a time as a Christian in a Black church where people could go to get a little bit of God or a lot of Him if they needed to. Michael went to church but was otherwise noncommittal in his religious commitments. He was finding other ways to get out. Graduating seniors thus made their way through the theologically complex ways of American religious crosscurrents.

6

Political Domain: Democracy and Domination

The United States is a democracy where citizens are diverse yet equal and have the Constitutional right to participate directly or through elected representatives in deliberative government bodies established to formulate and implement policies, laws, and initiatives for the mutual benefit of individuals and their communities. This convoluted political ideal and its derivatives are communicated across the country and throughout the world as if they were accurate descriptions of matter-of-fact reality. But close scrutiny of American political arenas may uncover realities that are decidedly undemocratic. One of the most enduring educational missions of public high schools is to ensure that democracy gets realized as a matter of fact. But whether this occurs depends on how political crosscurrents are negotiated within classrooms and corridors.

This chapter describes political crosscurrents and how democratic education was pitted against the politics of domination in the three public high schools. As is shown, the tension between pedagogical ideals and everyday reality had profound consequences for how high school seniors came of age in the American political domain. The discussion begins with how the political self strives for recognition in the midst of competing ideologies.

THE POLITICAL SELF

The political self, like other identity facets, has psychological and cultural aspects. The most significant psychological aspect is the desire for recognition that Fukuyama (1992) explicated in terms of the Platonic concept

142

of *thymos*. Thymos is the value or worth that an individual attaches to him- or herself. It is the inner sense of self-respect "something like an innate human sense of justice" that is felt deep within the human psyche:

> People believe that they have a certain worth, and when other people act as though they are worth less—when they do not *recognize* their worth at its correct value—then they become angry. Conversely, when other people see that we are not living up to our own sense of self-esteem, we feel *shame*; and when we are evaluated justly (i.e., in proportion to our true worth), we feel *pride*. Plato's *thymos* is therefore nothing other than the psychological seat of [the] desire for recognition. (p. 165)

The desire for recognition is the most specifically political part of the human personality because of how it causes people to want to assert themselves over others. Ordinary Americans and, for that matter, Western social scientists do not normally construe political activities as competitions for recognition. But thymos can and often does supersede other interests as the most powerful motivating force in human political affairs.

How thymos is manifested in the personality is shaped by what Fukuyama (1992) referred to as the "moral dimensions" of human psychology. People may value themselves as morally equivalent or equally worthy to others. They may satisfy their desire for recognition through acts of magnanimous generosity, altruistic service, or courage where they literally risk their lives to save the lives of others. But thymos also may manifest itself as a megalothymic desire to dominate. This latter, darker side of political psychology is a catalyst for battles where a person's main intent is to establish his or her superiority over someone else. It is the most basic, primordial starting point for human political conflict.

There also is a cultural aspect to the political self. How thymos is expressed is affected by the powerful discursive forces of political ideologies as well as by the ideological elements of religious theologies, family prescriptions, and other worldviews. Lather (1991) conceptualized ideologies as "the stories a culture tells about itself" (p. 2). Such stories speak to both the determinant and progressive features of a culture and provide people with the commonsense categories, concepts, and images through which they interpret their existence as it is or might become. Another way to think about ideologies is to conceive of them as storylines that groups spin about their historical pasts, present conditions, and what the future will or ought to hold for them. Storylines are saturated with group interests and are passed along with or without the interests of other groups, or the common good, in mind.

The psychology of thymos and cultures of ideologies are intertwined in the formation of the individual political self. Thymos was a powerful force in how seniors sought recognition in the contexts of their schools. But ide-

ologies, especially dominant ones, also exerted important cultural influences on their political self-leanings.

DOMINANT IDEO(LOGICAL) LEANINGS

National, state, and local American politics are rooted in the storylines of
dominant political ideologies, commonly divided into liberal, conservative, and radical factions. There are directional bearings associated with
these ideologies, as well as major political parties. Liberalism is pointed toward the left and defined within the purview of the Democratic political
party. Its ideological storylines about the past emphasize the impact and
amelioration of inequalities, especially those affecting racial and ethnic
minority groups and women. Storylines for present conditions tell of the
progress that liberals have made through landmark legislation and government programs and how much more has to be done in the future to ensure equal opportunity, provide social services, and promote social justice.
Liberals also support the recognition of diversity and individuals' right to
choose their own family arrangements, religious expressions, and other
styles of life.

Conservatives lean to the right and typically align themselves with the
Republican party. The conservative ideological view of history highlights
the development of free markets, fair and open competition, and individual pursuit of socioeconomic mobility. Present conditions, according to
the storyline, could be much better if the government exercised less control over the affairs of citizens. Regulation of the economy should be mini-
mized while military defense systems should be kept at high levels of
readiness. Conservatives also maintain that the rights of minority groups,
women, and other people should not be promoted or privileged through
tax-supported social programs and Affirmative Action policies but, rather,
protected by the courts in keeping with the judicial maxim of equal treatment under the law. The best hope for the future is for people to advance
themselves in a free-market economic system where individual competition rather than group preferences prevail. People also should be assimilated into a common culture by learning Standard English and embracing
traditional nuclear family values, Judeo-Christian religious mainlines,
and other mainstream American conventions.

There also are far-left radicals influenced by Marxism, feminism, and
other ideologies that emphasize on-going struggles against various forms
of oppression. They have traditionally organized themselves into minority political parties, grassroots movements, and other kinds of coalitions.
Radicals in the past supported Communism or more socialistic systems of
government. They have concentrated in recent years on the deleterious
effects of capitalism on the environment, living conditions in postcolonial

countries, and the globalization of economic disparities. Radicals offer some of the most utopian visions for the future that go much farther in their recommendations for socially transformative change than do those promoted in liberal and conservative camps.

Graduating seniors, in their own political self-leanings, were greatly influenced by dominant liberal and conservative ideologies. None of them identified themselves as radicals and most had little awareness of, or an accurate read on, the ideological storylines of groups that were not tied to major political parties. Their ideological self-awareness was somewhat heightened by the fact that there was a presidential campaign underway during my fieldwork in 1996.[16] It also was affected by their racial, ethnic, religious, sexual, and gender locations. Gender turned out to be a particularly significant political pivotal point. Although I cannot make generalizations, the boys in this research were more attuned to the overall political scene whereas the girls, if they took any interest in politics at all, were more tuned into specific issues.

There also was a subjective logic or ideo(logic) to seniors' political self-positionings. The nature of their identifications depended on the extent to which ideologies fulfilled their thymic desire for recognition and whether storylines made cultural sense to them, their families, communities, and/or the country.

David, among all of the seniors, was by far the most passionate about politics. He kept abreast of national political issues and had an extraordinarily good read on the shifting American political seascape, as was evident in his synopsis of how different groups of people identify with dominant ideologies at different points in their lives.

> People on the right, you know, Republicans want small government and lower taxes. They usually cater to the upper middle class, to rich Caucasians. The left [Democrats] most of the time they want enough revenue to provide programs for the middle class and below middle-class people and Blacks, women, and disadvantaged people like that. The moderates in the middle go with Republicans on economic issues and Democrats on social issues. They maybe were hippies in college who wanted to change everything until they made a little money. They feel different about economic issues but can't give up the social stuff, you know, the we-got-to-save-people stuff.

As for himself, David "at the present time" was a liberal Democrat because "I'm young, don't have any money, and am an endangered Black male." Liberalism not only recognized his thymic self-worth as a young Black man, but its ideo(logical) stances on educational issues and policies like Affirmative Action made perfect practical sense for him. "The Democratic party appeals to me because they like Affirmative Action and like to throw money at schools and programs for Black guys like me. It works for me at this point in my life." David also predicted that his political self-leanings would change if he did manage to achieve middle-class status. "I'll probably end up becoming one of those moderates in the middle worrying about the economy and, like, wondering when all those hippies are gonna grow up. "

Adam was disillusioned with status quo politicians like the incumbent president who was, in his estimation, more interested in being king than working for the good of the country. "I'd probably go with an independent, third-party person the way I feel right now. It seems like the people in office right now, like the president doesn't really work at it. He doesn't work at trying to fix problems. He just lets it go. He just wants to sit up there like a king." When I asked what problems needed to be fixed, he chose issues and ideo(logical) solutions that made sense to him:

> I agree with some of the tax issues and the budget and stuff like what Bob Dole [a Republican presidential candidate] says about reducing taxes and balancing the budget. But sometimes you got to realize like George Bush [a former Republican president] that sometimes you have to raise taxes otherwise the country probably would have gone under. I think [like Democrats] the government should find some way to give people health care 'cause if you're poor and sick and dying you need to go somewhere and get something, get some help.

He also felt Affirmative Action was a big problem because it did not recognize him or other young White males as equal or worthy of fair treatment. "It's wrong," he exclaimed. "It's definitely not fair and should be eliminated."

Most of the other boys also positioned themselves on the ideo(logical) continuum in ways that reflected their individual desires for recognition as well as group social and cultural locations. Stuart lived in a staunchly Republican district yet identified himself as a loyal Democrat. Members of his family contributed financially and in other ways to Democratic politicians because they supported regulations that helped small businesses and recognized Jewish people and Jewish causes. "They are big supporters of Israel," he said, "and I think they do a lot to stop hate talk, like, anti-Semitism in this country."

Peter, who lived in the same district as Stuart, was a diehard Republican who thought the government should eliminate liberal social programs and build up the defense budget:

> Welfare, get rid of it. Social security, get rid of it. All middle-class entitlements, get rid of them, too. All of those programs take up too much of my paycheck. They are supporting more people than they were ever

meant to support. The government should beef up the defense budget. There's a lot of crazy people out there in these countries these days. You have no idea what's going to happen. Castro is still in power. He could do a lot of damage to this country if he wanted to. So throw money at the military and get rid of all the programs that are doing things people should be doing for themselves.

He also was attracted to the conservative stance on success through competition. "They believe that no matter who you are, Black, White, Chinese, a girl, or whatever, you can make it if you're the best." You can or at least ought to be able to earn recognition regardless of your race, gender, or, in his case, ethnic background.

Michael had been employed as a clerical assistant in city hall where he discerned a rather lackluster effort on the part of local politicians. He explained how politicians functioned just like a "regular workforce" slacking off until the boss comes around:

> It's like they were working a regular job. When the big boss comes around, that's when you get your store looking good and stuff. When the boss isn't around, you slack off. But as soon as it's mentioned that the boss is coming, you try and hurry up and rush to do stuff you haven't kept up with. Like what I'm saying is that when elections come around, politicians try to do a lot of good things. That's when they pump in the hogwash. Once they get elected, they slack off until the next election rolls around.

He quit paying attention to politics after he quit his job at city hall, largely because of the political "hogwash" of slack-offs who don't care about the opinions of people like him. "I look at politics now and then like when the city talks about raising taxes to build new stadiums. But all the other stuff I don't pay attention to it until election time rolls around and all the hogwash comes pouring in and even then I don't care too much about it. They don't care about what I think anyway."

All of the girls initially claimed to have little or no interest in politics. When I asked Christina about politics, she said "They kind of bore me. I think if issues were really, really important to everyone, um, to me and all of the people, politics would be more exciting. Like in the 60s how you could be drafted but couldn't vote. We need more of those kinds of issues." When I encouraged her to come up with at least one important issue, she said "Well, there's always women's rights. Women's rights used to be recognized more like in the past. Sometimes I like blow it off, like I'll say 'yeah, we have equality.' But then I sometimes realize that there isn't equality. There's actually male dominance. Men have the high ranking jobs and everything like that." Although she picked an issue that was relevant to how she and other women were being recognized and treated in relation to men, Christina was neither aware of, nor particularly concerned about, the intricacies of ideological discourses involving women's rights. She was apathetic if not thoroughly detached in her political self-expressions.

Cassandra also claimed to have no interest in politics until I mentioned the controversial issue of legalized abortion. She spoke out in vehement opposition to abortion, unleashing a resoundingly conservative stance that essentially affirmed her own hoped-for thymic self-recognition as a teenage single mother who deserves the utmost respect for the responsibility she took for the life of her child. "I had my baby. I went through it. I do not want to have an abortion. It's not a method of birth control. That's what girls need to get through their heads. If they don't want to have babies, if they're not ready, then they need to stop having sex right now. But if it does happen, then they need to take responsibility. Let the child live and take some responsibility." Her conservative views on abortion were intertwined with, yet somewhat circumscribed by, the strands of Protestant theological mainlines. Although she insisted that abortion violated God's law, she also felt that state laws should not prevent women from exercising free choice. "Abortion should be up to the individual woman. There shouldn't be no law on it. But there's God law, you know, the laws of the Bible women should think about when they decide. If they think about that, they would have to be pro life. They would believe that you should let that baby live. If you don't want to keep that life then give it to someone who will love and worship that baby instead of you sittin' there using abortion as a method of birth control 'cause you don't care about that baby's God-given life."

Lona also did not pay much attention to politics. Even though politics were "confusing" to her, she agreed with her Black, working-class mother that the dominant ideologies of major political parties clearly benefitted some groups at the expense of others. "I pretty much go along with my mother who says Republicans are for all of the rich people and the Democrats are for all the middle-class people. They may say they're for poor people, Black people, but, you know, nothing really happens for them. They should focus more on the lower class people and help them, but the last I heard they were talkin' about takin' out welfare and everything for them. So I guess my mother is right." She also felt that political parties do not care about young people, which is why she and other young people generally do not care about them. "When you're younger you don't care. It's all about adult ideas. I haven't been payin' that much attention to like the Presidential campaign mostly because I'm still in school and don't have the personal life, social life, you know, the life that candidates say they gonna make better or [laughter] worse. I think a lot of kids are like that."

When I asked Lona about her views on specific issues, none of them struck her as "important in my head" with the exception of those involving intimate relations and the right to adopt alternative family-life styles. These issues understandably were of most ideo(logical) concern to her and her friends. Chief among them was gay rights. "I care about that. I heard something on the news last night, I actually watched the news [laughter] and, um, [Republicans] Pat Buchanan, Bob Dole sounded like they were swaying people to be, how should I say this, um, kind of like an antigay kind of thing. I mean people saying things like that on the news, I totally disagree with that."

Nay, in an evasive, somewhat contradictory remark, said that she did and did not pay attention to politics. "I don't really pay any attention to politics. Because every time you look around there's something new. Oh, no. I don't pay no attention. I mean I listen and read up on it, but I don't pay no attention to it. Change the subject."

When I discussed politics with Monica, she said there was no reason for her to take an interest in them since "the Japanese are taking over" and all politicians seem to care about is other countries:

> The Japanese are taking over this country. Like I'm paying them three dollars to do my nails. If I want color, I pay five. I mean, why can't we do this? Our political system it seems they're thinking more about other countries than what's going on here. I was listenin' to President Clinton and he's like askin' us to sponsor someone over there like go to another country and help people. I'm like why do you want a United States citizen do something over there? We need them to help out over here. He's more worried about what other countries are doing instead of what we're doing here and that don't make sense to me.

She also was not interested in a political system where Blacks and other people of color were not adequately recognized or represented in democratic governing bodies. In a monologue that revealed the liberal political self-positionings of many Black people, Monica spoke out in support of including more diverse voices of color on issues affecting "different people from ethnic backgrounds."

> It would be different if all different people from ethnic backgrounds could speak because then other people would see different lights on issues. You know I can't, I don't understand how a White person could really represent me when they really don't know me. You know what I'm saying? I would prefer a Black person because they know where I'm coming from, where we came from. They know what we've been through and everything. I think that needs to be changed, like they need to be more open about electing a Black President or Hispanic or whatever.

Despite her disillusionment, Monica and, for that matter, other seniors in their ideo(logical) leanings, remained well within the borders of
dominant American political discourses. Whatever awareness they did
have of radical ideologies were rife with negative misconceptions. Most
of the girls acknowledged gender inequities yet none of them identified
with feminists. They had a distorted view of feminist ideologies as, in
Cassandra's words, "man hating [and] out to convince women to be lesbians and not having kids and crazy stuff like that." Other radical views
were dismissed or misunderstood as dangerous for the country, especially those containing vestiges of Marxism. David, who actually had a
pretty good feel for contemporary Marxist thought, explained how most
Americans reject "hippie thinking" because it "spreads the evil seeds of
Communism."

> Most hippies, you know, the dudes who want to turn the world on its head
> are into stuff that isn't strictly Communist, you know, Lenin, Mao, all that.
> Their thinking has changed but most Americans believe hippie thinking,
> no matter what, it like spreads the evil seeds of Communism. They are
> scared of Communism, not like in the 50s but they don't want to have any-
> thing to do with it.

And yet, as a girl at Ridgewood High pointed out, both of the major political parties seemed to be headed toward Communism because of how
they pressure people to conform to their storylines. "The parties they are
like heading more towards communism than anything else just because of
how they expect everybody to conform. Everybody has to be this way or
that way. They just want everybody to be like them because they're in
power or want to be in power." Her and other seniors' concerns (or lack of
concern) about the power of the people in power were affected even further by political movements that made them wonder whether or not they
really had a cause for interest in national politics.

CAUSE FOR INTEREST
IN POLITICAL MOVEMENTS

Common Cause to Special Interests

Seniors, in our discussions about politics, noted a drastic liminal shift in the
political climate from the 1960s to the 1990s. Their impressions of the
1960s was that it was a period when liberal politicians and grassroots orga-
nizers were at the helm of political movements that promoted common
causes for profound social change. Political activity was driven by issues
rendered in terms of what policies, laws, and programs would provide the
greatest benefits in the interest of the common public good. Peter said that
was when "they were trying to lobby for equal rights for everyone." David

told of the "incredible progress" Blacks had made during the decade's civil rights movement. Monica spoke about how college students "got out onto the streets" to protest the Vietnam War and the entire concept of war as a solution to international conflict. But those times were gone as seniors perceived a major sea change that has rerouted political currents in a manner that has not necessarily been in the overall interest of society.

Political movements with overarching common causes have been replaced, in seniors' minds, with big government run by politicians catering to narrow special interests. As Stuart put it, "I think the government is getting a little too big [and] powerful people are a little bit too powerful these days. Somebody needs to step in and downsize the government because the country is supposed to be run, um, ruled by the people for the people. The definition of democracy is getting pretty impossible."

Michael felt that the old ideological distinctions that once divided the two major political parties were becoming muted or blurred to the point where it was no longer clear what if any major changes or reforms they envisioned. "I can't really say what they really stand for and sometimes I think they, I mean, the Democrats and Republicans, don't know either." Whatever new distinctions were being made were being subsumed under political discourses of special interests that, according to Peter, boiled down to whether or how much big government should be involved in giving individuals and groups whatever they happen to want at that particular moment in their lives:

> The political system used to be a lot smaller. Now it's starting to get bigger and people want more and more, they want the federal government to be more involved in their lives. But they don't want them too involved in their lives. I mean, see, I don't think there's really much wrong with our political system if you look at it like politicians are doing just what the people want them to do. If you want to remedy the political system, what you need to do is shape up the people and say, "Here, you idiots. Tell us what you want. Don't change your mind in like two seconds." People say "Yes, I want welfare" then they turn around and say, "No, I don't want welfare." The problem is they are looking at what's good for them at the moment instead of what's good for everyone down the line.

David noted the discursive shift and was concerned about how special interests, especially those represented by powerful White males occupying congressional and judicial positions, might wipe out the incredible progress made by Blacks:

> I don't want to play the race card but race has become like a silent political issue instead of out in the open. There are people on the Supreme Court and in the Senate and the Congress who seem to be against some of the gains of civil rights like Affirmative Action. It seems like they want to go

back, like what they feel is that White males, certain special interests have-
n't gotten their fair shake. That's not the case but that's what they feel. So
like race in the 1990s you don't talk about it. If you don't talk about it, if
nobody mentions it, it's not there. It goes away they hope.

He also believed that there was an even larger ideological conspiracy at
work that affected everyone including Whites. Politicians might talk
about how they want to shrink big government by lowering taxes and getting rid of social programs like welfare. But what they are really doing is
tricking the American people:

> They talk about lower taxes, less government, catch phrases like that. If
> you really think about it, you know they are not really serious about getting
> rid of big government 'cause they'd be out of the job if they did. They have
> tricked the American people into wanting more by giving less and getting
> less. They tell us that if taxes are cut you'll still get services. But it doesn't
> really work like that. How it really works is that politicians get more money
> into the pockets of their rich friends and then they say, "Oh, sorry, I guess
> we really can't provide services. Too bad. You're on your own."

Members of Lona's clique were even more cynical, as was evident in
Ashley's biting summation of what she thought were the typical positions
of politicians. "They are power hungry, money-grubbing, antigay, racist,
stupid idiots who only care about themselves, their friends, and getting re-
elected." Her own special interests certainly were not being served nor did
she see any common causes in the offing that would have benefitted her or
members of other marginalized groups. She and many other seniors found
themselves politically adrift, much like the popular cultural rebels who are
portrayed as having no causes, especially truly good ones.

Rebels Without Good Cause

The mythical image of the young American rebel without a cause was produced in a 1950s movie featuring a restless young actor named James
Dean. It remains as something of an icon in popular culture although its
relevance has waxed and waned in the decades following the release of the
film. Young rebels in the 1960s had plenty of causes. But by the 1990s, as
a Black girl at Central City High explained, there were no longer any
causes for her and other young people to fight:

> The thing about us is that we have all this, what's the word, everything we
> have inside us, you know, we can be anything. We're like rebels but we're
> fighting for the wrong cause. I don't think we even have any causes to fight
> for. When I say that we're like rebels without a cause I feel we have drive,

we have push, we have knowledge, all those things we have in us but we don't know what it's for yet. We don't know how to use it and there aren't any good leaders or politicians or whatever to show us the way. They are like dead or dead in the head.

Rebels in the popular cultural productions of the fabled 1960s and 1970s were "hippies," "Black panthers," "Women libbers," and other activists who brandished peace signs, wore Afro hairstyles and African-style clothes to symbolize collective Black identity and opposition to White rule, and made female fashion statements expressing freedom from male oppression. They listened to popular music with antiwar, antiestablishment lyrics. Plays, movies, television programs, and other shows idolized young heroes and heroines fighting or leaving a status quo that waged unjust wars, perpetuated racial discrimination, and otherwise violated the most fundamental principles of democracy.

But these popular cultural productions dissipated in the 1980s when, in the wake of the postindustrial capitalistic boom, young people became the "me generation," presumed to be more interested in getting rich and consuming goods than in making the world a better place. A decade later, they were relabeled "generation X" as if they no longer had an identifiable sociopolitical signature. Seniors were well aware of the tag and talked about what they thought the "X" meant. Three Black students at Central City High thought it indicated "something unknown," "something people don't understand," and "something kids probably don't know about themselves." Monica interpreted it to mean that kids were being "Xed off."

Our generation, we're gone. We're generation X and that to me means we've been Xed off. The sad part is that the ones coming up beneath us, the generation under us is looking up and saying, 'Is that what we should do?' They don't know what to do and that means they're gonna get Xed off, too.

The popular cultural X-ness of youth positionings was made even worse by media depictions of adult politicians. Most of what seniors knew about politics was what they saw on television. What many of them saw were politicians tainted by real or fabricated undertows of corruption. The impression that Lona had was that most politicians were "rich White guys" who do the bidding of "high classes and middle classes 'cause they got the money." She also made the rather astute observation that how media portrayals of politicians are interpreted depends on people's social location. "There's nothin' wrong with what they are doing if you have money and give it to them and they give you what you want. But if you don't have money, then everything they're doing is wrong because you don't get anything. So rich White people love 'em and poor Black girls like me think they're crooks doing a crappy job."

Poor Black girls like her were turned off by White "crooked" politicians and inclined to turn off the TV when they came on. But some of the afflu-ent White teenagers at Ridgewood High had a completely different take on media coverage. A member of the Young Life Club talked about how exposing corruption was bound to improve politics because the politi-cians she supported were more likely to win elections:

> Last year I took AP history and we learned so much stuff that made me think that politics will eventually improve just because throughout his-tory whenever there's been too much corruption the media exposes it and politics improve. Give it twenty five years and I bet things will be much better, um, because the bad people will be swept out of office by voters and better ones like Dole will get in. They might not get in right away, but they will get in.

Cassandra, like Lona, had a more negative interpretation of media ef-fects. What she saw on TV were politicians who constantly lied about their intentions to improve the country:

> I don't really like politics because of how they lie so much. They lie right there on TV. I hear them doing it and they don't care that I hear them. I mean they say they're going to do something, if you say you're going to do it, do it. If you're not intending to do something then don't say it. If you say something knowing you aren't going to do it then you're lying. Those peo-ple lie all the time.

She also noticed how democratic deliberations were corrupted by politicians who used the media to launch vicious attacks on one an-other's personalities and personal lives rather than invite thoughtful debates on issues:

> The reason why I think a lot of people don't vote is because they don't know the issues. All they hear on TV is politicians attacking each other on their personalities and dumb stuff they did a long time ago. They don't stress the issues except in one or two debates at the end and even then they are careful about what they say. 'Cause they feel that it will give them the upper hand if they say something bad about that person. It must work be-cause people are like "My God, is he really like that?" If they vote against someone, it's not because of issues but because the other party made the guy look really bad as a person.

In the absence of good causes and politicians, graduating seniors—es-pecially those from low-income, working-class, Black, female, or other less wealthy, politically influential groups—felt Xed out. The Black girl who spoke about how her generation were rebels without any causes made an interesting point. When young people do not have any politically noble rallying points or leaders for positive social change, they are more apt to fight for their own narrowly self-interested causes in ways that can be socially destructive. "Right now," she said, "in my neighborhood the rebels with a cause are the gang members."

> Some of them are so intelligent like you know they would have done some good if someone had like shown them how. Now they draw up their own combat plans, you know what I mean? They fight their own people. That's misplaced anger. They could use that anger and direct it towards something else that's good but instead they hurtin' each other.

Whereas rebels in her neighborhood fought for their own self-interested causes, teenagers in other places were growing up in families with political cultures that had their own local causes and particular means for pursuing special interests.

Local Family Interests

Conventional wisdom in the United States is that the electorate is divided more by religion, ethnicity, and race than by social class, although the latter factor certainly influences ideo(logical) leanings. The sector that has traditionally provided the strongest support for conservative Republican positions are White, Anglo-Saxon Protestants (WASPs) with middle- to upper-middle-class status. Catholics, Jews, racial and ethnic minorities, and unionized workers constitute the political base for liberal Democrats, although defections are occurring, especially among Catholics. Be that as it may, political assimilation begins and sometimes ends in the family, where children encounter more localized special interests.

Families define their particular interests with reference to the more general agendas laid out by politicians and political parties. Nowhere was this more apparent than in Stuart's account of his family's involvement in the Democratic party. Jews for decades have provided overwhelming electoral support for Democrats as is indicated by the fact that in the 1992 and 1996 Presidential elections, over 78% of them voted for Democratic candidates. Adult members of the Lyon family not only voted for Democrats, but also contributed to the financing of political campaigns. Stuart's grandfather, father, and uncles had given so much money to the Democratic party that they were routinely invited to exclusive fund-raising events for prominent politicians, including those held for the incumbent President. They had adopted what Stuart described as a "donating theory" that was partly charitable and mostly political:

When it comes to charities, my dad, grandpa, and my uncles have a theory about donations like how important they are. They all donate a lot of money. My grandfather does it anonymously. My uncle likes to get his name on plaques. My Dad gets upset with my uncle for doing that 'cause he's more like my grandfather. But he lets the Democrats know he's donating to them 'cause he thinks they do a better job of supporting small business. He doesn't mind if they know he's giving them money, you know, so they will support him, his interests, and stuff.

Stuart intended to follow his forebears' footsteps and perhaps go a step further by joining the Young Democrats. He understood that by doing so he would learn a great deal about what it takes to be an active insider in the dominant political system. He would be taught some of the same lessons that his counterpart Republican classmates were learning in their families and local political organizations.

In the case of Christina's family, Chicano ethnic interests collided with Catholic religious convictions. Members of the Sanchez family were not directly involved in political parties and campaigns, but they did vote. Like most other Mexican-Americans, they voted for Democrats because of the party's traditional advocacy for ethnic minorities. But like a growing number of Catholics, they were troubled by Democrats' pro-choice stance on abortion. Christina said that although her parents were still inclined to vote for Democrats because of their work with Hispanic immigrants, they "aren't sure what to do about the abortion thing. It's like a choice, a terrible choice between voting for people who help you or voting for someone who doesn't think there's anything wrong with killing babies. My parents discuss it and I can tell it bothers them like they aren't sure what to do about the abortion thing." The party's stances created something of a moral dilemma for her parents. As for Christina, she also opposed abortion, but because of the influence of her family and the local Hispanic community, she could not in all good political conscience vote for Republicans. So she decided not to vote at all.

Other seniors talked about how their parents would discuss politics and vote but otherwise limit their involvement in political processes. David said he and his parents discussed the upcoming elections quite a bit and all of them planned to vote for Democrats. But they were not planning on donating any money or volunteer service to the party. The percentage of the Black vote for Democrats is just as high as the Jewish vote. But unlike Jews, Blacks are much less likely to go to the polls or become active participants in political processes. None of the Black senior girls planned to vote nor did their adult kin. The cynicism they expressed in response to my queries about their interest in politics was shared by family members, especially by Black mothers who felt they had been written off by White politicians. As Monica explained, "My mother, most mothers I know, what do they hear? They hear White [politicians] saying it's all their fault they are poor, ignorant people with too many babies. Like there's nothing else out there but them to blame for their situation. Or they say, 'We'll help you if you vote for us.' So they vote for them and nothin' happens. So why vote? Why should they even care to vote when those people don't care about them?"

Monica did not "care to vote." Nor did Nay, Lona, and Cassandra. They were not the only ones who were politically alienated. Michael had become disenchanted after his employment experiences in city hall. Adam was quite disillusioned with the two major political parties and felt it was time for a third one to arise. As far as he could tell, the politicians currently in power cared more about "self interest than public interest. They don't seem to be all that interested in our problems. They might say they are. They might say those words but they aren't. It seems like what they want is money. They fly around the country and say 'I want money' instead of 'Here's how I'm going to help you out.'" The cynicism in these attitudes was disturbing in a country that touts its political system as being for the people and by the people. It certainly posed challenges for public high schools, where the ideals of democratic education clashed with the everyday politics of domination.

DEMOCRATIC EDUCATION

Pedagogical Legacies

Democratic education as a pedagogical ideal has been an important feature of American educational thought since the founding of the public school system (Hemmings, 2000c). Horace Mann, the 19th century Massachusetts educational leader who played such an instrumental role in the establishment of publicly funded schools, was adamant that a common political creed had to be instilled in children in order to head off political conflicts as the immigrant population grew and suffrage was extended (Spring, 1994). School children ought to be socialized into the creed not so much through curriculum taught in classrooms but through social interactions aimed at reducing tensions between groups.

A century later, James B. Conant (cited in Rury, 2002) issued a series of influential reports on U.S. high schools where he extended Mann's vision of public education as an effective if not necessary instrument for sustaining democracy. Even though students may be tracked into different courses of study, high schools can bind them together through a common institutional ethos and a required curricular core that would provide students with ample opportunities to participate in democratic discussion, debate, and other modes of deliberations.

Deliberative processes moved to the forefront of democratic education after the politically turbulent years of the 1960s. Gutmann (1987), in her widely cited work, encouraged teachers to engage high school students in deliberative processes premised on principles of nondiscrimination and nonrepression. The principle of nondiscrimination maintains that educable students be educated in both the processes and content of democratic deliberations, whereas the principle of nonrepression ensures students' freedom to consider diverse views, however controversial. Both of these principles should permeate pedagogy as well as classroom relations.

Educational anthropologists contributed to the discussion with a succession of theories and teaching methods that recognize cultural diversity as vital for democracy.[17] They emphasize the importance of acknowledging cultural differences in ensuring the well-being of all people, resolving intergroup conflict, and facilitating the free exchange of ideas. Difference ought to be bridged in public schools through instructional approaches that affirm students' native cultures and transmit common cultural understandings that cut across groups.

Hovering over the long and protracted history of democratic education are the progressive ideals of John Dewey, who conceived a vision of a democratic society as one where individual growth is nurtured and constructive social change is realized. The most democratic educational ideal in the Deweyan view is one that releases students' potentialities in "the realization of a form of social life in which interests are mutually interpenetrating, and where progress, or readjustment, is an important consideration" (Dewey, 1916, p. 87). Schools should model democracy as modes of social life where students with diverse backgrounds and talents participate in joint deliberations and collaborative actions to solve economic, social, and other problems. Such a model encourages students to think about their own interests and behaviors in relation to one another and to do so in a manner that contributes to "the breaking down of those barriers of class, race, and national territory which kept men from perceiving the full import of their activity" (p. 87).

All of these variants of democratic education have left a legacy in public high schools even as newer ones begin to emerge.[18] The common political creed espoused by Horace Mann is a staple feature of liberal educational rhetoric. High school students, as recommended in Conant's reports, are required to take classes on U.S. history and American government. They may sign up for curricular electives, join extracurricular debate clubs, or run for offices in student government, where they are given plenty of opportunities to participate in democratic discussions and debates. Teachers have gone along with the suggestions of Gutmann or other experts by facilitating nondiscriminatory and nonrepressive deliberative processes in their classrooms (Dillon, 1994; Preskill, 1997). Dewey's ideals spurred reforms that led to the establishment of small high schools conducive for sustaining democratic models of education where teachers, administrators, and parents collaborate in the design and implementation of progressive programming (Ayers, Klonsky, & Lyon, 2000; Clinchy, 2000; Meier, 1995; Sizer & Sizer, 1999). The theoretical insights of educational anthropologists contributed to the development of a variety of pedagogical approaches that bridged cultural differences (Banks & Banks, 2001; Gay, 1994; Nieto, 1992; Sleeter, 1991). And they were part of the legacy of the high schools in this study, even if they were not completely or even largely realized in the political lessons taught in classrooms.

Politically Explicit/Implicit Lessons

The most basic, universally recognized purpose of all renditions of democratic education is to prepare students for responsible citizenship by integrating them into the dominant political system. This purpose is fulfilled through various methods of political socialization where students are taught democratic values, norms, and creeds; are familiarized with institutionalized political and governmental roles and processes; and learn how to participate in democratic deliberations and decision making in a thoughtful, lawful manner. At the three high schools, most of the socialization was done in required classes such as those in U.S. history and government. Teachers in these classes not only taught explicit curricular fare, but also conveyed implicit lessons about their students' political positionings and likely involvement in the dominant political system. Implicit lessons constituted a hidden curriculum of political assimilation that was very much influenced by teachers' perceptions of the local political culture of the communities they served. Localized assimilation often supplanted the larger ideals of democratic socialization contained in explicit curriculum.

Explicit and implicit political lessons were evident in the U.S. government classes that seniors were required to take at Ridgewood High. I observed a number of sections of this class taught by different teachers, but the overall instructional pattern was the same. Students were exposed to standard curriculum on the U.S. Constitution, three branches of government, legislative process for passing laws, and other knowledge. They were told about how every citizen has the equal political right to choose and debate his or her own position on issues, vote, and otherwise get involved in political processes. But lessons did not end there. Students also learned implicit, as well as blatant, lessons that assimilated them into, and prepared them for active participation in, political processes intended to promote the right-wing conservative Republican leanings of the people who resided in the district.

I was in a government class where a teacher spelled out exactly where Ridgewood High students were situated in terms of the surrounding district's socioeconomic demographics and political geography. He explained how the voting district was 90% White with a median income of $80,000. It was, he claimed, "the most Republican major metropolitan area in the United States." The district was such a staunch Republican enclave that prominent Republican politicians would travel there to give speeches and raise money. Ridgewood High was frequently selected as the site for these speeches. The 1996 Republican presidential candidate had spoken at the school the year before. The district's Republican U.S. congressman visited the school the year I was there. Classes were canceled so that students could go to the gymnasium to listen to what the congressman had to say.

As I sat through other government classes, I observed teachers who facilitated classroom discussions where students were provided with ample opportunities to participate in democratic deliberations. But there often was a conservative slant in deliberations that effectively silenced or constricted more liberal or radical perspectives. The slant surfaced during a discussion on how the rights guaranteed in Constitutional amendments were not absolute. The teacher began by stating that all rights are limited by the courts. He and students then engaged in a lively debate on how none of the first amendment rights pertaining to the religion clauses, free press, and other matters were absolute. But when they started to discuss the second amendment on bearing arms, conservative positions took over the discourse as the most vocal discussants maintained that citizens had an absolute right to own guns. They forged, or more accurately, enforced a consensus in the class that most gun control laws were unconstitutional. If there were opposing views on the issue, no one dared to air them.

Supposedly progressive methods of instruction also were adopted where students were invited to participate in model or real-life democratic processes involving collaborative political actions. But although these methods were implemented in the guise of Deweyan ideals of democratic diversity, they were in actuality rather effective means for realizing the district's mostly homogeneous conservative, upper-middle-class political agendas.

I watched one day as a government teacher began class by asking students if they would work as volunteers at polling stations for the upcoming November election. A few of them said they would. He then asked if anyone was working for political campaigns. Two students said they were working for the Republican campaign and a couple of others were involved in the Republican congressional campaign. "If you don't want to volunteer at the polls or aren't involved in a campaign," he said, "then I strongly encourage those of you who are 18 or over to vote."

The teacher then proceeded to hand out newspapers published by the local chapter of the League of Women Voters. The paper contained detailed information about candidates and issues scheduled to appear on the ballot of upcoming elections. He explained to students how they would be participating in a "mock election" before the actual election and wanted their votes to be informed. Students were then divided into groups and told to list the pros and cons of the state and county issues on the ballot. One of the issues involved the legalization of gambling, where a proportion of casino proceeds would be used to fund public schools. Another one was a proposal to raise taxes to implement new programs in children's social services. The groups deliberated and eventually presented their arguments to the class. The cons apparently presented a stronger case than the pros because both issues were defeated in the mock election. They also were defeated in the actual election in keeping with the district's conservative positions against gambling and raising taxes even if revenues were generated for schools and programs for children.

I would often glance at senior participants during these lessons. Cassandra and Peter were usually attentive, whereas Christina would stare out the window, doodle, or sit with her eyes half closed in somnolent boredom. Stuart also was somewhat inattentive, although he would sometimes speak up in playful defense of more liberal positions. Most of the other students were more or less inclined to go along with prevailing political lines.

Political lessons were more fractured at Jefferson High. Seniors had taken their required U.S. government classes during their sophomore year and did not have much to say about them except that they were "a nice time to take a nap" (Lona) and teachers "made us learn stuff that I've pretty much forgotten" (Adam). But they had a lot of positive things to say about the lessons they learned in a U.S. history class taught in their junior year by a teacher named Mr. Cameron. Mr. Cameron was described by almost every senior as the best instructor they had ever had. Lona said he was "unusual" in how he got to know students and went beyond the textbook in his coverage of material. David described him as the best teacher not only because he cared about kids, but also because of how he facilitated rousing classroom discussions. When I asked David to give me an example of a discussion, he recalled a memorable one on race relations that took place during a unit on the civil rights movement. The discussion had gotten out of hand until Mr. Cameron stepped in and got it under control:

There were these White girls saying that racism was going away and these Black girls who said it wasn't. They were really going at it, getting emotional and everything. But Mr. Cameron was real cool, like how he calmed the girls down and got them listening to each other instead of screaming 'I'm right and you're totally wrong.' He got them to see where each was coming from like, you know, White people and Black people see things differently because of everything that happened in the past.

What was "real cool" about Mr. Cameron was how he was able to engage students in nondiscriminatory, nonrepressive deliberations that bridged or at least mollified differences. He chose topics that were directly relevant to students' political experiences and tackled them in a way that uncovered the underlying subjectivities of students' perspectives. He understood that racism and other forms of prejudice mattered much in the political culture surrounding the school. It certainly mattered to David, whose own political self-positioning was very much geared toward the amelioration of social inequalities. He liked Mr. Cameron precisely because "he wasn't afraid to talk about stuff like [racism] even though he's a White guy."

With the exception of Mr. Cameron's U.S. history class, Jefferson High seniors could not recall any other teacher addressing issues that most directly affected them as low-income, working-class, White, or Black youths. Nor did anyone encourage them to vote, work at local polling stations, or get involved in political campaigns. Although there were elections held for offices in student government, there were no mock national elections prior to the actual one held in 1996. The implicit lesson, to which Mr. Cameron was the notable exception, was that teenagers like them are pretty much on their own when it comes to whether or how they would become integrated into the dominant political system. Without adult sponsorship or encouragement, odds were high that they would not get involved in the system at all. David was something of an anomaly in a school where students were more apt, in Lona's words, "to not vote and do other junk like that."

Students at Central City High were even more politically disenfranchised as far as national politics were concerned. Like their counterparts in other public high schools, they were required to take classes with explicit curriculum framed by the pedagogical ideals of democratic education. But what, if any, lessons they learned about democracy were often overpowered by the everyday politics of domination.

DOMINATION AND EVERYDAY SCHOOL POLITICS

Horace Mann recommended over a century ago that school children be socialized into the democratic creed through social interactions that reduce intergroup tensions. Dewey, Gutmann, and other proponents of democratic education also emphasized the critical importance of fostering relations in schools that enable diverse students to bridge their differences and work together in mutually beneficial enterprises. But such relations often go unrealized in high schools, especially those serving students alienated by or within national political arenas. Students, like powerless people in all organizations, often pursue their self-interests by engaging in a politics of everyday life that operates outside of formal governing structures. They vie for thymic recognition and the raw power that will get them goods, status, money, sexual partners, and other desired things. And they do so by establishing, fighting, or going along with individual domination at the ground level of day-to-day social relations. These politics are played out in ecologies of games in classrooms and corridors that are anything but democratic. The particular game dynamics in the three high schools are described next in some detail because of the profound consequences they had for seniors' identity and integration work in the political domain, indeed, in every domain of American community life.

Ecology of Games

Anyone who has ever taught or observed high school classes is well aware of the give-and-take of social relations between teachers and students. These relations are the starting point for the politics of everyday life in classrooms. The phrasing and analytical dynamics of these politics were introduced by an educational anthropologist, R. P. McDermott (1974), in his ethnographic work on the reading achievement patterns of Black elementary school children. McDermott viewed classrooms as arenas where teachers, as part of their official duties, determine the organization of achievement hierarchies. Politically, the organization works smoothly if students agree with or are used to the criteria for determining rankings. But if criteria do not make sense or are applied erroneously, students usually put up a resistance and attempt to reorganize the situation in a fashion that is more commensurate with their own perceived statuses, identities, and abilities. They produce their own hierarchical social organizations that counter those of the teacher.[19]

Teachers and students within their respective social organizations, adopt what McDermott (citing Long [1958]) described as an "ecology of games." To play the achievement game within the teachers' ecology is to follow directions, complete homework assignments, study for tests, and accept all of the statuses, identities, and judgments of ability that go along with these actions. The game within students' peer-group organization is to thwart or ignore teachers' orders, not pay attention to printed materials, and otherwise learn how not to learn what is being taught. Students who play this game well achieve high status (thymic recognition) and other social benefits in relation to their peers. They also achieve school failure, often in keeping with the self-fulfilling prophecies of their teachers.

In high school classes, especially those serving large numbers of alienated youths, the politics of everyday life may escalate into what McDermott termed "war games." Teacher games clash with student peer-group games as everyone chooses sides and figures out what moves to make within the battle zone. Alliances and tactics are important as stakes are very high. Which games ultimately prevail determines how power is distributed and exercised. The winners of these games move to the top of the social hierarchy where they can assert their dominance. They become the recognized leaders who run or continue to win subsequent plays. What happens during the entire length of the game may be beneficial for both teachers and students. But the particular ecology of games that prevails also may result in the production of on-going classroom war scenes where there are no clear winners and undeniable losses.

CLASSROOM POLITICS: WINNING LOSING WARS

Graduating seniors, by the time they had reached twelfth grade, were well versed in everyday classroom politics. The prizes they sought in the ecologies of games they played were passing or high grades, diplomas, and other indicators of academic success. Obtaining these prizes via teachers' games was not easy because it often meant completing ungratifying assignments and accepting a hierarchical organization that limited the number of achievers and guaranteed a proportion of failures. Seniors were so close to graduation that they felt it was not in their best self-interest to put up a resistance that would have completely overthrown their teachers. It made more strategic political sense for them to play peer-group games that eased teachers' demands or created paths of least resistance through the schoolwork regime. Their games were often playful, if not downright fun. But they also could be cruel in their tactics.

Thymic recognition was pivotal. Students who did well in teacher or peer games won recognition as individuals who deserved coveted educational and other prizes. Teachers, in their games, demanded recognition as adult authority figures in charge of directing the classroom drama, including the determination of who is or is not an achiever. Recognition in every game was about getting and keeping respect. Garnering social respect and self-respect was absolutely necessary for classroom actors to assert their dominance or superiority. Respect was the prize that preceded the prize.

Teacher games and peer games were not necessarily in opposition. They could be virtually the same or blended in ways that resulted in mutually acceptable compromises. This was largely the case at Ridgewood High,

where the mostly White middle-class student population was quite accli-
mated to, and supportive of, the school's college preparatory milieu.
There was a level of restlessness in many classes as students eased the te-
dium or stress of their teachers' directions by kidding around, passing
notes, or chatting quietly with their friends. Teachers tolerated the play so
long as students did assigned work. Occasionally students would become
angry and openly challenge teachers, especially if they thought they were
being graded unfairly or too low. But out-and-out classroom warfare was
rare as students gave their political assent to a regime they judged to be in
their best interests.

The games played at Central City High and Jefferson High were much
more contentious. A large percentage of students in both schools were
Black teenagers, White working-class youths, and other teenagers who
did not feel they were getting the respect they deserved. Classroom war
games were frequently on-going like the ones that occurred over and over
again in an Advanced Placement (AP) English class I observed for several
weeks at Central City High. Nay, Monica, and Michael were enrolled in
the class. The teacher, Ms. Thomas, was a White woman who was a re-
placement on the instructional team assigned to the senior class. Ms.
Thomas's primary goal was to prepare students for the AP English exam.
To accomplish that end, she adopted what she regarded as a typical upper-track approach, where students read literary classics and interpreted
texts through classroom discussions and independent writing assignments. But rather than go along with the teacher's regime, students spent
most of the period talking with their friends and otherwise playing
peer-group games. Ms. Thomas would tolerate the play until it reached a
point where she felt compelled to impose the rules of her game. Then the
battles would begin.

One of the most self-deflating battles for Ms. Thomas took place in a
class where students were asked to write an essay based on a sample AP
exam question. Ms. Thomas told the class to pick a book from a list of literary classics and write about a character whose brief appearance had a
profound impact on the plot. She provided the example of King Hamlet,
whose fleeting appearance as a ghost set off the chain of events in Shake-
speare's play *Hamlet.* Shortly after she had given the instructions, students started to talk. Some, like Monica and Nay, would alternate
between talk and work. They would write a few words, talk with their
friends, and then write a few more words. Others did not write at all. All
they did was talk. Michael was the only student who worked quietly on
the essay.

After a few minutes of chatter, Ms. Thomas decided it was time for her
to take control. She began by asking for respect. "Please listen to me," she
said. "I'm the teacher, okay? Be quiet and listen up. " She asked students if

they had found an example of a character. A girl immediately blurted out
that she was "going to do the guy who raped that girl in *The Color Purple.*"
She then proceeded to describe the rape scene in gross, somewhat embel-
lished detail. Students laughed uproariously as Ms. Thomas stood in
stunned silence. The girl had effectively defeated the teacher's assertion
of dominance through a hilarious but devastating display of disrespect.
The tactic was particularly effective because while it toppled the teacher,
it was technically within bounds of the teacher's directions. The girl essentially did what she had been told to do.

Ms. Thomas persevered a few days later. She was half-way through another set of instructions when a boy walked in late with a bag full of do-
nuts. Ms. Thomas glared at the boy and ordered him to "go to the office
and get that food out of my class." The boy laughed at her and kept eating
in an overtly provocative act of disrespect. Ms. Thomas became enraged.
In a fit of anger, she grabbed the boy by the shirt and demanded that he
leave the room. It looked for a tense moment as if the boy was going to
lunge at her. He was literally poised to get into a physical fight over the
public challenge to his thymic-self respect. Instead of fighting, the boy
backed off, got up, and walked out of the room. The teacher had won that
round. But there were many more to come.

Sometimes the rules of the games were reversed. Mr. Harrison, a
teacher at Jefferson High, was a White man in his late 40s who taught an
AP psychology class that Adam and Lona were taking. Rather than follow
AP instructional protocols, he made a mockery of curriculum and his position as an adult authority figure. He would dedicate most of the class period to off-color discussions on sex, sexuality, and what he called "theories
of love." On one occasion, he asked students, "What does intimate
mean?" A boy answered, "It's smooching without fondling." Another boy
said it was "cuddling, kissing and light petting on top of the pants instead
of inside them." Mr. Harrison, in as serious a voice as he could muster,
said, "Yes, yes that's a good way to feel it out."

Although some students went along with Mr. Harrison's inversion of
the teacher game, others lashed out against it. A boy demanded that Mr.
Harrison "cut the crap. " A girl told him how he "was a disgrace to his profession and offensive as hell." Adam was thoroughly fed up with the
teacher and might have become a more vocal defender if he had not been
so determined to stay out of trouble. He merely dismissed the class as a co-
lossal waste of time. As one of his friends put it, "Horny Harrison's class is
over before it starts and we're the ones who are getting screwed."

The give-and-take of everyday classroom politics did not always play
out to such extremes. There were classrooms where teachers and students
managed to negotiate game rules founded on mutual respect. Mr.
Cameron's classes at Jefferson High were like that. So were the classes

taught by Ms. Hathaway, a mathematics teacher at Central City High. Ms. Hathaway was described by just about every senior as one of the most respected teachers in the school. "She makes everyone sit up straight when she walks in the room," Michael said. "Like no one gives her any crap." What set Ms. Hathaway off from Ms. Thomas was how she made the rules for learning explicit and practically manageable for students. She would march her classes through lessons in a step-by-step, this-is-how-you-do-it fashion and provide whatever direct assistance students needed to complete assigned tasks. Something else that set Ms. Hathaway off was the high level of civility in her relations with students. Students were never rude to her nor did they make jokes or otherwise sabotage lessons with disrespectful remarks. The respect shown to this teacher was expressed in recognition of her instructional competence and respect for inner-city Black kids as students who can and will learn if they are shown exactly how.

But there was a discouraging fact of everyday life in Ms. Hathaway's classroom. Although she was a teacher held in high regard, the attendance rates in her classes were among the lowest in the school. Students routinely cut her classes because of the unrelenting pace of the teacher's regimen. And, perhaps, because of the everyday politics of corridor life.

CORRIDOR POLITICS: (RE)GAINING RECOGNITION

The politics of everyday life also were played out in corridors. A number of students, especially at Jefferson High and Central City High, utilized communication codes and practices in their games tactics that constituted what I have described elsewhere as a youth culture of hostility (Hemmings, 2000a, 2002). Students, in their youth cultural productions, built up or tore down dominance hierarchies as they vied for status and showed off their distinctive abilities. They also engaged in identity politics that sometimes went to megalothymic extremes as students satisfied their insatiable desire for recognition as powerful people deserving the utmost respect. Corridor politics of recognition were mired in competing discourses of respect as teenagers representing diverse racial, ethnic, gender, religious, sexual, and other sociocultural locations fought for control within and over their relations. These politics could be enormously destructive for individual teenagers or so divisive that there was little chance that students could or ever would work together for the common good. But they also could be quite liberating as students, including the graduating seniors in this research, struggled hard for recognition as worthy, self-respecting young men and women.

Respectability and Reputation

Respect in the corridors at Jefferson High and Central City High was a social commodity students absolutely had to have. Having respect was imperative for garnering the power necessary to assert, challenge, or neutralize
social controls in relations with peers. To lose respect was to become powerless, subordinate, and vulnerable to abuse. How students earned and kept
respect was very much influenced by what Gordon (1997) described as the
opposing twin discourses of respectability and reputation. Focusing in particular on Black men, Gordon traced the discursive roots of respectability to
the patriarchal cultural practices of African traditions and more contemporary codes of mainstream, middle-class propriety. A Black man seeking respectability adopts conservative styles of self-presentation in his dress and
demeanor. He adheres to the conservative values of "hard work, economic
frugality and independence, community commitment and activism, mutual help and uplift, personal responsibility [and] religious faith" (p. 41).
He also adopts the elaborated speech codes of formal standard English,
which not only enables him to communicate within schools, businesses,
and other institutions, but also marks him symbolically as a respectable
middle-class man (Bernstein, 1971).

Reputation, in marked contrast, is acquired by limited use of standard
English, standing up to authorities, showing up male rivals, and controlling women through multiple sexual conquests and harassment. It may
also be acquired by adopting the restricted speech codes characterizing
street talk. These codes have become important markers for some young
Black men residing in impoverished, insulated urban neighborhoods not
only as signs of their dominance, but also as reinforcers of their
Black-American identities (Ogbu, 1999).

Black teenage boys who want to build up a reputation also may follow
what Anderson (1998) referred to as the code of the streets. This code
arises in places where the influence of police, teachers, and other adult authority figures ends and where personal responsibility for one's safety and
socioeconomic advancement begins. Among the main features of the code
are verbal expressions of disrespect toward competitors or people who
come off as easy prey. Disrespect also is shown by stealing another person's possessions, messing with someone's woman, pulling a trigger, or
tearing someone's ego apart with slashing insults. If a man loses respect,
he has no choice but to try to regain it even if he has to get into a fight or
resort to other forms of violent retaliation.

Fights for respect were common in corridors at Central City High. Amber, a youth advocate employed in the school, described fights as
"planned performances" that usually began with a public announcement
where a challenger would yell insults laced with profanities at a targeted

opponent. The yelling of insults was the clarion call for other students to form an audience. Once an audience was assembled, combatants would commence the fight. The performance would end with the arrival of security guards who separated the fighters and led them ceremoniously down to the office where they were awarded suspensions.

Nay felt there were way too many fights because far too many boys were "runnin' their mouths" in never-ending exchanges of disrespect. "They be dissin' each other and talkin' trash. They talk too much They say something bad about a person and when that person hears about it they come after them, you know, they are lookin' for a fight. They got no choice. If they would shut up and care more about respectin' each other there wouldn't be so many fights."

But not every boy ran off his mouth or got into fistfights. Michael had never been involved in serious verbal or physical confrontations, which was remarkable given his politically precarious position as an academically high-achieving White boy in a school full of reputation-minded Black boys. He desired recognition as an upwardly mobile, respectable man. But he also wanted to be just as "cool" as the playas and other street hustlers who looked rich, acted tough, and otherwise cultivated reputations of control and being in control. How Michael accomplished this symbolically tricky feat was by engaging in crafty, chameleon-like identity politics where he would switch codes in accordance with the social situations in which he found himself. He projected a cool playa image by coming to school dressed in expensive designer jeans, gold jewelry, and the exact same brands and colors of athletic shoes worn by his Black male peers. When he was in corridor spaces, he would play fight with other boys, talk hip-hop Black street talk, and behave as if he were abiding by the code of the street. But when he entered the classroom, he would instantly transform himself into an altogether different image. He spoke flawless Standard English, worked hard, and otherwise accommodated to the codes of the respectable (Black) man. Michael moved between and within the opposing twin discourses of respectability and reputation with amazing agility and managed in the process to win the games in corridors as well as in his classes.

Boys at Central City High were not the only ones straddling the currents of opposing discourses. Fighting had become something of a rite of passage for David and Adam at Jefferson High, who felt they had to secure some kind of reputation in their relations with other boys. David underwent a rather heroic passage in his journey to manhood. It began in his sophomore year when his father was diagnosed with a potentially fatal illness. "It was weird," David recalled. "When my dad got sick I thought I had to be the man, you know, the guy in charge." He became angry and was socially disposed at the time to establish his reputation as "the man" by getting into fights. He was a good fighter and by his own account could be "intimidating as hell." Everything changed one fateful day when he was viciously attacked in an ambush carried out by a group of boys under a school stairwell. David was beaten up "pretty bad." But what hurt most of all was his pride. "God, that hurt."

It was at that point that David decided to become a more respectable man. He gave up fighting and became involved in more democratic modes of politics. He got elected to the student council and in his senior year was elected as the class president. He became intensely interested in national politics, especially issues with implications for the advancement of Black people in general and Black men in particular. He also assumed democratic positionings in his relations with peers. Expressions of intergroup and interpersonal hostilities were more than evident in the everyday politics of corridor life. But David dismissed them as he exchanged cheerful greetings, jokes, and other pleasantries with Blacks, Whites, and other students. He made a point of getting along with everyone and earned a lot of respect in the process. "Most important of all," he said with a grin. "I got my self-respect back."

Adam also navigated respectability and reputation, but his approach was shrouded in the discourses of loss that have caused many young White men to feel decentered, under siege, and no longer able to secure the socioeconomic positions once held by their forebears (Fine & Weis, 1998). Adam's feelings of frustration were exacerbated by the perception that unfair advantages have been extended to Black people and other groups. These discursive forces all came into play in his interpretation of, and approach to, everyday corridor politics.

Adam as a sophomore had earned a reputation in a fight that had gotten him suspended from school. When he came back, he did his best to stay out of trouble, including staying out of fistfights. But his resolve was constantly being tested by Black peers who showed disrespect toward him and his White friends. Blacks kids, according to Adam, were much more disrespectful to Whites than Whites were to Blacks. They also were more likely to get away with it because of the preferential treatment they received. He reiterated the point in a class we attended together. The teacher told students to take out their textbooks. Adam looked for his book in his backpack only to discover that it was missing. He turned around and spotted a Black boy who had taken it. The boy laughed loudly and handed the book over to Adam. Adam then turned to me and said, "See what I mean? He took my book. Everyone knows he took my book. I get put down but I have to put up with it 'cause I'll get in trouble if I don't. He gets away with it. They all get away with it. That's how it is around here."

One of Adam's friends described the disrespect among Blacks and Whites as more of a two-way than a one-way pattern of interaction. "Like it's back and forth. It's not like, oh, the Black people is on the Whites or all the Whites on the Blacks." White kids would call Black kids "niggers" and "jungle bunnies," while Black kids would call Whites "honkies," "crackers," and "wimpies." Another girl gave an example of a volley of insults she heard at one of the school's baseball games. "Our baseball team went out on the field and Black kids were like yelling 'You White honkies. You all White team.' Our team was yelling 'Shut up, you niggers. You're going to the jungle.' Crap like that."

It was very difficult under such circumstances for either side to maintain respectable relations. Situations could be even more challenging for girls, who had the added burden of defending their bodies. As girls sought respectability and/or reputation, many of them engaged in sexual politics that simultaneously positioned them as docile and not-so-docile female bodies (Adams, 1999). They would attempt to force disrespectful boys to maintain more respectful relations with them while simultaneously projecting images as tough girls with reputations for being just as capable as boys of asserting dominance through physical strength, aggression, and fearless counterattacks.

So it was within Lona's clique. Lona once had a widely recognized reputation as a tough girl. Her school records indicated that she had been suspended for fighting and was issued reprimands for other infractions. Her record was much cleaner after her introspective period of self-reckoning. Not only did Lona regain her self-respect by re-forming herself, she also became an enforcer of mutual respect among clique members despite their differences in race, gender, sexual orientation, abilities, and disabilities. A few of her friends went out of their way to show respect for other kids, especially those most vulnerable to victimization. I watched one day as a girl in the group walked up to a mentally disabled boy in a wheelchair, gave him a hug, and spoke to him in the kindest of words. "See," she told me, "I'm special education friendly."

And yet, a few days later the same girl viciously attacked another boy. The boy sat next to her in a class and proceeded to fondle her breasts and buttocks. She repeatedly told him to stop, that is, to be respectful of her body. When he kept molesting her, the girl changed her tactics. She toughened up and yelled, "Get the fuck off me" in a voice loud enough for the teacher to hear. The teacher did nothing to intervene so she kicked the boy in the face when he leaned over to touch her again. The boy sat up with a huge bruise on the side of his head. The fondling finally stopped as the girl managed to regain control of her body with a fierceness that matched her determination to show respect for people who could not fight back.

Lona did not want to have to fight like that. But she said she would do it to help a friend like Randy, the disabled boy in the clique who had incurred a traumatic brain injury. Randy had been an object of cruel ridicule until Lona took him under her wing. "Kids would call him 'doofus' and set him up so he did stupid things they could laugh at. He needed a friend so there I was. I keep a constant eye on him and if, say, some guy comes along and picks on him, I come to the rescue. I'm kind of big so they usually back off."

She did not want to get into a fight on Randy's behalf, but she would do so if that is what it took to make sure that he was getting the respect he deserved. Fighting was more than a matter of establishing control in one's own relations, it also meant extending assistance to friends and acquaintances. This was important in a school where loss of respect carried such dire social consequences.

The main issue for Black senior girls at Central City High was their desire to be recognized as respectable Black women with middle-class aspirations. I listened to Monica and Nay as they talked about their plans to go to college, enter professional careers, and achieve social success in middle-class society. Yet both of them, in apparently contradictory fashion, came to school looking like fly girls who had reputations in the street as women who knew how to use their bodies and guile to acquire money, goods, status, and, above all else, respect. Fly girls wore sexy designer clothes and draped themselves in expensive gold jewelry. The height of social status for them was to be seen in the fancy car of a successful street hustler. A few fly girls had rougher, meaner reputations as prostitutes, accomplices in drug trafficking, or women involved in other illicit or dangerous ventures.

Although Monica and Nay, to the best of my knowledge, did not engage in fly-girl activities, they did project a fly-girl image. When I first met Monica, she had on a skin-tight dress hemmed halfway up her thigh. She wore three gold rings, a gold bracelet, and a gaudy gold watch. Nay arrived in a very revealing short-sleeve shirt, white miniskirt, white panty hose, and shiny black shoes. She had on several gold rings, some with diamonds, two gold chains, and sported a gold front tooth. The girls thus conveyed the outward trappings of reputations that not only allowed them to get around in the streets, but also afforded them symbolic dominance in their relations with peers at school. They sent signals that they were women who possessed everyday political power when it came to dealing with men, handling female competitors, and otherwise taking care of themselves within their immediate or most intimate relations with others. These signals were juxtaposed against their desires to be respectable women who wanted to move beyond the life of the streets. Both girls thus maneuvered through codes in a manner that got them the respect they needed for survival in the streets and to move beyond the streets into middle-class society. And they accomplished all of that without getting into any real fights.

Manipulating the Mark

The corridor politics of recognition at Ridgewood High involved qualitatively different styles of play although the objects of the game were generally the same. One object was to be recognized as someone with a distinguishing mark. Another was to target and ultimately hit the marks of individual desire. Both were reached through mostly nonviolent tactics where players attempted to set their thymic-self value and otherwise manipulate their marks through words, bodily gestures, and other discursive maneuvers.

One of Stuart's friends explained during lunch about how critical it was to have a distinguishing mark in the predominantly White middle-class milieu in and around Ridgewood High. "If you don't have it," he insisted, "you're a complete nobody." The distinguishing starts in the home, is nurtured in schools, and ideally comes to fruition in the most preeminent economic, kinship, religious, and political sectors of society. The boy pointed at an athlete wearing a football jersey. "That guy is the quarterback of the football team." His distinguishing mark was that of a star player who, like a military general or corporate CEO, leads the charge to win recognition as well as territory, goods, wealth, and power. He pointed at another boy. "That guy is a genius." He was an intellectual who might become a university professor, scientist, or some other recognizable personage in control of the production and dissemination of consequential knowledge. Then he pointed out a couple of girls. "That girl is a cheerleader. That one is a musician." One was distinguishing herself as a woman willing to cheer on and hopefully be recognized by the men distinguishing themselves on exalted fields of competition. The other was marking herself as a musician who might acquire recognition and success on the basis of her own public performance.

Stuart and Peter also cultivated distinguishing marks. And they adopted tactics of interpersonal domination where they attempted to manipulate peers into fulfilling their personal desires. Stuart let it be known that he was the descendent of prominent businessmen and that he was himself destined to become a man of affluence and influence. Peter tried to distinguish himself as an aspiring military officer who would one day be in command of his own troops. Although Peter was much less successful than Stuart in his bid for recognition, he used similar everyday political means to reach his desired ends.

Both boys talked about how they used their eyes to gain recognition, wield social control, and get what they wanted out of people. Suckers are born every minute, according to Peter. "Just look in their eyes and that's how you find out what you can get out of them. When I was using drugs, it was easy to get money to support my habit. I would read people by looking into their eyes. That's how I found out if I could get what I wanted out of them. I don't think I'd have any trouble killing people in the Army. The key is not to look into their eyes."

Stuart also manipulated people with his eyes. "I make eye contact with them, lock them in, and they're mine." In addition to eye tactics, he used charisma to control relationships with women and make vulnerable peers believe what he wanted them to believe. "Give me 25 kids that are younger than me or a bunch of insecure people and then give me something to talk about and I've got enough charisma to make them believe anything. They don't make decisions for themselves. I tell them 'This is good, this is bad' and they believe it." His manipulations were politically well calibrated as was evident in the social dominance he enjoyed in the preppie corridor scene. He called the shots, with some exceptions in his relations with girlfriends, and was regarded by other students as an outgoing, somewhat overbearing fellow who usually got his way.

Cassandra, as she made her mark, was determined to regain the recognition she had lost after falling into the depths of the worst White middle-class stereotypes of Black women. She was a single teenage mother who had been impregnated by a Black boy sentenced to jail for committing a violent offense. Her status and future prospects had plummeted, especially in relation to her preppie peers. As she surveyed the situation, Cassandra felt that in order to raise herself and her son up, she had to redeem her thymic-self worth by accommodating to the most conservative codes of Black respectability. In doing so, she took full advantage of counseling sessions and other school-sponsored avenues of recovery. She became a devout, churchgoing Protestant with the belief that she could very well be among the (s)elect few sitting next to God. She talked, dressed, and acted like a competent, professional Black woman who could be successful even in workplaces dominated by White people.

And she adopted a style of outreach in everyday corridor politics that effectively repositioned her as a recognized leader. Cassandra, as she journeyed through hallways, would approach students in her capacity as a peer mediator. She would stop and talk to Black, White, Asian, and many other kids about how or what they were doing to elevate themselves. She had achieved such a high level of redemption that she became a redeemer with the power of experience to save other fallen middle-class adolescents.

Christina was so repelled by such manipulations of the mark that she did not want to be associated with, or recognized as, a preppie. Preppies, in her estimation, were "snobs" who looked down on everyone except themselves. She distanced herself by adopting the countercultural distinguishing marks of 1960s hippies who rebelled against White middle-class domination. Among these marks were those borrowed from druggie subcultures as signs of the devil feared most by preppie parents. But she also cultivated the image of the artist on the creative fringes of middle-class so-ciety. Christina the artist arranged and rearranged the disparate facets of her self. In one of her art classes, she produced what she described as her "masterpiece." It was a figurine of a Chicana woman molded out of clay. The woman, dressed in festive Mexican attire, was wearing a hat with its brim bent backwards as though it were pushing against the forces of strong prevailing winds. I could see Christina in her shining-glazed brown eyes looking ahead at the many possibilities to come.

7

Reaching Shore

PARTICULAR ANSWERS
TO A PERENNIAL QUESTION

Working Through Crosscurrents

So, did the U.S. public high schools in this research enrich individual human potential and allow young people to achieve a good life? The usual approach to this perennial question is to define and explore student potential and achievement in rather narrow academic terms. But such a tack ignores the fact that high schools are and always have been established to facilitate coming of age processes in the broadest cultural sense. They are sites where adolescents realize their potentials through complex identity formation and seek the good life through integration into economic, kinship, religious, and political community domains. When this two-pronged process of identity and integration work is examined through (post)anthropological lenses, it becomes quite evident that coming of age in U.S. public high schools cannot be understood, nor can answers to critical educational questions be found, without careful consideration of American cultural crosscurrents.

Crosscurrents are comprised of fluid, shifting, conflicting discourses and attendant practices. As is summarized in Table 7.1, the currents described in this study flowed through community domains as multilayered pressures on individual and group adaptations.

Economic currents in contemporary America are manifested in discourses of money and occupational gratification. Dominant versions emphasize the importance of the American work ethic while reinforcing divisions of labor with their customary ethnic, racial, classed, and gendered workplace

176

TABLE 7.1
Crosscurrent Descriptors

	Economic	Kinship	Religious	Political
Dominant Culture	Work ethic and labor divisions	Traditional nuclear family	Judeo-Christian mainlines	National ideologies
Liminal Trends	Postindustrial prospects	Alternative family-life styles	Secular tides	Special interests
Popular Culture	Cool image	Popular sex	New/ancient age	Rebel cause
Undertows	Hustler pursuits	Gender antagonisms	Pastoral sacrilege	Political corruption
Ethnic Tributaries	Economic niches	Community linages	Havens/harbors of faith	Sociocultural coalitions
Local Family Worlds	Securing employment	Prescribing obligations	Localizing beliefs/practices	Defining interests
Youth Culture and Subcultures	Licit and illicit gains	Connections and disconnections	Sanctuaries and netherworlds	Respectability and reputation

positionings. Despite their historical grip, these versions are being unsettled by a momentous liminal shift in postindustrial economic prospects ushered in by an explosion in global consumerism, a rapid succession of developments in electronic technologies, and policies for the equalization of equal opportunity. Popular cultural currents also are flooding the cultural seascape with their commodified, media-generated "cool" images of wealth and power. Competing with these expansive versions are more particular ones spun within ethnic communities and local family worlds. Whereas some are aimed at securing ethnic strongholds in occupational niches, others are meant to ensure the intergenerational financial well being of family members. Flowing beneath these discursive variations is an underground economy fueled by the glamorous yet destructive undertows of fast money and instant gratification. Undertows were infused along with other discursive versions of money and occupational gratification into youth cultures and subcultures produced by high school students in their own pursuit of il/licit economic gains.

Dominant *kinship currents* are those that uphold traditional nuclear family arrangements. These arrangements are widely regarded as ideal, but there is a liminal change underway in the societal acceptance of single parenting, same-sex partnerships, and other once unacceptable alternative family-life styles. Although the change is tolerated in public discourses, it is often stifled or constrained within ethnic communities and local family worlds where "good" family connections are governed by prescriptions intended to normalize family relations and extend lineages. Despite these pressures, there has been a steady rise in the popularity of popular cultural sex, as well as more destructive surges in sexual predation and harassment aroused by undertows of gender antagonisms. High school students who experienced family disconnections, or threats to their family connections, often retreated into peer cliques where they constructed subcultures that forged family relations and ties among friends.

Judeo-Christian theologies are paramount in U.S. *religious currents*. For centuries, dominant Protestant, Roman Catholic, and Jewish theological mainlines defined American beliefs in the supernatural, fostered or restricted religious critical consciousness, delimited morality, and guided modes of spirituality. These discourses are now being circumscribed by a liminal tide of secularism that has removed overtly religious expressions from public rites, rituals, and celebrations. Many people have found solace in communal ethnic havens and harbors of faith or are sustaining their religious commitments through the localized beliefs and practices of their families. Others are consumers of popular cultural, new/ancient age movements or refuse to buy into religion altogether. Many Americans, as they seek freedom of or from religion, turn to churches that uphold their religious convictions and disparage religious leaders and parishioners who succumb to sacrilegious undertows. Young people, in their own religious quests, often worked out or against commitments within the confines of their own peer sanctuaries and netherworlds.

Political currents are spread out across a continuum of democratic ideals and the reality of domination in everyday politics. Dominant discourses in the United States are firmly entrenched in the ideals presented in national liberal and conservative ideo(logies). There was a perception among seniors that these ideo(logies) have shifted over time from an emphasis on the common interest to more attention paid to the special interests of powerful individuals and groups. They also noted how popular cultural productions, now more than ever, are portraying young people as X-ed out rebels with no good causes. The situation was made even worse by image of politicians as self-serving, inattentive, or operating within the undertows of political corruption. Many ethnic, racial, and religious groups have responded by carving out their own sociocultural political niches. Powerful families are looking after their own localized interests, whereas families with less influence are politically apathetic or thoroughly alienated. Teenagers may or may not be interested in national politics, but many are caught up in everyday politics of domination where they vie for power and control over themselves and others through opposing discourses of respectability and reputation.

High school students, as they come of age in the midst of these crosscurrents, engage in complex identity work that revolves around the formation of an enduring or "true" psychocultural self. This self is a multifaceted subjectivity that has economic, familial/sexual, religious, and political aspects. It reflects individual proclivities as well as ethnicity, race, class, gender, and other social locations. And it is something that evolves over time as young people mature and circumstances change.

But coming of age is much more than the formation of a viable true self. It also involves situating or integrating the self into community domains. Community integration in the United States is essentially about achieving some kind of good life characterized by economic prosperity, desirable family arrangements, comprehensible religious commitments, and participation in political processes that address common and individual interests. It also is about forging good community relations with others. But such integration can be extremely difficult, especially for teenagers who must navigate crosscurrents that may or may not be compatible with their emergent sense of self. An adolescent's integration work may proceed smoothly, but it can also lead to intense conflict where the true self becomes endangered, chances for successful integration are severely limited, and/or relations with parents, teachers, employers, clergy, peers, and others become strained, hostile, or completely broken.

Whether a true self that enriches human potential is formed and a good life is achieved very much depends on how identity and integration work unfolds in sites like public high schools. It is within these sites that crosscurrents are transmitted to, and became construction material for, the cultural adaptations of youths.

School Transmission and Construction Sites

At the surface level of educational programming, all three of the high schools in this study appeared to following a basic common educational script. Jefferson High, Ridgewood High, and Central City High had similar academic requirements as well as programs and classes geared more specifically toward preparing students for economic occupations, family life, and political participation. They all avoided explicit religious instruction in compliance with the law. But it became very evident during my fieldwork that this script was not being followed in the same manner by teachers, administrators, and support staff who, in the particular contexts of their schools, had to find particular answers to the perennial question of enriching human potential and achieving a good life. Their search for answers was complicated by a paradoxical cultural imperative embedded in the question that endorses, on one hand, egalitarianism in service to the common good where students are to be treated the same and, on the other hand, individualism where students are to be treated differently (Page, 2000). Educators in each high school generally approached the first part of the imperative by reaffirming dominant culture and, to some extent, recognizing liminal trends. Handling the second part meant dealing with the characteristics of students who had their own individual and group adaptations not only to dominant culture, but to other crosscurrents as well.

Solving the paradoxical imperative was complicated at Jefferson High where changing student demographics and growing public neglect made answers uncertain. The school for many years had served the mostly White middle- and working-class people residing in surrounding neighborhoods. But these circumstances changed when a court-ordered desegregation plan opened the doors to low-income Black students and other adolescents once kept at bay. Tensions were sparked as newcomers clashed with old-timers in ways that exacerbated racism, sexism, and other divisive social prejudices.

Along with the heightening of social tensions was a steady lowering of public support for public schools. Voters in the district repeatedly refused to increase tax levies for school building maintenance, textbooks and classroom supplies, and other operational costs. Signs of physical neglect were everywhere inside the dilapidated interior of Jefferson High. Other more symbolic signs were communicated to students, many of whom were convinced that the public really had written them off.

Teachers under such conditions certainly had their work cut out for them. Some invested an enormous amount of energy into the transmission of standard curricular fare. Such was the case with an English teacher who pranced around her classroom in a determined effort to arouse student interest in classic literary texts. Others tried to relate to students by acknowledging ethnic heritages (the art teacher who presented colorful slide shows on African-American painters), indulging in vulgar popular culture (the AP psychology teacher with his off-color references to sex), recognizing local worldviews (the history teacher who encouraged open discussion about Black and White perspectives), and crossing into other cultural currents. Still others simply gave up through virtual abdications of their teaching roles.

Although teachers worked to provide egalitarian educational opportunities in their classes, there was a sense among many students that they were not being treated as individuals who deserved more direct, differentiated adult attention. Teachers hunkered down in their classrooms and administrators were often unavailable or nowhere to be seen as students struggled with identity conflicts, uncertainty about their future in the community, and other problems that were especially acute among White working-class youths and impoverished Black teenagers.

The situation was qualitatively different at Ridgewood High where affluent parents expected teachers and administrators to make sure that students stayed the cultural course set for them. Egalitarian education in this school meant preparing every student for college and affirming the predominately White, upper-middle-class, politically conservative, Judeo-Christian bearings of the people who resided in the district. Most of the adolescents who attended the school were preppies who formed identities with distinguishing middle-class marks and accommodated to pressures intended to integrate them into middle-class economic niches, intact nuclear families, American political arenas, and, perhaps, mainline religions. Coming of age for them was a voyage chartered by adults determined to keep teenagers on course, even if it meant going to great lengths to rescue those who fell overboard.

Ridgewood High teachers were well supplied with curricular materials, computers, and other instructional materials as they proceeded to teach students how to acquire or build up dominant cultural capital. Counselors offered programs designed to provide more individualized assistance to students with academic, social, or psychological problems. Although there were students like Christina who felt they were not getting the attention they needed, most understood that help was available to any individual who had trouble adjusting to the common educational milieu.

Central City High was located in the socially insular, economically impoverished, mostly Black, urban community of the Upper Banks. Beyond the Upper Banks was a White-dominated, middle-class world that presumably could be reached by anyone willing and able to cross through its currents. Most teachers and many staff at Central City High would have liked nothing better than to move as many students as possible up within or out of the Upper Banks. They felt an obligation to prepare students for college or participation in the legitimate workforce, salvage dysfunctional families, and quell the everyday politics of domination. But many of them settled for less ambitious approaches as they adjusted to minimalist or alienated Black students whose own adaptations did not necessarily include unequivocal accommodation to schooling as a feasible or even desirable way to move between or out of what, for many of them, were opposing worlds.

Classrooms in all three schools were sites where teachers attempted to transmit dominant and liminal currents to varying degrees and through a variety of means. But corridors were just as important if not more critical cultural "construction sites" (Weis & Fine, 2000). It was in hallways, lunchrooms, bathrooms, and other relatively unsupervised corridor spaces where students engaged in some of their most significant identity and integration work. Through processes of bricolage, they took symbolic material from dominant and liminal currents and combined it with ethnic traditions, popular culture, and/or undertows into their own distinctive youth cultures and subcultural productions. These productions enabled them to express and defend their true selves and community ties during the course of peer relations that in some instances were marred by hostilities and in other situations were marked by more harmonious social bonds. The tactics students used to position themselves in corridor scenes could be socially destructive and divisive or positively creative and unifying. And they had very real consequences for graduating seniors as they struggled with their own particular answers to the question of how they might or ought to come of age.

REFLEXIVE LOOK BACK

Seniors, as they looked back on their years in high school, portrayed themselves as teenagers who had accomplished a great deal despite daunting obstacles or nearly ruinous setbacks. Academic accomplishments were important to them. But even more significant was what they had achieved in their identity and integration work. Such was the case with Adam Willis, Lona Young, and David North, whose most remarkable feat at Jefferson High was the re-formation of themselves and their life trajectories after perilous times of trouble.

Adam was a White, working-class boy who as a freshman got into trouble in a school that, in his opinion, lacked discipline and was full of "disrespectful" students. He had been a victim of petty crimes and was losing ground in his peer relations, especially in his encounters with Black students. Adam felt he was pretty much on his own as teachers retreated into their classrooms and administrators often were nowhere to be found. So he assumed the posture of a tough kid willing to fight for himself, even if it meant being suspended from school.

Although Adam managed to project the image of someone able to hold his own within immediate circumstances, it was not an image that gave him much direction in the long run. He eventually took stock of his situation and decided to re-form his self into a better student and, more vitally important from his point of view, a better person. By the time he was scheduled to graduate, Adam had raised his grades and was maintaining more respectful relations with peers. He was settin his sights on becoming a landscaper, making definite plans to marry his high school sweetheart in traditional family fashion, and was someone who in his politics and religion could be relied on to "help out whenever and wherever I can."

Lona and David also went through troubling times but for different reasons. Lona got into trouble when her self-assertions led to real and symbolic breaches with her family, church, and school. She passed through what she described as a "very bad phase" where she was admittedly at risk of becoming a loss or danger to the community. David's troubles began when his father was diagnosed with cancer. His graphing of the years that followed reveals an undulating series of ups and downs that ended with him on the upward slope:

> If you would graph my years in school, you would see that I peaked in ninth grade and plunged in tenth grade, then things got better again. Tenth grade was my weird year. My dad had cancer and I had a hard time with the transition to high school. I got every form of punishment they have. I was suspended twice. I was in ISS once. I skipped school and got into those fights I was telling you about. Then I got beaten up pretty bad by some guys. Everybody knew about it. It took me a couple of months to get over the pain and humiliation. But instead of going after those guys, I turned my life around. I decided that wasn't the way to go. I worked through my problems and did it by myself. Counselors didn't help me. My mother was angry and yelled at me but she couldn't tell me what to do. By the end of the year, I got a job, a car, and the weather got nicer. I turned my life around. Most important of all, I got my self-respect back.

He and Lona both reached a critical turning point. David, as he turned his life around, re-formed himself into a respectable young Black man who abandoned the everyday politics of domination and became more actively involved in democratic political activities that ultimately led to his election as senior class president by overwhelming majority. He also developed an interest in computers and applied for, and was admitted to, a computer engineering program in a major university. He was a self-proclaimed agnostic who nevertheless had faith that things usually work out for the best. David felt that in his own best work, he had became someone who "makes a difference instead of the guy you better watch out for."

Lona turned her life around after an introspective period of self-reckoning. "I looked at myself," she said. "And hated what I saw." She underwent intense re-formation work and carried a number of other troubled teenagers along with her (Hemmings, 2000b). Within the safe social space of her peer clique, she and her friends mended fractured identities, rebuilt sociocultural linkages with their families, schools, and peers, and forged ahead into more true-self-affirming realms of economic, family, religious, and political life. As for Lona herself, she was not exactly sure where she would end up in her own coming-of-age journey, but she was taking steps toward reconciliation, or reaggregation, into community domains.

Coming of age was not accomplished in such classic stages by the key senior participants at Central City High. Monica Reese, Nay Wilson, and Michael Meyer regarded themselves as having been set off from the most marginalized students in their school. Michael explained how the "good" students in his set enrolled in advanced classes, thereby limiting their interactions with the other set of "kids who think they are too big for school." Although they sought positionings as good students, Michael and many other members of his set performed balancing acts where they juggled identities and conflicting cultural codes. They came to school expressing the language, dress, and normative Upper Banks street codes of fly girls and playas. At the same time, they conjured a semblance of accommodation to the White, middle-class world beyond by signing up for advanced classes as if they really were upper-track students destined for the upper echelons of society.

Monica, in her balancing act, was able to convey a fly-girl reputation that earned her respect among her Black peers. But she also tried to integrate her self into the world beyond by joining a White Protestant church, getting a part-time job in a White-owned marketing firm, and ultimately gaining admission to a predominately White college. Nay was much more firmly entrenched in her female-headed family network and the churches and other Black institutions in her neighborhood. Yet she had aspirations of becoming gainfully employed, getting married, and "doing what I got to do to do it right." As she considered her next move after graduation, she looked no farther than across the street from Central City High, where there was a vocational college. The college had a nursing program that, she reasoned, "would give me something I can do wherever I live," even if she continued to live right where she was.

The balance that Michael maintained could very well have been complicated by his status as a high-achieving White boy had he not been so adept at positioning himself in both worlds without jeopardizing his positions in either world. He understood that to be a cool White kid meant hanging out with cool Black kids. Michael had several Black friends with whom he would play along in playa style in corridors. But when he was in classrooms, he would switch over to his other academically successful, valedictorian, college-bound self. Unlike most of his classmates, Michael went well beyond semblances as he followed his teachers' directions, did his homework, and earned high marks. In doing so, he put himself in a position where he could pursue his dreams of becoming an engineer and eventually settling down into a good life in other community domains.

Ridgewood High served its constituency well as teachers, administrators, and support staff tried to assure parents that they were keeping their children on the mainstream, middle-class course set for them. Despite such assurances, the voyages of Stuart Lyon, Cassandra Sommers,

Christina Sanchez, and Peter Hsieh did not always go as planned. Stuart experienced the smoothest passages mostly because there was cultural congruence between his family's, school's, and his own identifications and integrative maneuvers. He was exceptionally good at fitting into the preppie social scene despite religious and political ideological differences. He also had a strong familial identification with the Lyon family, whose male members had not only taught him the importance of extending the lineage, but also how to make money and succeed in middle-class professions. He enjoyed his cruise through adolescence and had every reason to believe it would continue on to even better, more pleasurable destinations.

Cassandra had fallen off course in her freshman year and spent her remaining years in high school trying to redeem herself with the help of adults who were more than eager to rescue her. "They're so humane in this school. They help students like me who, you know, need help. They really show they care. All of the staff basically. Like the counselors, principals, everyone. They aren't like, "Oh well, do what you want. Go ahead and do drugs and whatever." They try and stop it. They try and prevent it and help you when you go ahead and do it anyway."

Cassandra eventually became a higher academic achiever, a more devout member of a Black Christian church, a devoted single mother, a staunch supporter of conservative family values, and someone who planned to go to college and find a decent middle-class job. And she became a redeemer who lifted up other fallen students.

Peter stayed the course, at least in terms of his academic achievement, until he plunged into the dark recesses of drug addiction. He eventually recovered but was unable to get back on course as a well-integrated student and community member. He was never able to gain the social acceptance of his preppie peers, even though he participated in counseling sessions on how to build better relations. He felt like a foreigner in the Chinese Christian church his parents attended and clung to conservative political stances that, he believed, supported the interests of hard-working people regardless of their backgrounds. He was an outsider among insiders who kept trying to fit in even as he retreated into his own new/ancient Chinese faith, longed for a happy family life, and felt he could have more control over himself and others by moving into the inner circles of military command.

Christina's voyage was as intentionally resistant as it was tentatively accommodating. She was a Mexican-American girl brought up in the communally warm havens of a close-knit family and Hispanic Catholic church. Like many other children of upwardly mobile immigrants, she was expected to assimilate into mainstream America, at least to an extent where she would be able to find a good job, establish her own family, remain Catholic, and be a good, responsible citizen. As much as she reveled in her ethnic havens and understood the benefits of assimilation, Christina, as she came of age, was not ready to fully commit herself to either world. She had a strong identity as a Mexican-American Catholic yet was somewhat reluctant to adopt practices associated with what she referred to as the "Catholic lifestyle," much less a distinctively Mexican one. She understood that integration into mainstream middle-class America meant staying the course set in her school. Yet she resisted the preppie image by projecting a rebellious, 1960s pop-art image of herself and claiming to have ties with the underworld druggie subculture. But she managed in the end to adapt just enough to graduate from high school and keep future channels open.

Seniors, in their reflexive look back, made it repeatedly clear to me that they regarded themselves as the primary agents who ultimately defined who they were and where they would end up in their treks through American crosscurrents. Although they were subjected to powerful discursive pressures and restrictive disciplinary practices, they did what they could to lay out their own courses of action with or against the currents that swirled around them. There are those who would argue that their agency was illusory, as their positionings within currents made "chosen" lines of action seem like the best or only possible ones for them (Davies, 2000). But seniors experienced a more self-empowering sense of agency as they accepted, rejected, modified, or invented meanings in ways that enabled them to come of age.

Seniors also regarded themselves and other adolescents as both part of the problem of, and solution to, the dilemmas of schooling. Their sense of agency within, knowledge about, and astute interpretations of U.S. cultural crosscurrents should be taken into account in efforts to find particular answers to perennial educational questions. To leave high school students out of the effort is to ignore the fact that teenagers, as they reach the shores of adulthood, are the next generation poised to make a difference. This fact certainly was not lost on at least one graduating senior, who spoke these final words as he looked back on his coming-of-age passages and looked ahead toward possibilities to come:

> We're the turnaround generation. The turn that we take is going to determine generations to come. If we're worse than what the country is right now, it's going to be bad for a long time. If we're better, then everyone will feed on us and things will get better and better. It's all up to us.

Endnotes

1. The names of cities, schools, and research participants have been changed to ensure anonymity and protect confidentiality.

2. In addition to Foucault's (1979, 1990) germinal writings, some of the best, most accessible introductions to poststructural analyses of discourses as language systems can be found in the work of Davies (2000); Kritzman (1988), Lather (1991), and Weedon (1997).

3. The main emphasis in the 1960s and 1970s on identity research in educational anthropology was on conflicts experienced by ethnic minority students. Wax (1976), during her groundbreaking fieldwork on the Pine Ridge Reservation, found that schooling threatened the cultural identities of Oglala Sioux youths. Sioux students protected their identities in the classroom through "unanimous inattention" (p. 218). Similar patterns were documented among second- and third-generation Mexican-descent students in California (Matute-Bianchi, 1986) and Navajo Indians in a racially polarized high school (Deyhle,1992). Other studies indicate that ethnic identity conflicts do not necessarily lead to academic failure. Research on Iranians (Hoffman, 1988), French Algerians (Raissiguier, 1994) and Mexican-Americans (Foley, 1991) provides examples of students who achieved in school while sustaining an identity that kept them connected to their ethnic heritages. Identity also has been addressed in studies focusing on students' race (Fordham, 1996; Fordham & Ogbu, 1986; Miron & Lauria, 1995, 1998), gender (Gilligan, Lyons, & Hanmer, 1999; Lesko, 1988b), social class (Brantlinger, 1993; Willis, 1977) or some combination of sociocultural factors (Fraser, Davis, & Singh, 1997; Heath & Mc Laughlin,1993; Hemmings, 1998; Herr & Anderson, 1997; Kinney,1993; Mehan, Hubbard, & Villanueva, 1994).

4. Examples of subcultures constructed around the nexus of class include the "lads" in Willis's (1977) classic study, neo-Nazi skinheads, and other working-class White boys who affirm their class origins by minimizing their efforts in school, looking mean, or showing outright animosity toward Blacks,

187

immigrants, or other groups. Middle-class kids may produce more overtly political subcultures like hippies and yippies in the 1960s or form off-beat "Bohemian" groups with an intellectual or artistic bent (Brake, 1985). Or they may become freaks and druggies who resort to mind-altering substances to escape societal controls. Racial and ethnic minority youths have generated oppositional subcultures in response to racism, job ceilings, and other types of White discrimination (Ogbu, 1978, 1987; Ogbu & Simons, 1998). Gender and sexual orientation also are impetuses for subcultural opposition. "Burnout" girls in Lesko's (1988a, 1988b) study openly defied patriarchal, self-restrictive images of the good girl with dirty language, provocative dress, and outrageous makeup and hairstyles. Gay, lesbian, bisexual, and transgendered youths are coming out with styles indicating that they no longer are willing to "stand alone, outside, despised, and ripe for discrimination" (Unks, 1995, p. 3).

5. Amber Solomon (not her real name) was a former graduate student who wrote an exceptional masters thesis on students at Central City High. She played an instrumental role as an insider who helped me to gain entree into the school.

6. Fordham (Fordham & Ogbu, 1986), in her published research on an all-Black high school, offered a succinct description of what it means for Black youths to "act white" or in ways deemed inappropriate for them or that accommodate to the White enemy. For students in Fordham's study, it meant:

> (1) speaking Standard English; (2) listening to white music and white radio stations; (3) going to the opera or ballet; (4) spending a lot of time in the library studying; (5) working hard to get good grades in school; (6) getting good grades in school; (7) going to the Smithsonian; (8) going to a Rolling Stone concert at the Capital center; (9) doing volunteer work; (10) going camping, hiking or mountain climbing; (11) having cocktails or a cocktail party; (12) going to a symphony orchestra concert; (13) having a party with no music; (14) listening to classical music; (15) being on time; (16) reading and writing poetry; and (17) putting on "airs." (p. 186)

To act Black was to resist or invert these behaviors as expressions of a collective oppositional Black social identity.

7. There was a surge of research in the 1970s and 1980s on how and why high school students resisted schooling. Many scholars embraced sociological, cultural, and feminist resistance theories to explicate the active and passive rejection of schooling among low-income and working-class youths (Metz, 1978; Willis, 1977), girls (Lesko, 1988a, 1988b; McRobbie & Garber, 1976), African-Americans (Fordham & Ogbu, 1986; Ogbu, 1978, 1987; Ogbu & Simons, 1998), Mexican-Americans (Matute-Bianchi, 1986, 1991) and other historically marginalized groups. The thrust in recent years has been to construe student adaptations as a politics of resistance and accommodation to dominant White middle-class schooling (Brantlinger, 1993; Fordham, 1996; Miron & Lauria, 1995, 1998; Valenzuela, 1999). Although this literature offers critical insights into how teachers and other factors may incite student resistance, it often ignores the inherently unpleasant nature of

school work. Schoolwork is, and always will be, an imposition on the young. Following a path of least resistance is one way for kids to deal with an imposition that stands between them and economic advancement.

8. Learning what is "deliberately taught," Erickson (1987) wrote, is form of political assent on the part of students who not only experience various kinds and degrees of pressures, but who also judge the "legitimacy of teachers' authority" (p. 36). Students like those at Ridgewood High, who were under tremendous pressure to do assigned schoolwork, were nevertheless poised to withdraw their assent if they perceived their teachers to be incompetent or unqualified. White middle-class students are especially likely to test their teachers' intellectual authority before they go along with instructional directives. Other students also want good teachers, but their assent is often circumscribed by pressures that convince them that their interests are not necessarily advanced by doing schoolwork. These pressures, coupled with the fact that schoolwork often is intrinsically ungratifying, make it very difficult for teachers, including the most experienced and educationally qualified ones, to exercise their authority. This is especially true in schools serving mostly low-income or working-class youths and students of color.

9. McNeil (1983, 1986) documented the instructional patterns of high school teachers who engaged in what she calls "defensive teaching." Defensive teachers reduced their instruction to "simplistic ... information that required no reading or writing by the students, little or no student discussion, and very little use of the school's resources" (McNeil, 1983, pp. 115–116). They did so in order to maintain classroom control. McNeil noticed that when students saw minimal teaching, they responded with minimal classroom effort. As far as control was concerned, it was not necessarily forthcoming as was the case in many of the classes I observed.

10. Appleton (1983) offered a related theoretical perspective on how ethnic groups in pluralistic societies form and sustain cultures in response to economic conditions. Increasing urbanization and the expansion of electronic media has caused a "clash of contact" between previously isolated ethnic communities. Contact has broken down symbolic barriers and led to widespread behavioral assimilation as more people adapt to dominant cultural patterns. But behavioral assimilation by no means has eradicated cultural conflict or differences. Cultural divisions persist as groups defend their most cherished values and compete for wealth and socioeconomic status. Group cultural systems thus reflect group interests and constitute the new "indigenous" ethnic cultures in contemporary America.

11. Stone (2001), in her edited volume *New Directions in Anthropological Kinship,* included several chapters by feminist scholars on the history of kinship studies, biology, and culture in the study of kinship, kinship and reproductive technologies, kinship and gender, new family forms and formulations, and kinship and the politics of nations. The book offers excellent, comprehensive coverage of how research on kinship is being transformed, or if one prefers, resurrected from the ashes.

12. The book I was referring to is *Reviving Ophelia,* which was a national best-seller during the initial year of my fieldwork. Written by Dr. Mary Pipher, a clinical psychologist, the book is based on therapeutic work with

predominantly middle- and upper-middle-class White girls whose physical, emotional, thinking, academic, and social selves were being falsified or crushed by dysfunctional family relationships, divorce, depression, drugs, and alcohol. Although I take issue with the exclusive focus on affluent White teenagers and the sweeping characterizations of these and other adolescent girls as, in one reviewer's words, "saplings in the wind," I did find reference to the book to be an effective technique for starting discussions with seniors about their own multifaceted, historically evolving and, above all else, individually rendered sense of a "true" enduring self.

13. Educational anthropologists generated cultural difference theories in the 1960s to refute cultural deficit theories that essentially "blamed the victim" for persistent academic achievement gaps between majority White and ethnic/racial minority students. The cultural difference framework rests on the premise that the values, beliefs, and norms children internalize in their native home environments can be quite incongruent with those transmitted in schools. Home cultures and school culture are conceived as distinct systems, divided by symbolic borders and boundaries that children must cross in order to achieve academic success (Erickson, 1987). Ethnographic studies supported the framework by describing how academic troubles occurred when children's learning, motivational, language, and literacy styles did not match teachers' expectations for appropriate classroom behavior (Au, 1980; Cazden & John, 1971; Delgado-Gaitan, 1987; Gallimore, Boggs, & Jordan, 1974; Heath, 1983; Phelan, Davidson, & Yu, 1998; Philips, 1983). Many contemporary anthropologists have abandoned the concepts of borders and border crossings and instead are exploring symbolic terrains and travels within "borderlands" that blur lines between group cultural systems.

14. McCarthy (1985) provided a thorough historical analysis of church/school/state relations in the United States and how Supreme Court rulings have effectively eliminated prayer, Bible scripture readings, and other explicitly Protestant religious instruction and practices in public schools. She also had an interesting discussion on the discrepancy between American principles of religious liberty and the actual practice of religion in public institutions. It is a discrepancy that has yet to be resolved, especially in public schools.

15. In my original research design, I had identified coming of age in economic, kinship, and political domains as my main areas of inquiry. I had a fourth community domain that focused attention on churches, clubs, volunteer associations, and other organizations. It was about half-way through my fieldwork at Jefferson High that I realized how important religion was to students. It was at that point that I added questions to my interview guide and expanded my focus in field observations in order to conduct more in-depth explorations of graduating seniors' identity and integration work in the religious domain.

16. The Presidential campaign in 1996 pitted the incumbent Democratic President, Bill Clinton, against Bob Dole, the Republican challenger. The media was inundated with coverage of candidates' positions on reforming welfare, lowering the national debt, shoring up the defense budget, and other economic and military issues mentioned by seniors. Media also spotlighted

hot-button cultural values issues such as abortion, gun control, and the environment. Gay rights and some of the other issues that mattered to members of Lona's clique were not covered as much and appeared to be matters of least concern to candidates.

17. Theories in educational anthropology on cultural pluralism have the most direct implications for democratic education. They have evolved over time, as have the educational policies and pedagogical recommendations associated with them (Davidson & Phelan, 1993; Hemmings, 1998). Classical theory on cultural pluralism views modern industrial societies as patchworks of bounded ethnic communities with equally valuable cultural traditions. When a community's traditions are disrupted through conquest or forced assimilation into another culture, members suffer enormous psychological harm and other setbacks. Educational policy in democratic societies should preserve the integrity of distinctive cultures through legal protections that guarantee the right of ethnic communities to control the schooling of their children. This theoretical view was modified over time. Modified versions of cultural pluralism retain the classical position that ethnic community cultures should be preserved, but they also promote the transmission of common cultural competencies. Cultural conflict is regarded as detrimental to democracy, and teachers can help to bridge differences by adopting pedagogies that affirm students' native cultures *and* transmit a common culture (Au, 1980; Au & Jordan, 1981; Trueba, 1988; Trueba, Spindler, & Spindler, 1988). Theories in the new cultural pluralism depart from earlier versions in how they emphasize the critical relationship between cultural diversity and social stratification. Ethnic communities no longer are conceived of as bounded communities where members practice relatively stable patterns of life. Group cultures are evolving systems that may reflect long-held ethnic traditions but also contain elements of a dominant culture that is itself constantly changing as a result of intergroup appropriations, resistance, and accommodations (Appleton, 1983; Marcus & Fischer, 1986; Newman, 1973). Social conflict leads to cultural conflicts that are not necessarily destructive in democratic societies. Conflict can be and often is a catalyst for positive sociocultural change.

18. Among the emergent variants of democratic education are those that emphasize the indispensability of identity and the many dangers of ideological dogmatism tied to identity work (Kyle & Jenks, 2002). The phrases "identity politics," "politics of identity," and "politics of identification" are coming into vogue as more educators look for "ambiguity, relativity, fragmentation, particularity, and discontinuity" in identity rather than clarity, continuity, and wholeness (Crotty, 1998, p. 185). Identity is treated as decentered and constantly under construction as individuals are encouraged to work with and against the grain of ideologies in their relations with others. A truly democratic education promotes a "politics of liberation" that recognizes how the identities of poor people, people of color, women, gays, lesbians, and other marginalized groups are inscribed with oppressive, self-debilitating discourses, whereas those of privileged people have exclusions built into them that sustain their superiority (Lather, 1991). Liberation comes about when marginalized people unsettle and take control of the meanings inscribed on their identities and when privileged people interro-

gate their identity exclusions in a manner that causes them to question and ultimately change their positions.

19. Erickson (1987) also wrote about the everyday politics of classrooms. He pointed out that when people say that students are "not learning," what they mean is that they are not learning what teachers intend them to learn as a result of intentional instruction. Learning what is deliberately taught is a form of political assent. Not learning is a form of political resistance. Student assent is "a leap of faith" that involves:

> trust in the legitimacy of the authority and in the good intentions of those exercising it, trust that one's own identity will be maintained positively in relation to the authority, and trust that one's own interests will be advanced by compliance with the exercise of authority. (p. 36)

If the leap isn't made or is broken, teachers and students end up in regressive relationships where mutual trust is sacrificed and on-going classroom political conflict ensues.

References

Adams, N. G. (1999). Fighting to be somebody: resisting erasure and the discursive practice of female adolescent fighting. *Educational studies, 30*(2), 115–139.

Adams, W. R. (2000). Introducing this volume. In W. R. Adams & F. A. Salamone (Eds.), *Anthropology and theology: God, icons and God-talk* (pp. 1–31). Lanham, MD: University Press of America.

Anderson, E. (1998). The codes of the street. In L. C. Mahdi, N. G. Christopher, & M. Meade (Eds.), *Crossroads: The quest for contemporary rites of passage* (pp. 91–97). Chicago: Open Court.

Appleton, N. (1983). *Cultural pluralism in education: Theoretical foundations.* New York: Longman.

Au, K. H. (1980). Participant structures in a reading lesson with Hawaiian children: Analysis of a culturally appropriate instructional event. *Anthropology & Education Quarterly, 11*(2), 91–115.

Au, K. H., & Jordan, C. (1981). Teaching reading to Hawaiian children: Finding a culturally appropriate solution. In H. T. Trueba, G. P. Gutherie, & K. H. Au (Eds.), *Culture and the bilingual classroom: Studies in classroom ethnography* (pp. 139–152). Rowley, MA: Newbury House.

Ayers, W., Klonsky, M., & Lyon, G. (2000). *A simple justice: The challenge of small schools.* New York: Teachers College Press.

Banks, J., & Banks, C. M. (2001). *Handbook of research on multicultural education.* San Francisco: Jossey-Bass.

Barth, F. (1969). Introduction. In F. Barth (Ed.), *Ethnic groups and boundaries: The social organization of cultural difference* (pp. 9–38). London: Allen and Unwin.

Bellah, R. N., Madsen, R., Sullivan, W. M., Swidler, A., & Tipton, S. M.. (1985). *Habits of the heart: Individualism and commitment in American life.* New York: Harper & Row.

Berns McGowen, R. (1999). *Muslims in the diaspora.* Toronto: University of Toronto Press.

Bernstein, B. (1971). *Class, codes and control* (Vol. 1). London: Routledge & Kegan Paul.

193

Bettis, P. J. (1996). Urban students, liminality, and the postindustrial context. *Sociology of Education, 69,* 105–125.

Bowles, S., & Gintis, H. (1976). *Schooling in capitalist America.* New York: Basic Books.

Brake, M. (1980). *The sociology of youth culture and subcultures.* New York: Routledge & Kegan Paul.

Brake, M. (1985). *Comparative youth culture: The sociology of youth culture and youth subcultures in America, Britain and Canada.* London: Routledge.

Brantlinger, E. A. (1993). *The politics of social class in secondary school.* New York: Teachers College Press.

Cazden, C. B, & John, V. P. (1971) Learning in American Indian children. In M. L. Wax, S. Diamond, & F. O. Gearing (Eds.), *Anthropological perspectives on education* (pp. 252–271). New York: Basic Books.

Chaudhry, L. N. (2000). Researching "my people," researching myself: Fragments of a reflexive tale. In E. A. StPierre & W. S. Pillow (Eds.), *Working the ruins: Feminist poststructural theory and methods in education* (pp. 96–113). New York: Routledge.

Clinchy, E. (2000). *Creating new schools: How small schools are changing American education.* New York: Teachers College Press.

Cohen, A. (1974). *Two-dimensional man: An essay on the anthropology of power and symbolism in complex society.* New York: Routledge & Kegan Paul.

Crotty, M. (1998). *The foundations of social research: Meaning and perspective in the research process.* Thousand Oaks, CA: Sage.

Davidson, A. L., & Phelan, P. (1993). Cultural diversity and its implications for schooling: A continuing American dialogue. In A. L. Davidson & P. Phelan (Eds.), *Renegotiating cultural diversity in American schools* (pp. 1–26). New York: Teachers College Press.

Davies, B. (2000). *A body of writing: 1990–1999.* Walnut Creek, CA: Altamira Press.

Delgado-Gaitan, C. (1987). Traditions and transitions in the learning process of Mexican children: An ethnographic view. In G. Spindler & L. Spindler (Eds.), *Interpretive ethnography of education: At home and abroad* (pp. 333–359). Hillsdale, NJ: Lawrence Erlbaum Associates.

Denzin, N. K., & Lincoln, Y. S. (2000). Introduction: The discipline and practice of qualitative research. In N. K. Denzin & Y. S. Lincoln (Eds.), *Handbook of qualitative research* (pp. 1–28). Thousand Oaks, CA: Sage.

Dewey, J. (1916). *Democracy and education.* New York: Macmillan Company.

Deyhle, D. (1992). Constructing failure and maintaining cultural identity: Navajo and Ute school leavers. *Journal of American Indian Education, 32,* 24–47.

Dillon, J. (1994). *Using discussion in classrooms.* Buckingham, UK: Open University Press.

Dimitriadis, G. (2001). "In the clique": Popular culture, constructions of place, and the everyday lives of urban youths. *Anthropology & Education Quarterly, 32*(1), 29–51.

Douglas, R. (1996). *Playing the future: How kids' culture can teach us to thrive in an age of chaos.* New York: HarperCollins.

Epstein, J. S. (1998). Introduction: Generation X, youth culture, and identity. In J. S. Epstein (Ed.), *Youth culture: Identity in a postmodern world* (pp. 1–23). Malden, MA: Blackwell.

Erickson, F. (1987). Transformation and school success: The politics and culture of educational achievement. *Anthropology & Education Quarterly, 18,* 335–355.

Fine, M., & Weis, L. (1998) *The unknown city: the lives of poor and working-class young adults.* Boston: Beacon Press.

Fitzgerald, J. (1997). Linking school-to-work programs to community economic development in urban schools. *Urban Education, 32*(4), 489–511.

Foley, D. E. (1991). Reconsidering anthropological explanations of school failure. *Anthropology & Education Quarterly, 22,* 60–86.

Fordham, S. (1996). *Blacked out: Dilemmas of race, identity, and success at Capital High.* Chicago: University of Chicago Press.

Fordham, S., & Ogbu, J. U. (1986). Black students' school success: Coping with the "burden of acting white." *Urban Review,18,* 176–206.

Foucault, M. (1979). *Discipline and punish.* New York: Pantheon.

Foucault, M. (1990). *The history of sexuality.* New York: Vintage.

Fraser, J., Davis, P. W., & Singh, R. (1997). Identity work by alternative high school students. *International Journal of Qualitative Studies in Education, 10*(2), 221–233.

Fukuyama, F. (1992). *The end of history and the last man.* New York: The Free Press.

Gallimore, R., Boggs, J., & Jordan, C. (1974). *Culture, behavior and education: A study of Hawaiian Americans.* Beverly Hills, CA: Sage.

Gamoran, A. (1987). The stratification of high school learning opportunities. *Sociology of Education, 60*(3), 135–155.

Gamoran, A. (1992). Is ability grouping equitable? *Educational Leadership, 50*(2), 11–17.

Gamoran, A., & Berends, M. (1987). The effects of stratification in secondary schools: Synthesis of survey and ethnographic research. *Review of Educational Research, 57*(4), 415–435.

Gay, G. (1994). *At the essence of learning: Multicultural education.* West Lafayette, IN: Kappa Delta Pi.

Geertz, C. (1973). *The interpretation of cultures.* New York: Basic Books.

Gergen, M. M., & Gergen, K. J. (2000). Qualitative inquiry: Tensions and transformations. In N. K. Denzin & Y. S. Lincoln (Eds.), *Handbook of qualitative research* (pp. 1025–1046). Thousand Oaks, CA: Sage.

Gibson, M. A. (1988). *Accommodation without assimilation.* Ithaca, NY: Cornell University Press.

Gilligan, C., Lyons, N., & Hanmer, T. (1999). *Making connections: The relational worlds of adolescent girls at Emma Willard School.* Cambridge, MA: Harvard University Press.

Giroux, H. A. (1998). Teenage sexuality, body politics, and the pedagogy of display. In J. S. Epstein (Ed.), *Youth culture: Identity in a postmodern world* (pp. 24–55). Malden, MA: Blackwell.

Gordon, E. T. (1997). Cultural politics of black masculinity. *Transforming Anthropology, 6*(1 & 2), 36–53.

Gutmann, A. (1987). *Democratic education.* Princeton, NJ: Princeton University Press.

Hacking, I. (1999). *The social construction of what?* Cambridge, MA: Harvard University Press.

Hale-Benson, J. E. (1986). *Black children: Their roots, culture and learning styles.* Baltimore: John Hopkins University Press.

Heath, S. B. (1983). *Ways with words: Language, life and work in communities and classrooms*. New York: Cambridge University Press.

Heath, S. B., & McLaughlin, M. W. (1993). *Identity and inner-city youth: Beyond ethnicity and gender*. New York: Teachers College Press.

Hemmings, A. (1996). Conflicting images? Being black and a model high school student. *Anthropology & Education Quarterly, 27*, 20–50.

Hemmings, A. (1998). The self-transformations of African American achievers. *Youth & Society, 29*, 330–368.

Hemmings, A. (2000a). The "hidden" corridor curriculum. *The High School Journal, 83*(2), 1–10.

Hemmings, A. (2000b). Lona's links: Postoppositional identity work of urban youths. *Anthropology & Education Quarterly, 31*(2), 152–172.

Hemmings, A. (2000c). High school democratic dialogues: Possibilities for praxis. *American Educational Research Journal, 37*(1), 67–91.

Hemmings, A. (2002). Youth culture of hostility: Discourses of money, respect and differences. *International Journal of Qualitative Research in Education, 15*(3), 291–307.

Hemmings, A., & Metz, M. H. (1990). Real teaching: How high school teachers negotiate national, community, and student pressures. In R. Page & L. Valli (Eds.), *Curriculum differentiation: Interpretive studies in U. S. secondary schools* (pp. 91–111). New York: State University of New York Press.

Herr, K., & Anderson, G. L. (1997). The cultural politics of identity: Student narratives for two Mexican secondary schools. *International Journal of Qualitative Studies in Education, 10*(1), 45–61.

Hoffman, D. M. (1988). Cross cultural adaptation and learning: Iranians and Americans at school. In H. Trueba & C. Delgado-Gaitan (Eds.), *School and society: Learning content through culture* (pp. 163–180). New York: Praeger.

Hoffman, D. M. (1998). A therapeutic moment? Identity, self and culture in the anthropology of education. *Anthropology & Education Quarterly, 29*(3), 324–346.

Jacobson, J. (1998). *Islam in transition: Religion and identity among British-Pakistani youth*. London: Routledge.

Jen, G. (1997, April 21). Who's to judge? *The New Republic*, 18–19.

Kinney, D. A. (1993). From nerds to normals: The recovery of identity among adolescents from middle school to high school. *Sociology of Education, 66*, 21–40.

Kliebard, H. M. (1987). *The struggle for the American curriculum 1893–1958*. New York: Routledge & Kegan Paul.

Kohlberg, L. (1975). The cognitive-developmental approach to moral education. *Phi Delta Kappan, 56*, 670–677.

Kohlberg, L. (1976). Moral stages and moralization: The cognitive-developmental approach. In T. Lickona (Ed.), *Man, morality and society*. New York: Holt, Rinehart & Winston.

Kritzman, D. (1988). *Michel Foucault: Politics, philosophy, culture*. New York: Routledge.

Kyle, K., & Jenks, C. (2002). The theoretical and historical case for democratic education in the United States. *Educational Studies, 33*(2), 150–169.

Lambeck, M. (2002). *A reader in the anthropology of religion*. Malden, MA: Blackwell.

Lamphere, L. (2001). Whatever happened to kinship studies? Reflections of a feminist anthropologist. In L. Stone (Ed.), *New directions in anthropological kinship* (pp. 21–47). Lanham, MD: Rowman & Littlefield.

Lather, P. (1991). *Getting smart: Feminist research and pedagogy with/in the postmodern.* New York: Routledge.

Lesko, N. (1988a). The curriculum of the body: Lessons from a Catholic high school. In L. Roman & L. K. Christian-Smith (Eds.), *Becoming feminine: The politics of popular culture* (pp. 123–142). New York: Falmer Press.

Lesko, N. (1988b). *Symbolizing society: Stories, rites and structure in a Catholic high school.* New York: Falmer Press.

Levi-Strauss, C. (1966). *The savage mind.* Chicago: University of Chicago Press.

Lincoln, C. E, & Mamiya, L. H. (1990). *The Black church in the African American experience.* Durham, NC: Duke University Press.

Lincoln, Y. S., & Denzin, N. K. (2000). The seventh moment: Out of the past. In N. K. Denzin & Y. S. Lincoln (Eds.), *Handbook of qualitative research* (pp. 1047–1065). Thousand Oaks, CA: Sage.

Lipkin, A. (1995). The case for a gay and lesbian curriculum. In G. Unks (Ed.), *The gay teen: Educational practice and theory for lesbian, gay, and bisexual adolescents* (pp. 31–51). New York: Routledge.

Long, N. (1958). The local community as an ecology of games. *American Journal of Sociology, 64,* 251–261.

Lucas, S. R. (1999). *Tracking inequality: Stratification and mobility in American high schools.* New York: Teachers College Press.

Maffly-Kipp, L. (2002). African-American religion in the nineteenth century. *Black and Christian.* Retrieved from www.blackandchristian.com

Marcus, G., & Fischer, M. (1986). *Anthropology as cultural critique: An experimental moment in the human sciences.* Chicago: University of Chicago Press.

Matute-Bianchi, M. E. (1986). Ethnic identities and patterns of school success and failure among Mexican-descent and Japanese-American students in a California high school: An ethnographic analysis. *American Journal of Education, 95,* 233–255.

Matute-Bianchi, M. E. (1991). Situational ethnicity and patterns of school performance among immigrant and nonimmigrant Mexican-descent students. In M. A. Gibson & J. U. Ogbu (Eds.), *Minority status and schooling: A comparative study of immigrant and involuntary minorities* (pp. 205–247). New York: Garlan Publishing, Inc.

McCarthy, M. M. (1985). Religion and public schools: Emerging legal standards and unresolved issues. *Harvard Educational Review, 55*(3), 278–317.

McDermott, R. P. (1974). Achieving school failure: An anthropological approach to illiteracy and social stratification. In G. D. Spindler (Ed.), *Education and cultural process: Toward an anthropology of education* (pp. 82–118). New York: Holt, Rinehart and Winston.

McNeil, L. (1983). Defensive teaching and classroom control. In M. W. Apple & L. Weis (Eds.), *Ideology & practice in schooling* (pp. 114–142). Philadelphia: Temple University Press.

McNeil, L. (1986). *Contradictions of control: School structure and school knowledge.* New York: Routledge and Kegan Paul.

McRobbie, A., & Garber, J. (1976). Girls and subcultures: An exploration. In S. Hall & T. Jefferson (Eds.), *Resistance through rituals* (pp. 209–229). London: Hutchinson.

Mead, M. (1928). *Coming of age in Samoa.* New York: Morrow Quill Paperbacks.

Mehan, H., Hubbard, L., & Villanueva, I. (1994). Forming academic identities: Accommodation and assimilation among involuntary minorities. *Anthropology & Education Quarterly, 25,* 91–117.

Meier, D. (1995). *The power of their ideas: Lessons for America from a small school in Harlem.* Boston: Beacon Press.

Metz, M. H. (1978). *Classrooms and corridors: The crisis of authority in desegregated secondary schools.* Berkeley, CA: University of California Press.

Metz, M. H. (1990). Real school: A universal drama amid disparate experience. In D. Mitchell & M. Goertz (Eds.), *Education politics for the new century: The twentieth anniversary yearbook of the politics of education association* (pp. 75–91). Philadelphia: Falmer Press.

Metz, M. H. (1993). Teachers' ultimate dependence on their students. In J. W. Little & M. W. McLaughlin (Eds.), *Teachers' work: Individuals, colleagues and contexts* (pp. 104–105). New York: Teachers College Press.

Miron, L. F., & Lauria, M. (1995). Identity politics and student resistance to inner-city public schooling. *Youth & Society, 27,* 29–54.

Miron, L. F., & Lauria, M. (1998). Student voice as agency: Resistance and accommodation in inner-city schools. *Anthropology & Education Quarterly, 29,* 189–213.

Morris, B. (1987). *Anthropological studies of religion: An introductory text.* Cambridge, England: Cambridge University Press.

Munoz, V. I. (1995). *"Where something catches:" Work, love, and identity in youth.* New York: State University of New York Press.

Newman, W. A. (1973). *American pluralism: A study of minority groups in social theory.* New York: Harper & Row.

Nieto, S. (1992). *Affirming diversity: The sociopolitical context of multicultural education.* White Plains, NY: Longman.

Noddings, N. (1984). *Caring, a feminine approach to ethics and moral education.* Berkeley: University of California Press.

Noddings, N. (1992). *The challenge to care in schools: An alternative approach to education.* New York: Teachers College Press.

Oakes, J. (1985). *Keeping track: How schools structure inequality.* Birmingham, NY: Vail-Ballou Press.

Ogbu, J. U. (1978). *Minority education and caste: the American system in cross-cultural perspective.* New York: Academic Press.

Ogbu, J. U. (1987). Variability in minority school performance: A problem in search of an explanation. *Anthropology & Education Quarterly, 18,* 313–334.

Ogbu, J. U. (1999). Beyond language: Ebonics, proper English, and identity in a Black-American speech community. *American Educational Research Journal, 36*(2), 147–184.

Ogbu, J. U., & Simons, H. D. (1998). Voluntary and involuntary minorities: A cultural-ecological theory of school performance with some implications for education. *Anthropology & Education Quarterly, 29,* 155–188.

Ortner, S. B. (1991). Reading America: Preliminary notes on class and culture. In R. G. Fox (Ed.), *Recapturing anthropology: Working in the present* (pp. 163–189). Santa Fe, NM: School of American Research Press.

Page, R. N. (1991). *Lower-track classrooms: A curricular and cultural perspective.* New York: Teachers College Press.

Page, R. N. (2000). The tracking show. In B. Franklin (Ed.), *Curriculum and consequence: Herbert M. Kliebard and the promise of schooling* (pp. 103–127). New York: Teachers College Press.

Parsons, T. (1959). The school class as a social system: Some of its functions in American society. *Harvard Educational Review, 29*(4), 297–318.

Parsons, T. (1964). *Essays in sociological theory.* Chicago: Freepress.

Phelan, P., Davidson, A. L., & Yu, H. C. (1993). Students' multiple worlds: Navigating the borders of family, peer, and school cultures. In P. Phelan & A. L. Davidson (Eds.), *Renegotiating cultural diversity in American schools* (pp. 52–88). New York: Teachers College Press.

Phelan, P., Davidson, A. L., & Yu, H. C. (1998). *Adolescents worlds: Negotiating family, peers, and school.* New York: Teachers College Press.

Philips, S. U. (1983). *The invisible culture: Communication in classroom and community on the Warm Springs Indian Reservation.* New York: Longman.

Pipher, M. (1994). *Reviving Ophelia: Saving the selves of adolescent girls.* New York: Ballantine Books.

Preskill, S. (1997). Discussion, schooling, and the struggle for democracy. *Theory and Research in Social Education, 25,* 316–345.

Purpel, D., & Ryan, K. (1976). *Moral education: It comes with the territory.* Berkeley, CA: McCutchan.

Raissiguier, C. (1994). *Becoming women, becoming workers: Identity formation in a French vocation school.* Albany, NY: State University of New York Press.

Redfield, R. (1963). *The social uses of social science.* Chicago: University of Chicago Press.

Rury, J. L. (2002). Democracy's high schools? Social change and American secondary education in the post-Conant era. *American Educational Research Journal, 39*(2), 307–336.

Schneider, D. M. (1968). *American kinship: A cultural account.* Chicago: The University of Chicago Press.

Schneider, D. M. (1995). *Schneider on Schneider.* Durham, NC: Duke University Press.

Shweder, R. A. (1991). *Thinking through cultures: Expeditions in cultural psychology.* Cambridge, MA: Harvard University Press.

Simon, S. B., Howe, L., & Kirschenbaum, H. (1972). *Values clarification: A handbook of practical strategies for teachers and students.* New York: Hart.

Simon, S. B., & Kirschenbaum, H. (1973). *Readings in values clarification.* Minneapolis: Winston Press.

Singleton, J. (1974). Implications of cultural transmission. In G. Spindler (Ed.), *Education and cultural process: Toward and anthropology of education* (pp. 26–38). New York: Holt, Rinehart & Winston.

Sizer, T., & Sizer, N. F. (1999). *The students are watching: Schools and the moral contract.* Boston: Beacon Press.

Sleeter, C. E. (1991). *Empowerment through multicultural education.* Albany: State University of New York Press.

Smith, C. L., & Rojewski, J. W. (1993). School-to-work transition: Alternatives for educational reform. *Youth & Society, 25,* 222–250.

Spindler, G., & Spindler, L. (1978). *The making of psychological anthropology.* Berkeley: University of California Press.

Spindler, G., & Spindler, L. (1989). Instrumental competence, self-efficacy, linguistic minorities, and cultural therapy: A preliminary attempt at integration. *Anthropology & Education Quarterly, 10,* 36–50.

Spindler, G., & Spindler, L. (1992). The enduring, situated, and endangered sel in fieldwork: A personal account. In B. Boyer (Ed.), *The psychoanalytical study of society* (pp. 23–28). Hillsdale, NJ: The Analytic Press.

Spindler, G., & Spindler, L. (1993). The processes of culture and person: Cultural therapy and culturally diverse schools. In P. Phelan & A. L. Davidson (Eds.), *Renegotiating cultural diversity in American schools* (pp. 27–51). New York: Teachers College Press.

Spring, J. (1994). *American Education.* New York: McGraw-Hill, Inc.

Stack, C. B. (1974). *All our kin: Strategies for survival in a Black community.* New York: Harper & Row.

Stone, L. (2001). *New directions in anthropological kinship.* Lanham, MD: Rowman & Littlefield.

Taylor, M. (2000). "Spirit" in the researching of cultural worlds: On theology's contributions to anthropology. In W. R. Adams & F. A. Salamone (Eds), *Anthropology and theology: God, icons and God-talk* (pp. 33–45). Lanham, MD: University Press of America.

Trueba, H. (1988). Culturally based explanations of minority students' academic achievement. *Anthropology & Education Quarterly, 19,* 270–281.

Trueba, H., Spindler, G., & Spindler, L. (1988). *What do anthropologists have to say about dropouts?* New York: Falmer Press.

Turner, V. (1969). *The ritual process: Structure and anti-structure.* Chicago: Aldine.

Turner, V. (1977). Variations on a theme of liminality. In S. Moore & B. Myerhoff (Eds.), *Secular ritual* (pp. 36–52). Assen, Netherlands: Van Gorcum.

Turner, V. (1982). *From ritual to theater: The human seriousness of play.* New York: PAJ Publications.

Unks, G. (1995) *The gay teen: Educational practice and theory for lesbian, gay, and bisexual adolescents.* New York: Routledge.

Valenzuela, A. (1999). *Subtractive schooling: U. S.-Mexican youth and the politics of caring.* New York: State University of New York Press.

Valli, L. (1983). Becoming clerical workers: Business education and the culture of femininity. In M. W. Apple & L. Weis (Eds.), *Ideology and practice in schooling* (pp. 213–234). Philadelphia: Temple University Press.

Van Gennep, A. (1960). *The rites of passage.* London: Routledge.

Ward, J. (1995). Cultivating a morality of care in African American adolescents: A culture-based model of violence prevention. *Harvard Educational Review, 65*(2), 175–188.

Wax, R. H. (1976). Oglala Sioux dropouts and their problems with educators. In J. I. Roberts & S. K. Akinsanya (Eds.), *Schooling in the cultural context: Anthropological studies of education* (pp. 216–226). New York: David McKay.

Weber, M. (1958). *The Protestant ethic and the spirit of capitalism* (T. Parson, Trans.). New York: Charles Scriber's Sons.

Weedon, C. (1997). *Feminist practice and poststructural theory.* Malden, MA: Blackwell.

Weinstein, D. (1991). *Heavy metal: A cultural sociology.* New York: Lexington.

Weis, L., & Fine, M. (2000). *Construction sites: Excavating race, class and gender among urban youths.* New York: Teachers College Press.

Willis, P. (1977). *Learning to labour: How working-class kids get working-class jobs.* Farnborough, England: Saxon House.

Willis, P. (1990). *Common culture: Symbolic work at play in the everyday cultures of the young.* Boulder, CO: Westview Press.

Wilson, W. J. (1996). *When work disappears: The world of the new urban poor.* New York: Alfred A. Knopf.

Yon, D. A. (2000). *Elusive culture: Schooling, race, and identity in global times.* New York: State University of New York Press.

Zine, J. (2001). Muslim youth in Canadian schools: Education and the politics of religious identity. *Anthropology & Education Quarterly, 32*(4), 399–423.

Appendix

INTERVIEW GUIDE*

School

1. What are your general impressions of this school?
2. What are corridors like? Describe the "typical" student.
3. What are classes like? Describe the "typical" teacher.
4. If I were a new student and you were asked to take me under your wing, what advice would you give me?

Economic Domain

5. What are your impressions of the economy and employment opportunities? What's good or bad about the economic situation for young people?
6. Are there features of the economy that are changing? Will men, women, Blacks, Whites, and other groups do the same kinds of work they did in the past or are there new trends?
7. Describe economic activities in your family and community.
8. As you look into your own future, what is the most ideal occupation for you?

---

*The original interview guide did not contain a separate section on religion. There were questions about involvement in community agencies such as churches that led to rather extensive discussions about religion. Halfway through my fieldwork at Jefferson, the first research site, I modified the interview guide and added the questions about religion. I also began to focus more attention on religion in my fieldwork observations.

Kinship Domain

9. What are your impressions of family life in America? What's good or bad about family life?
10. Is family life changing? Is marriage here to stay, or do you think more people will opt for alternative living arrangements?
11. Describe family life in your home and community.
12. What do you envision as the most ideal family arrangement for you?

Religious Domain

13. What are your impressions of religion in this country? What's good or bad about religion?
14. Has the nature or impact of religion changed? Are traditional religions like Christianity and Judaism here to stay or do you think people are more apt to explore other kinds of religions?
15. Describe religion in your home and community.
16. Is religion important to you? What religions or religious activities might you get involved in as an adult?

Political Domain

17. What are your impressions of the country's political system? What's good or bad about American politics?
18. Are there issues and other aspects of the political system that are or ought to be changing? Are the beliefs and activities of major political parties the same as they were, or are there new trends?
19. Describe whether or how people in your family and community get involved in politics.
20. Are you interested in politics? What kind of involvement in politics or political activities might you have as an adult?

Grand Finale

21. Overall, how do you feel about entering adulthood? What are the best opportunities and greatest challenges facing you and your generation?
22. How well has your school prepared you for the future?

Author Index

205

Subject Index